W9-AAF-227

JOURNEY TO JOY

SWAMI MUKTANANDA PARAMAHANSA, SIDDHA GURU

JOURNEY TO JOY

An Introductory Guidebook
to Siddha Meditation
by

ROBERT SHIARELLA

matrika publications

New York   1982

© 1982 by Robert Shiarella.

All rights reserved. No part of this book may be reproduced or utilized in any form or by any means, electronic or mechanical, including photocopying, recording, or by any information storage and retrieval system, without written permission from the publisher.

Matrika Publications, Ltd.
10 East End Avenue (Suite 1-K)
New York, N.Y. 10021

Cover and text design by Paul Segal.
Illustrations by the author.
Copyediting by Sheldon Lewis.
Proofreading by Karen Shiarella and Susan Baker.

International Standard Book Number: 0-943648-00-9
Library of Congress Catalog Card Number: 82-90157

Manufactured in the United States of America.

Dedication

There is an ancient brotherhood of rare, Enlightened Masters who, not content with merely seeking food and drink, have earned themselves a wondrous place forever free of hunger and of thirst. And yet, these blissful beings, having attained the unattainable, still choose to walk among us, guiding others to their lofty state. This book is dedicated to that exalted brotherhood.

Table of Contents

Introduction

There once was a beggar who spent his entire life on a tiny plot of barren land beside a busy roadway. His wedge of worthless property was all he owned, and it did not even contain a shelter to protect him from the elements. Each night he slept curled up beneath uncaring stars, and his days were spent squatting in the dust beside the roadway, begging for crumbs from passersby. The years of his life dragged by like an endless parade of dreary ordeals, filled with constant loneliness, hunger, pain and ill health, and the only way he found the necessary strength to survive them all was by incessantly spinning a host of elaborate daydreams in which he would imagine a future time when every conceivable pleasure would be his to enjoy without restriction.

In such a manner did this miserable wretch pass seventy interminable years, and the closest thing to real pleasure he ever experienced was an occasional abatement of his chronic hunger pangs, thanks to some half-eaten morsel tossed his way by an itinerant stranger. Finally, the Lord of Death showed mercy and came down to liberate him from his tortured existence, but even then the fool fought desperately to embrace his worthless life in the futile hope that someday all his fantasies would still come true.

And so, miserable to the very end, he was wrenched away into the world of ancestors, leaving the local authorities with the distasteful task of disposing of his pitiful remains. Deciding that it would be easiest and most fitting to simply bury his body in the place where he had spent his entire life, they began to dig a grave in the middle of that tiny piece of wasteland. When they had dug no deeper than a few feet, however, their shovels suddenly broke through the ceiling of an ancient underground vault which contained an enormous mountain of buried treasure!

Thus, that woeful derelict had lived seventy years of needless agony, begging for crumbs his whole life long, tragically unaware that all the while he had actually been the rich and powerful lord of a magnificent estate.

Perhaps it will come as a shock to some of us, but this tale is a classical analogy employed by the science of metaphysics to describe the life of *every human being*. Though at first we may become a bit indignant at being compared to that tragic figure portrayed above, the ancient science which we are about to examine is founded upon the unqualified assertion that each and every one of us is exactly comparable to that poor devil. If we don't happen to feel particularly miserable right now, we're told, it's because we simply do not know what we are missing. The venerable sages of this ancient science assure us that, compared to what we could be if we ever fully realized our hidden potential, even the greatest king who ever lived was a miserable beggar.

Though most of us would find it rather difficult to admit with much conviction that we are in reality a "rich and powerful lord of a magnificent estate," we might at least own up to feeling a subtle but constant gnawing awareness that somehow our life should be a great deal better than it is right now. In fact, if we were not feeling some measure of disappointment in our present existence and its promise for the future, we would probably not have bothered to look between the covers of this book.

Now what could an average member of modern society possibly have to feel miserable or even dissatisfied about? We are currently enjoying the highest standard of living in the history of humankind; we are better housed, better fed, better clothed, better educated, better paid, and better cared for medically than any other citizens in history. We have more political freedom, more personal rights, more leisure time, more material comforts and more labor-saving devices than our ancestors dreamed possible; and yet, for all our wealth, luxuries and freedom, we must still be counted among the most unhappy and unhealthy people ever to walk the earth.

At this very moment no less than ninety percent of contemporary civilization is in the process of committing gradual suicide through one or more self-destructive addictions such as alcohol, tobacco, caffeine, prescription and nonprescription drugs, narcotics, and junk food. Our bodies, which medical science assures us are built to last at least 600 years (provided our cells can eliminate their waste matter and reproduce properly), are instead ravaged by heart disease, cancer, arthritis, allergies, ulcers, tooth decay, malnutrition, obesity, influenza, chronic head- and backaches, failing eyesight and hearing—the list is endless—and if we're somehow lucky enough to avoid most of these illnesses, we are certain to fall prey to the universal disease, old age, which is nothing more than the body suffocating in its own waste matter. If we do manage to live past the age of sixty-five, we are rewarded by being labeled obsolete by a youth-oriented society which has little use for those who can no longer keep up the high standards of production and consumption that this culture demands of its members.

One out of ten of us is in need of mental treatment, plagued by neurosis, frustration, anxiety, depression, emotional instability, inability to love, loneliness, rage, hate, compulsion, insecurity or outright psychosis. Socially and economically there is also chaos and decay: our divorce rate is up to fifty percent; we are suffering from public apathy, governmental corruption, monopolization by big business, and runaway inflations which are interrupted only by more disastrous depressions; and there are raging epidemics of crime, violence, racism, sexism, hedonism and perversion. Even if for us personally everything seems to be going rather well at present, how could any truly compassionate person ever claim to be satisfied with life while so many of our fellow human beings are quite obviously wallowing in abject misery?

Social reformers offer a multitude of reasons for this alarming state of affairs, but this book will maintain that there is only one reason: In our enthusiasm to pursue external "crumbs," we have forgotten that a treasure of inconceivable value lies buried right inside of us. In other words, we have lost the knowledge of our own true worth. In effect, we have forgotten who we really are, and the following pages will explain why this single fact is the sole cause of all our suffering, both personal and collective. The contention herein will be that loss of self-knowledge results in loss of self-esteem, and alienation from one's self results in feelings of alienation toward everything else in Creation as well.

Quite simply put, when human beings begin to feel worthless and alone, they begin to act that way. This is why all valid personal-growth disciplines insist that the only meaningful way any of us can contribute to the establishment of universal harmony is by eliminating disharmony within our own being, through the pursuit and attainment of true self-awareness.

The main purpose of this book, then, is not just to pinpoint the cause of our present predicament, but to thoroughly investigate an effective remedy as well—one which has already begun working for hundreds of thousands of people who once suffered from feelings of misery or dissatisfaction regarding the meaning and value of their lives. During its course, this presentation plans to accomplish the following objectives: (1) to present the evidence supporting the existence of a hidden reservoir of growth-potential within each human being and to divulge its exact nature; (2) to describe a specific technique which for thousands of years has been successfully employed to tap this secret reservoir; (3) to detail the precise process of personal evolution which then ensues, elevating us to the full expression of our highest potential at every level of our being; and (4) to carefully examine one particular system of personal growth which guarantees to activate this process, with ease and safety, in virtually every person who desires it.

Yoga

Whenever the term *Yoga* appears in this book, it will refer generically to the field of endeavor known in the West as "spiritual science"—a special breed of ancient discipline specifically designed to guide seekers of self-awareness. All valid systems of this type provide their guidance through a holistic approach which integrates such diverse fields as philosophy, psychology, religion and practical science.

Many Westerners mistakenly identify Yoga as an Eastern religion, equating it with Hinduism because of its similar trappings and the fact that it has its roots in Indian culture, which is traditionally Hindu. But to assume that Yoga is Hinduism just because its discoverers were Hindus is comparable to assuming that the theory of relativity is Jewish simply because Einstein was a Jew.

Though it is true that Yoga is related to the field of religion in that its concerns are primarily spiritual in nature, it is still first and foremost a science. This is attested to by the fact that it is currently being practiced by people of every religious persuasion, including ministers, priests, nuns, rabbis, and even atheists. Pure spiritual science gives each of us the space to follow the dictates of our own conscience throughout the exploration of our inner being. If, for example, we happen to be Christian, Yoga's goal is not to turn us into Hindus, but to help us to become better Christians.

Practitioners of yogic science are provided with a meticulous philosophy which instills in them an intellectual understanding of ultimate reality, including the true nature of their own being, the true nature of the entire Creation, and the true relationship between the two. In addition, Yoga encompasses true psychology (the word literally means "soul science") in that it offers us specific techniques of self-study through which we are brought to know and experience the depth and breadth of our entire being, thereby laying claim to all our dormant capabilities and putting them to work for us. Next, Yoga contains the very essence of religion, teaching us to love and serve the highest cosmic truth, and to disregard illusion.

To support us in this exploration for absolute truth, Yoga lastly supplies us with the sturdy framework of an exacting and pragmatic science. This science does not deal in mere hypothesis or dry intellectual concepts; it is a practical, empirical discipline which offers us precise step-by-step methodology leading to our personal validation of its doctrines through direct experience.

Siddha Yoga

While all valid spiritual sciences have a common goal, usually referred to as "Self-realization" or "Enlightenment," each offers us a unique approach to that goal, an approach which has been deliberately designed for those of us with a particular type of temperament and specific personal inclinations.

Siddha Yoga, the main topic of this book, is one such science. Although it was introduced to the general public little more than a decade ago, its practitioners already number in the hundreds of thousands, and there are hundreds of Siddha Meditation centers scattered across the globe.

Despite its recent appearance on the spiritual-science scene, however, the history of Siddha Yoga stretches far back into antiquity, and the reason its masters have at last made it available to the modern public is also the reason for its sudden phenomenal growth and popularity: its approach seems uniquely compatible with the needs and capabilities of today's seekers. In the first place, this is not a path for recluses, demanding that we turn our backs upon the world in order to attain our inner unfolding. On the contrary, Siddha Yoga is tailor-made for the worldly person who wants to pursue personal growth while at the same time enjoying a full and rich social, professional and family life.

Practitioners of this science strive to enjoy the best of both worlds—inner and outer—by including as aids to their psychic development things which other disciplines consider to be impediments. Hence, while some people think of Yoga practitioners as social dropouts, the average Siddha students are model contemporary citizens—with one notable exception: while outwardly living normal worldly lives, Siddha students are at the same time becoming inwardly transformed, gradually attaining self-awareness and activating all their dormant psychic powers as well, evolving into truly rare individuals with uncommon capabilities and enviable personal contentment.

Another specialty of Siddha Yoga is its complete lack of secrecy. Unlike most other spiritual sciences, which traditionally initiate new practitioners in solitude, initiation into Siddha Yoga is conducted in an open forum and involves no mysterious rites which must be veiled in secrecy. Moreover, every Siddha Meditation center throughout the world is open for public scrutiny at all times, and all Siddha students are encouraged to speak freely and openly about their personal experiences resulting from the practice of this Yoga.

Such an up-to-date approach does not in any way compromise the effectiveness of this ancient science because these features are not ones which have been recently imposed simply to attract more students; rather they are an integral part of this Yoga and its basic philosophy, Kashmir Shaivism, which also dates back untold thousands of years. Exactly why such a venerable philosophy is suddenly becoming "ultra-modern" will be explained in the course of this text, and also included will be sections which compare the ancient assertions of this philosophy with the recent findings of contemporary science.

The final point which must be made here regarding Siddha Yoga is the one which most clearly sets it apart from other disciplines expressly designed to instigate within us an organic process of psychic development. An almost universal characteristic of all valid spiritual sciences is that the average initiate is generally required to spend many years performing special practices preparatory to the actual activation of this inner process; but in Siddha Yoga the process becomes activated in a single instant, right at the very outset of our practice, with complete safety and without any personal effort on our part.

The lone factor responsible for this incredible free boost in our ascent toward Self-realization is the Siddha Guru, a fully perfected Yoga master of such rare power and purity he can actually accomplish for us in one brief moment what is traditionally expected to take many years of self-effort.

Siddha Yoga literally means "Yoga which is received through a Siddha Guru," whose responsibility it is to activate the process of inner unfolding within us, and then to guide us through that entire process to completion, prescribing for us at every step along the way the precise techniques which will accelerate our progess to the maximum extent possible, according to our individual capacity.

The Yoga we will be investigating throughout the following pages is a simplified encapsulation of a monumental system of philosophy, psychology, religion and practical science, all integrated into a cohesive, comprehensive discipline of personal evolution.

This ancient science is the product of an elite lineage of consummate spiritual technologists whose current patriarch is Swami Muktananda Paramahansa. The title of *swami* indicates that he is a member of a particular order of yogic monks, and during initiation into this order he also left his family name behind to be called *Muktananda,* a Sanskrit term meaning "the bliss of Liberation." Then, after a period of intense study and practice, his Yoga master awarded him the highest honor in the field of yogic science —the accolade of *paramahansa*—which signifies the attainment of complete and permanent Self-realization.*

Muktananda, affectionately called "Baba" (Father) by those who follow his spiritual guidance, is the world-renowned Siddha Guru who has brought this unique science to Western shores. Now in his seventies, Baba is still a veritable dynamo of spiritual power, a living embodiment of the universal truths he teaches; and, according to the testimony of current Siddha students, he is actually able to transmit to those in his presence an experience of the state that he himself has attained, giving them a preview of what their own lives will be like once they fully activate all their dormant capabilities.

As our study unfolds throughout the following pages, we will discover exactly what makes Baba Muktananda's Siddha Yoga a safe, natural, easy and spontaneous route to Self-realization, a path which he assures us can be followed by virtually any one of us with guaranteed success, regardless of our age, background, credo, or previous experience with spiritual science.

*NOTE: A guide to the correct pronunciation of the yogic terms employed throughout this text will be found on pages 319 and 320.

About This Guidebook

The quest for Self-realization is often likened to scaling a mountain, with each valid spiritual science a different pathway leading to the summit. Though all such paths take us to the same pinnacle, each wends its way there by a unique route, covering peculiar terrain and requiring special skills of its climbers. Therefore, it is not only essential for each of us to locate a pathway guaranteed to lead us to the highest peak, it is also imperative that we find one which truly suits us.

With this in mind, the following presentation has been styled in such a way that each of us, regardless of our background, might come away with a basic understanding of both spiritual science in general and Siddha Science in particular, thus enabling us to competently determine whether or not this path seems worthy of further exploration. The teachings which will be presented during the general survey section of our text are assertions commonly encountered among the many valid schools of yogic science, while those chapters which deal exclusively with the Siddha Path will focus mainly upon the teachings of Baba Muktananda and his lineage.

This said, our overview of the entire mountain now begins at its very base, with an examination of the single most essential technique in the field of spiritual science: the practice of meditation.

Part One

Why Meditate?

1. Our Quest for Happiness

The musk deer is a small animal inhabiting central and eastern Asia. Near the navel of the male, there is a special gland which produces a delightful, odorous secretion known as musk, used extensively in perfumes. Though this secretion is designed primarily to attract the female deer, the male himself is also intoxicated by its aroma—but he can't figure out where it's coming from.

He first experiences this intoxication as a fawn, feeding from his mother's breast, so naturally he assumes that the sublime aroma is coming from his mother: he associates intoxication with maternal care. Then, as a youngster gamboling through the meadows, he catches whiffs of the divine essence from time to time, when the wind is just right, and he decides that it's connected somehow with play. As an adolescent, he watches his father posturing magnificently on the crest of a hill, and the yearling becomes intoxicated once again, this time associating it with power and status. While munching meadow flowers or sipping sweet water, the growing deer catches occasional whiffs of the ambrosial scent and concludes that it is also connected with food and drink. As he matures, he finds intoxication in the company of female deer; and when he mates, the body-warmth of the sexual act increases the potency of his secretion and sex becomes synonymous with bliss.

He spends his days pursuing all the various activities he has learned to associate with the intoxicating scent he loves so much, but the problem is that none of these activities guarantees him an experience of drunken bliss each time; it all depends upon which way the wind is blowing. His desires become more and more fragmented; one moment he's chasing after food, and the next it's sex, power or recreation. He runs this way and that, changing directions with the wind, until finally he collapses, exhausted, to the forest floor.

His weary head hangs down until his nose is at his navel, and then, just when he least expects it, he experiences the most powerful, uninterrupted dose of divine aroma that he has ever had. In that incredible instant, he realizes that what he has been seeking frantically in other things for his entire life, has been coming from his very own being all along.

Silly deer. We're much too clever to make such a foolish error, aren't we?

Like the musk deer, we all catch whiffs of divine intoxication from time to time. Examples of this are legion: the shudder of ecstasy that sweeps over us at the first taste of a culinary masterpiece; the warm, comfortable sense of well-being we get when permitted to sample magnificent luxury; the satisfaction which comes when we finally possess an object of great desire; the feeling of fulfillment which follows a flash of inspiration; the buoyant rapture brought on by great music or beautiful scenery; and so on. In almost every instance, these all-too-brief moments of divine intoxication are experienced in conjunction with some external relationship or activity; but the biggest mistake we can make in life is to conclude from this that happiness can be received from some external source.

When we eat a piece of chocolate cake, for example, the pleasure we derive is not baked into the cake; rather, the cake somehow causes a feeling of satisfaction to well up from inside us. Even the memory of some delightful food eaten long ago can elicit a little of that same satisfaction in us. If delight were "baked right in," then everyone who eats chocolate cake would experience the same satisfaction every single time, when the fact is, many people actually dislike chocolate cake. Similarly, some people get great satisfaction out of smoking, while others find it nauseating; an acquaintance whose company we find enjoyable may impress other people as being very boring; we all find certain activities to be pleasurable one day, and a complete drag the next. If satisfaction were built into such objects, relationships and activities, then we'd all like the same things, all the time, and this is obviously not the case.

In reality, external things are only tools which we employ in the hope of eliciting satisfaction from a source which exists somewhere deep inside our own being. If we fail to understand this, we become like the puppy who chases his own tail, intent upon capturing an elusive, tantalizing phantom always glimpsed out of the corner of his eye, and which always seems to zip away at the exact moment he lunges for it. Most of us have witnessed the perplexity on a puppy's face when he finally clamps that phantom in his snapping teeth; incredulous, he learns a painful lesson: that he has just been running around in circles all the while, chasing himself.

A person who believes that happiness can be extracted from any outside source is like an animal chewing on a dry bone; as the fossil splinters and cuts its mouth, the animal feels satisfaction, not realizing that the juice it's swallowing is really just its own blood.

It is undeniably true, however, that contact with external things can result in the tapping of our inner source of satisfaction, but this approach carries with it a host of annoying, built-in restrictions. The first is that of *time*: pleasurable experiences are always temporary—they have a beginning, a middle, and an end—and when they're over, we're left to search for gratification elsewhere.

Another restriction is *availability*. Things which elicit satisfaction in us aren't always available when and where we want them. For example, we crave a chocolate cake, but the bakery is closed; we are attracted to another person, but that person isn't interested in us.

Desensitization is a third restriction to seeking happiness in external things. An object "gives" us pleasure for a while, but eventually we become bored with it; after five minutes in the presence of a delightful odor, we can no longer smell it; too much chocolate cake—or anything else—turns our gratification into repulsion, exhaustion, and even illness.

A fourth restriction is *cost*; the most pleasurable things often require a great deal of effort to obtain, and frequently they are not worth the price we have to pay for them.

Competition is still another restriction. The most satisfying things are in great demand and short supply—things such as success, power, recognition—which means we must compete for them with others; and there are always a lot more losers than there are winners.

Next, there's *indecision*. Often we just don't know what will give us satisfaction, and even when we think we know, we're often wrong.

In addition, many pleasurable pursuits are dangerous, unhealthy, illegal or immoral. Let's face it, the list of restrictions seems endless. There must be a better way.

The Better Way

According to spiritual scientists, the basic goal in life for every human being is the complete elimination of suffering and the permanent experience of happiness. Every single thing we do each day is done in the hope that it will help us to get more satisfaction out of life. To increase our pleasure and attain personal fulfillment we pursue a profession, enter into relationships, educate ourself and take part in recreational activities. Even when we eat and sleep, bathe and clothe ourself, we do so because we realize that an attractive, well-cared-for body is an essential asset in our pursuit of happiness.

As we have already learned, however, uninterrupted satisfaction is impossible to obtain through the pursuit of external things, due to the many restrictions outlined above. Such a course requires us to constantly alternate between sporadic satisfaction and periods of pain or frustration.

At this point, it becomes almost irresistible to conclude that the goal of human life as stated above is simply unattainable—that some people get closer than others, but no one is ever completely successful. This belief is very fashionable nowadays, but despite its popularity, it is false. In fact, countless people have succeeded throughout history, and millions more are presently on the road to complete success.

The method is simple. Instead of seeking to taste our inner wellspring of bliss through contact with external things, why not just eliminate the middleman and tap the inner source directly? This way, all restrictions are removed and our experience of complete gratification becomes undiminished and continuous. At the same time, we cease to identify with that part of our being which is subject to pain, thus achieving a state of total bliss, completely free of suffering. Moreover, this goal is obtainable *right now,* in this very lifetime—not in some heavenly hereafter.

The process through which one attains it is commonly known as spiritual science or *Yoga,* and the specific practice which activates this process is called *meditation.*

What we are discussing here is not mere conjecture. Yoga is a very exacting science, though admittedly a subjective one whose research is conducted in the laboratory of our own body rather than in the outside world. Though not a religion, it is decidedly "spiritual" in nature, meaning that its primary concern is with that part of our being which cannot be labeled as either "body" or "mind."

A valid scientific experiment is one which, when performed in a specific manner, produces the same results every time, regardless of who performs it. In Yoga, too, predictable results are guaranteed, provided the practitioners conduct their systematic inner research with proper guidance and in the prescribed manner laid down by the *Rishis* of India—the ancient spiritual scientists who pioneered this field.

Through meditation, many of the world's greatest beings have explored the inner realm before us—beings such as Socrates, Confucius, Milarepa, Buddha, Lao Tsu, Shankaracharya, Zoroaster, Patanjali, Nanak, Mohammed, and Jesus. Most of our religions have been built around the teachings of such masters, but when they were alive they did not teach religious dogma, they simply shared what their inner explorations had revealed to them, and their descriptions of that realm all agree on several vital points:

1. The source of all happiness, love, peace, power and wisdom lies within our very own being.

2. The essential nature of this inner wellspring is *absolute existence* (it exists eternally, without beginning or end),

absolute consciousness (its awareness is cosmic, having no limitations or restrictions), and *absolute bliss* (since it is actually made of pure joy, its pleasure is unlimited, uninterrupted, and not dependent upon anything else).

3. Once we gain access to this inner kingdom, we will attain perfect satisfaction, permanent contentment, and an end to all our pain and suffering.

4. In addition, the moment we enter this realm of supreme truth, we will perceive that everything in Creation—ourself included—is rooted in a single reality; we will come to know that the universe is a living, knowing, joyful entity, and that the essence of this cosmic entity is contained in each and every one of its innumerable parts.

5. This experience, which has been shared by countless great beings throughout history, may be enjoyed by any one of us, through meditation.

What Is Meditation?

Meditation is easy—we do it all the time. It is nothing more than being completely absorbed in whatever we happen to be doing. Remember how often we've sat with our eyes glued to a movie screen? The idea of being "glued to something" is a perfect description of total absorption, to the point where there is no longer any separation between us and the object of our concentration. When we are "glued to" a thrilling book or "glued to" the road while driving in bad weather, we are meditating; and when children are so "glued to" television that they don't hear when they are called, they too are experiencing meditation.

Our effectiveness at work, study, recreation or any other area of life is directly proportional to the level of concentration we are capable of achieving in anything we do. If we could maintain complete mental absorption constantly, in even a single area of endeavor, we would all be geniuses. The fact is, people who are not good meditators are not very successful at anything in life. It's unnatural *not* to meditate, and there is only one small difference between the kind of meditation we practice in our daily life and the kind prescribed by Yoga: When the object of our complete engrossment is outside of us, we call it "worldly involvement," and when the object is within, it's known as "meditation."

Spiritual meditation is not to be confused with prayer. In prayer, we communicate internally with a deity who is perceived to be separate from the part of us that's praying, and the existence of this deity is accepted primarily through faith. Prayer becomes meditation when this sense of separateness vanishes and we experience total union with our inner deity, whose existence then becomes verified to us through personal contact with it.

The Self

In yogic terminology, the *Self* denotes our essential nature, the central core of our entire being. Western psychology speaks of the Self in similar terms, and in other traditions throughout the world it is referred to by names such as the soul, spirit, *Atman*, anima, psyche, etc. According to Yoga, this inner Self is the *real us*, our very essence which has become suppressed due to our compulsive preoccupation with our body and our mind—the more superficial aspects of our being.

To reunite with this estranged inner Self is to tap the hidden wellspring of love, peace, power and wisdom which flows within the heart of every human being. This is not mere conjecture, but the verified experience of countless meditators over many thousands of years.

Meditation is the act of dipping into the Self for the purpose of regeneration. If each of us did not do this daily, the Rishis tell us, we could not survive. No matter how much pleasure we experience in the outside world, no matter how much wealth, power or status we accumulate, at the end of each day we are worn out. No matter who we are, at the end of each day we must renounce our worldly existence, forget all our titles and possessions, strip off our clothing, pull down the shades, turn off the lights and go to sleep.

Sleep is an inward turning, toward the Self, and only through it do we find the strength to meet the coming day.

Sleep, however, is a very inefficient, superficial contact with our inner treasure-trove. To enter its realm, we must leave our awareness behind, which is like being unconscious in paradise—we're there, all right, but we sure don't get to enjoy it much. The goal of meditation is far beyond the realm of deep sleep, and our object is to plunge into the Self with full awareness, so that all its treasures are at our command.

Will Meditation Make Me Weird?

The most-often-voiced objections to meditation have to do with the ideas that (1) meditation turns people into social "dropouts" and (2) meditation is a purely selfish act. Some people reason that since meditation is introspective, meditators therefore become introverts, social outcasts who purposely turn their backs upon all the problems of humanity in order to escape into their own little worlds and get high. Many people shun meditation because they fear it will turn them into unkempt, long-haired hippies whose only interest is in running off to live in some Tibetan cave.

Meditation is indeed introspective; it is the act of turning our awareness inward for a brief period each day in order to *enrich* our worldly life, not to escape it. Sleep is also introspective; it is the act of turning our awareness inward for approximately one-third of our entire life. Does sleep make us introverts, social dropouts, or selfish hippies?

Yoga teaches that just as everyone routinely goes to sleep each day in order to function effectively in the world, wise people also meditate for a short time each day, not only to enrich their spiritual lives, but also to further increase their effectiveness in the world. Sometimes it pays to withdraw from the world for a while, to learn how to function more efficiently in it. Going to college is a four-year withdrawal from worldly life, after which we return to society with an increased capacity for effective action in the world.

Unlike so-called self-improvement processes, which are imposed upon us from the outside, meditation is completely safe and natural, and its results are guaranteed. There is no need to be concerned that meditation might turn us into something we do not want to be. The process that works in meditation is exactly the same process that turns a flower bud into a blossom; just as that natural process could never turn a rose into a tulip, likewise meditation will never make us into anything but exactly what we already are. In other words, meditation simply helps us to blossom —to realize our fullest potential at every level of our being.

Many of our leading teachers, artists, scientists, politicians, athletes, clergy, doctors, lawyers and business people are meditators. Despite this obvious fact, some social activists decry meditation, shouting, "How can anyone sit at home in a closet meditating when there are wars, famines and countless other sufferings which need our attention *right now*?" To such people, the yogic sages present the following riddle:

> Imagine you are walking down a country road with a bucket in your hand. On a nearby hill, you see a house afire and there are people trapped inside. At the bottom of the hill a fire truck has stalled for lack of fuel. Your bucket is filled with liquid, but you can't tell whether it's water or gasoline. What should you do?

The fact is, we often do not know what long-term effect our actions will have in a given situation. The Bible tells us that the road to hell is paved with good intentions, which means that very often when we try to help, we end up only making matters worse. This is because we often do not see a situation clearly enough to know what action would be proper; all we can do is take an educated guess as to the correct course of action. Sometimes we're right, and sometimes we're wrong. Some of our actions help, while others, despite our good intentions, only hinder or have no effect at all either way. What, then, will be the resultant sum of all our actions? At the end of our life, when all our actions are balanced out, what total effect will we have had on the problems of humanity?

There will always be houses afire; there will always be opportunities to help others. What is really the wisest answer to the above riddle? If we take a chance and toss our liquid onto the fire, we face a fifty-fifty possibility of only making matters worse. If we empty our bucket into the fire-engine's gas tank, we might hopelessly foul it just before someone else arrives with gasoline. Either action would be impulsive and impetuous.

Is it possible to do *neither*, and still take positive action? Suppose we take our bucket home instead, determined to find out exactly what's inside before we try to serve humankind. If we elect this course, we may be accused of being a selfish dropout by some people, but those who are wise will say that we are acting with prudence and in the long run the positive effects of our action will be far-reaching indeed.

Meditation is the act of finding out what's in our bucket. It's the process of plunging into that part of our being which knows the proper action to take in every situation. Why? Because the inner Self is a part of the universal mind, which psychologists call the Collective Unconscious. Immersed in this Self, we can see the entire situation rather than just a fragment as we usually do; thus, we not only know exactly where each element is in the overall scheme of things, we can also see where it's been and where it's supposed to be going. In every instance we discern precisely what to do to help, and then we act, with force and confidence.

During the early stages of our meditation practice, some of us may indeed cut down on our external activity for a while, but this is only because we are performing fewer *negative* or *useless* actions. Temporarily we may be doing less, but with more positive effect than all our random activity produced before. There is a very important distinction between action simply for action's sake and proper action taken only when required. Gradually, as our meditations take us closer to the Self, our positive actions will increase as the negative ones continue to subside.

When we think about our daily life on a purely practical level, meditation makes sense. As everyone will agree, *homo sapiens* is a multi-dimensional being consisting of a body, a mind, and something more nebulous which is often referred to as "a spirit." We know that if we spend a little time each day exercising and nurturing our body and mind, our effectiveness in life becomes greatly increased. Clearly, then, this effectiveness must be impaired when we remain out of touch with the spiritual aspect of our being. Throughout the world, millions of modern-day people from every walk of life are discovering that a short time each day spent in inner contemplation is precisely what's been missing from their lives.

Many of us may be leery of meditation because we are afraid of what we may find if we look too deeply inside ourselves. Despite the assurances of all the great beings who have explored this path before us, we choose instead to believe the lesser-but-louder ones who take delight in telling us our hearts are filled with sin and evil. If we really and truly believe that, then we might as well just put this book away—it's not for us. Yoga teaches that the greatest evil, the worst sin, the most heinous crime is to have a low opinion of ourself. If we are going to take someone else's word for it regarding the true nature of our deepest being, why should we choose to believe the spiritual midgets instead of the giants? Better yet, why don't we simply look inside and find out for ourself?

Part Two

The Mechanics
of Meditation

1. Turning Inward

Even those of us who've had no personal experience with meditation can at least conjure up a mental image of what a meditator looks and acts like. Possibly, that image is of a rather kooky person sitting bolt-upright on the floor, petrified in a weird pretzel-legged position, lost in some kind of trance or chanting an eerie pagan tune, oblivious to everyone and everything around. It's true that meditation does involve some tactics which at first glance may seem absurd or meaningless; even experienced meditators often do not appreciate the full significance of the techniques which they themselves employ. As we examine the mechanics of meditation in this section, we will discover that the practices which Yoga recommends are neither bizarre nor arbitrary, but based upon solid practicality.

Over the past several-thousand years, countless writers and teachers have elaborated upon the terse instructions laid down by the ancient Rishis. Rather than improving upon these already perfect yogic precepts, however, the endless embellishments have only served to obscure the firm practical foundation upon which Yoga is built. This is why the beginning meditator today is often faced with a hodgepodge of contradictory information regarding the correct method of practice.

To eliminate this problem, we need merely get back to basics. In the brief sections which follow, we will emphasize only those aspects of meditative technique which are essential, explaining exactly why Yoga recommends them. Once we understand the solid practicality behind the yogic precepts, we will then know how to apply them creatively to our own practice for maximum benefit according to our specific needs.

The Golden Rule of Yoga

Yoga is a science. As such, its researchers are expected to examine its merits with a genuinely scientific attitude, meaning that we should be neither so gullible that we believe with blind faith everything we're told, nor so close-minded that we automatically reject ideas which seem new or unusual.

The Golden Rule of Yoga is this: *Use Your Discrimination*. In applying this rule to the technical aspects of meditation, we must understand that there is never just one right way to fulfill a condition recommended by Yoga; the "right way" is simply the one that works best for us, and it may change from time to time as our practice progresses. The Rishis advise us to never do anything which seems wrong to us, and to always try to accomplish the most with the least amount of effort.

The Inner World

When we enter a dark movie theater on a sunny day, for the first few minutes our eyes are so accustomed to the bright light outside that we cannot even discern which seats are occupied and which are vacant. Learning to perceive the Self is a bit like this, because our inner realm is very subtle compared to the solid physical world we're used to dealing with each day. When we begin to turn our awareness inward, some time and patience are required until our senses make the necessary adjustment.

Just as our outer world is easier to perceive than our inner world, the physical and mental aspects of our being are easier to experience than those which lie deeper. So, when we first begin to practice self-awareness, we might well be led to falsely assume that there is nothing more to us than just our body and mind. In ordinary states of consciousness, our self-awareness is mostly limited to our body and mind because their normal state is agitation—neither can keep still for very long—and their constant activity easily draws our attention away from the deeper, more quiet part of us. This incessant fidgeting becomes a great distraction when we attempt to experience that which lies beyond our body and mind.

In the initial stages of meditation practice, our primary goal is to minimize these distractions. Technically speaking, meditation is simply the process of learning to do nothing at all—to completely still both body and mind—so that the Self can be directly perceived. Each and every meditative practice is designed specifically to aid us in this endeavor.

2. Stage One: Body Control *(Asana)*

The body position which Yoga recommends for meditation is expressly designed to discourage fidgeting while at the same time permitting us to relax without feeling inclined toward sleep. Since we are already programmed to go to sleep when we lie down, it's preferable to use a sitting position when practicing meditation.

The most essential aspect of *asana* is that our spine be held erect without tension, thus encouraging the free movement of vital energy during meditation. The exact nature of this energy will be discussed later, so for now we need only point out that its axis in the human body is the spinal column. Poor posture (a rounded back) impedes the flow of energy, as does good posture with muscle strain (using the back muscles to hold the spine erect).

FIGURE I

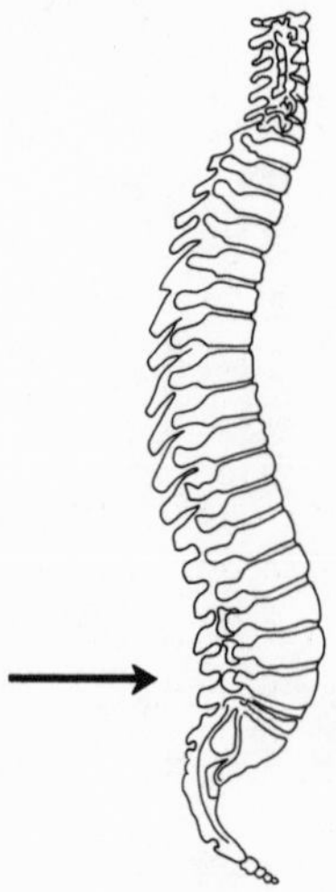

THE HUMAN SPINE

In Figure 1 we see that an erect human spine is not completely straight, but rather serpentine with a pronounced inward arch in the lower back, or lumbar, area.

The tapering thickness and curved structure of this spinal axis combine to make it an extremely strong supporting column. However, the spine is also very flexible, so it must be set properly before it becomes capable of supporting the entire weight of our head and torso without any help from the back muscles.

First, the top of the pelvis should be thrust forward with the abdomen relaxed; then the shoulders should be stretched backward, and relaxed. Unless we can completely relax in this position without slumping forward, muscular tension will cause backaches and inhibit the flow of energy. If some sort of back support seems necessary for us to achieve good posture without stress it should be used, and if back or leg tension makes it difficult to sit on the floor with a comfortably erect spine, we should improvise alternatives such as the following:

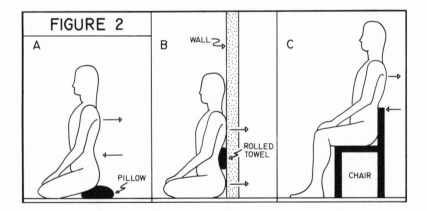

In extreme cases, when *no* sitting position is feasible, we may even meditate lying down. Though, as stated before, the supine position has drawbacks, many people still learn to meditate quite effectively this way.

Mudra

A *mudra* is a seal which prevents the loss of energy during meditation. The various leg crossings which Yoga recommends are mudras and are considered secondary in importance to good posture without tension. For those who find it comfortable to sit cross-legged, however, this is the preferred position, and for the few of us whose legs are extremely flexible, any good Hatha Yoga book will explain the more advanced positions and their added benefits.

A hand mudra serves the twofold purpose of sealing in energy and discouraging the hands from fidgeting during meditation. The mudra most often recommended for this purpose is called *chin-mudra*, shown in Figure 3. With the hands in this position, they may be placed comfortably anywhere on the thighs or knees, palms upward or downward. Meditation texts also describe other acceptable positions, such as simply folding the hands in the lap.

FIGURE 3

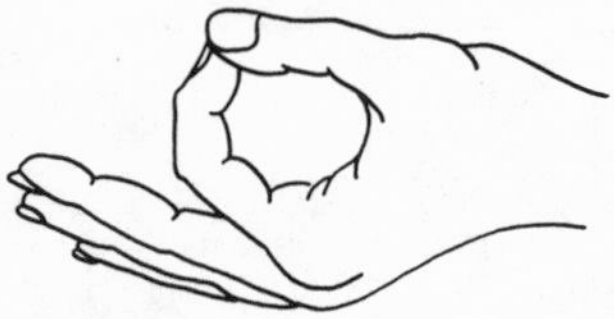

CHINMUDRA

Since energy can also escape from the mouth and eyes, these should be kept closed during meditation. Some yogic texts recommend more-difficult eye positions, such as staring at the tip of the nose or between the brows, which sound pretty silly until we accept the fact that exhaustive research has shown such positions to be effective methods of recycling energy emanating from the eyes. However, simply closing the eyes is also effective, and though it has the drawback of inclining us toward sleep, this mudra is better for most people than the more difficult ones, and it is the mudra employed by most successful meditators.

These are the basic elements of asana. When applied thought-fully and with discrimination, they provide valuable assistance in our practice of body control. Through repetition of a meditative posture, our body becomes increasingly more stable, and as soon as we are satisfied that a comfortable posture has been achieved, our attention can then move to the next level of meditation.

3. Stage Two: Mind Control

The ordinary human mind thinks about life but never experiences it. Instead of perceiving the present moment directly, our mind must rely upon information received from the sensory organs. Our senses pick up *ex*ternal vibrations and relay them to the brain in the form of *in*ternal vibrations; the brain then processes these, correlating and reconciling them with impressions already stored; and finally, the mind reacts, acknowledging and evaluating the event perceived. What our mind experiences as the present moment is really just the recent past, after it's been processed, refined, packaged and labeled. This "present moment" bears about as much resemblance to true reality as white sugar does to a living sugarcane plant.

When it's not busy processing incoming impressions, our mind busies itself by mulling over memories, creating and solving problems, and fantasizing about the future. Since the unstable mind functions only in the past and future, while the Self exists only in the eternal present, we can experience the Self only when the mind becomes stable.

A Stable Mind

A stable mind is one which has become completely free of all thought-agitations. In meditation the mind is encouraged to suspend its activity, and because of this some people assume that meditators become dull-minded. This could not be further from the truth, for in fact a stable mind is the exact opposite of a dull one. Such extremes often seem very much alike to us; for example, our eyes can see neither very low nor very high vibrations of light, so both conditions appear to us as "darkness," though in reality there is a world of difference between the two states. The difference between a stable mind and a dull one is like the difference between a spinning top and one which is slowing down, wobbling to a stop. The stable mind is completely vibrant, fully aware and perfectly balanced, so there is no agitation to obscure our perception of the inner Self which lies behind it.

To fully understand this difference, we need only think back to times when intense excitement forced our mind out of its past-future warp. Sensual indulgences, roller coasters, monster movies, daredevil feats—these are some of the things we utilize in order to stabilize the agitated mind just long enough for us to get a brief hit of exhilaration from our inner wellspring of bliss. Rather than feeling dull-minded at such times, the experience we have is one of *super*-consciousness.

By far, our very favorite method of stabilizing the mind in daily life is through the fulfillment of desire. Throughout our waking hours we constantly lapse into daydreams built around the desire for things we feel would make our life complete. *If only I could be a famous movie star, how happy I would be! If only I could possess that sex object, life would be pure heaven! If only I could get a promotion, all my problems would be over!*

Then one day the manager of our department tells us he is leaving and we are being considered to replace him. Suddenly our mind becomes obsessed with desire for that promotion; for days we can think of nothing else, and we are sure that we will *die* if we don't get it. We work harder at our present job; we "sell" ourself to the boss at every opportunity; we dream about the status that the new title would bring; and we make lists of all the wonderful things we would be able to buy with the additional income. All our other desires have become eclipsed by a single, all-pervasive want: DEPARTMENT MANAGER.

Finally, the boss calls us into his office and tells us that the promotion is ours! What perfect Bliss! What indescribable Joy! We have never been so Happy in our entire life! But gradually, as the days turn into weeks and the weeks into months, our daydreams return as persistent as ever, filled with the desire for all sorts of new things which we feel would make our life "more" complete.

Chances are each one of us has starred in countless little dramas such as this, always telling ourself, "This one is really *it*—this time I'll win some lasting happiness." In every instance we are convinced that the object we desire is the source of the happiness we seek, despite the obvious fact that the more we get, the more we seem to want.

In reality, the fulfillment of desire brings us happiness only to the extent that our mind becomes stabilized in the process. According to spiritual scientists, what really happened in the above episode is this: The mind began to dwell on just one desire, then suddenly that desire was fulfilled, and for a short time the mind became completely disarmed, stabilizing just long enough for a flash of bliss to burst through from the inner Self. As soon as the mind recovers from such shocks of satiation, however, it begins to function in its usual way again, becoming agitated with more desires. As long as we continue to be guided by the mind, we will spend the rest of our days chasing one thing after another; and our death will be tragic and painful, because even as we draw our final breath, the mind will urgently proclaim that our life has not yet been fulfilled.

Meditation and The Mind

In the second stage of meditation practice, our goal becomes to still all mental agitations so that we can reach beyond the mind and immerse ourself in the supreme bliss of our essential nature. The moment we succeed in transcending the mind and plugging into the inner Self, we need no longer seek to extract happiness from external things; instead, we will now be able to *inject* happiness into everything around us all the time.

Our meditation practice begins to focus upon the mind more and more as our body becomes less and less distracting to us; the quieter our body is in meditation, the more our attention is able to center upon the workings of our mind. At this point, we will probably discover that when we first begin to aim our full attention at the mind, it will suddenly become alarmingly hyperactive. This is a natural occurrence for which Yoga provides a spectrum of remedies, the main ones involving either willful force, the practice of witness-consciousness, or the repetition of a spiritual *mantra*.

1. Willful Force. Any of us who elect this course and attempt to still the mind willfully are certain to learn very soon that we have set ourselves an extremely difficult task. When most people try to still an overactive mind with force, they find that the situation only gets worse. If someone says to us, "Try not to think of a monkey," chances are that a monkey will immediately jump into our mind, and the more we try to oust the obstinate simian from our thoughts, the more it will obsess us. Trying to still the mind willfully is like trying not to think of a monkey. It's a course recommended only for those of us with iron wills or fairly quiet minds during meditation.

2. Witness-Consciousness. According to Yoga, one of the easiest ways to experience the deepest aspect of our being is to simply disregard the mind when we meditate. Just as the heart's job is to beat, the mind's job is to think; and just as we don't expect the heart to stop beating when we meditate, we need not expect the mind to stop thinking. Rather, we may choose to equate our thoughts with clouds in the sky, obscuring the sun of the Self; instead of bothering about the clouds, we may simply concern ourself with looking past them, striving to glimpse the light which lies beyond. The technique of not identifying with our mind in meditation is called practicing witness-consciousness. This technique is much simpler than stilling the mind through forcible restraint, but to understand how it works we will have to take a moment to consider exactly to whom we refer when we use the pronoun "I."

Yoga tells us that the most important question a human being can ask is: "Who am I?" Until we thoroughly understand and experience the most accurate answer to this question, all other questioning is absurd, for how can we effectively understand the true nature of anything we examine if we don't even know the true nature of the examiner? Yoga is the process of understanding and experiencing the ultimate answer to the question "Who am I?"

The easiest way to illustrate that most of us do not have a clear idea about who we really are is to look at the ways we refer to ourselves in normal conversation. For instance, when we say, "I am John Doe," or "I am a doctor," we are identifying with our name or profession; but when we say, "My name is John Doe," or "My profession is medicine," we indicate that these labels merely *belong* to us—they are not who we really are.

When we say, "I am sick," "I am hungry" or "I'm too fat," we are identifying with the body; but when we say something like, "I almost broke every bone in my body," we are indicating that the body is just one of our possessions. Exactly what part of us is the owner implied by our statement?

Could it be the mind? We say, "I think such-and-such," "I remember so-and-so," "I'm smart (or stupid)," etc., indicating that indeed we are the mind; but what about the times we say, "My mind was a blank," "My mind's getting tired," or "I am trying to improve my mind"? Who is the owner of our mind to which we then refer?

Could it be the Self? Certainly not the self we speak of when we say, "I did everything myself," "I thought only of myself," etc., because there's that little possessive pronoun *my* again, indicating that our normal impression of "self" is nothing more than our most superficial characteristics—body, mind, name, job, etc. —all rolled into one. This "self" is but a shadow of its true owner, the pure, perfect, blissful inner Self—and how many of us really *know* this part of our being?

The practice of witness-consciousness is the subtle act of differentiating between the limited "self" and the limitless *Self* which lies beyond it. Once we clearly understand the difference between these two terms, the following statement should be clear as well: *Meditation is not being concerned only with yourself, it's being concerned only with your Self!*

The Self perceives the universe through both the body (senses) and the mind (ego-intellect). True Yoga teaches us to respect and care for both body and mind with great reverence because they are our most valuable possessions, but we are warned that these are valuable to us only if they are used as vehicles to help us seek the Self. If we become deluded into thinking that the body and mind are *us*, rather than our instruments, we become vulnerable to endless pain and anguish. Thus, Yoga tells us, it is imperative that we begin to identify with the Self rather than its instruments, and when we do this we are practicing witness-consciousness. Simply stated, witness-consciousness is looking at everything from the point of view of the Self.

How do we begin to get a handle on this elusive Self which lies beyond the mind, and why is it called a witness? If we have ever been in a state of extreme excitement due to anger, fear, sorrow or whatever, we may have noticed that no matter how upset our body and mind were, there still seemed to be some part of us which just calmly stood back and watched everything quite impersonally. At any rate, most of us have surely experienced occasions in which we were fast asleep and dreaming, while some other part of us remained aloof and reminded us that it was all a dream. This part of us which never sleeps is the witness who greets us when we awaken each morning and tells us whether we've dreamed or did not dream. This one who witnesses dispassionately from some point beyond our mind is the very Self which we seek, and it is through the practice of witness-consciousness that we become more and more established in the Self, making more and more of its treasures available to us.

3. Mantra. The easiest way of all to still the mind is by using the natural workings of the mind itself to lead our awareness to the Self. This is accomplished through the mental repetition of a yogic *mantra*. Since this subject is covered in detail later, we need only say a few words here to indicate how the science of *mantra* uses the mind to transcend itself.

In Mantra Yoga, sound vibrations are utilized to affect the energy structure of a person or object. Since all thoughts are vibrations, *mantra* meditation involves the constant mental repetition of certain syllables—special "thoughts" whose vibratory effect is to refine our awareness and modulate it upward to higher and higher levels of the mind until eventually the very limits of the mind are reached and transcended, leading us right to spontaneous witness-consciousness. Through mantra meditation, Yoga offers us a simple-to-use, highly effective means of bypassing many of the obstacles inherent in the quest for Self-realization, and exactly how this is accomplished will be our concern at a more appropriate point further on in our investigation.

4. The Ideal Environment for Meditation

If we were to walk into a discotheque right now, chances are the atmosphere there would not make us feel like taking a nap. In a cathedral, we'd probably not feel like shouting and chasing about. This is because environments have a distinct effect on the way we are inclined to behave. By the same token, there are certain surroundings which make it easier for us to meditate, and Yoga provides us with some valuable guidelines in that regard.

It is not necessary for everyone to adhere rigidly to all the recommendations discussed below; rather, we should each feel free to create our own uniquely personal meditation environment, using the guidelines for general reference. If our present living situation makes some of the recommendations seem impractical, or if our religious or philosophical beliefs make us feel uncomfortable about some of the tools which Yoga recommends, we should simply disregard these for the time being. Remember, the techniques of Yoga are designed to help us *overcome* obstacles, not to burden us with more. With these precautions in mind, let's examine briefly what Yoga describes as the optimal environment for meditation.

Physical Environment

Since external distractions make it difficult to direct our attention inward, the place in which we meditate should be as dark and quiet as possible. Ideally, a small room should be set aside solely for meditation, but where this is impractical any comfortable area may be selected—preferably one in which no other activity will take place. Each time we enter a space in which we have performed only one activity repeatedly, we tend to be more easily drawn toward the performance of that same activity.

The decorations we choose for our meditation area should also be selected with the same idea in mind. Each of us should include whatever items best help us to feel closer to the inner Self. Some of us will prefer the more traditional form which includes a formal altar and pictures of great beings who have realized the Self through meditation; others will find that personal items which elicit love or devotion in us are the most effective.

This approach also applies to the clothing we wear for meditation. It is better to have a special outfit which is not used for any other activity, but beyond this, any loose-fitting, comfortable garment is fine.

Since all decorations and equipment used for meditation are either symbolic of the inner Self or representative of our intent to experience the Self, these items should be treated with great respect at all times.

Everyone who meditates experiences the fact that internal energy is amplified. Some spiritual sciences liken the human body to an electromagnetic core with the positive pole at the head and the negative at the feet. The energy field around this core is called the human aura, which can now be photographed by scientists. In the average person (Fig. 4-A) this energy field is weak, bottom-heavy due to the pull of gravity, and much of it is dissipated without being recycled. The person who meditates daily, however, produces a strong, positive aura which resists the pull of gravity and minimizes dissipation (Fig. 4-B).

In meditation, the polarity of the body is reversed and our energy is recycled with much greater efficiency. This reversed flow, however, is adversely affected by the energy field of the earth (Fig. 5-A) unless an insulating material is placed between the meditator and the ground (Fig. 5-B). The yogic Rishis tell us that the best material for this purpose is wool (preferably white) and it is for this reason Yoga recommends that we place a woolen mat or blanket beneath us when we meditate.

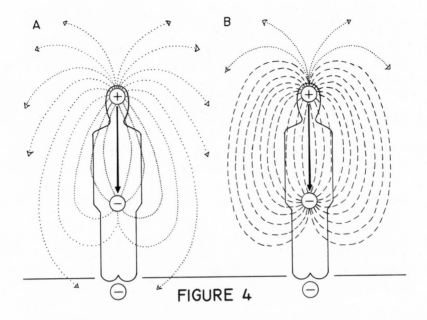

FIGURE 4

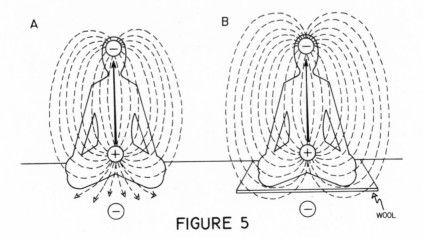

FIGURE 5

This sort of energy control is the basis of every physical technique of Yoga, and since most of us are not aware of the incredible swirling ocean of energy which surrounds and fills us, many of the recommendations Yoga makes in this regard seem strange to us. For example, we are told that the best direction to face during meditation is either East or North, if practical, and the best times of day for meditation are dawn and dusk. Each of these suggestions has to do with arranging the most favorable flow of energy, both within our own being and in relationship to the world around us. Even when we are advised to meditate with an empty stomach it's because after a meal so much energy is consumed in the process of digestion that little is available for meditation.

In short, to minimize the *physical* dissipation of energy during meditation, Yoga offers us advice in the following areas: (1) asana (including body posture and insulated seat), (2) compass direction, (3) time of day and (4) diet. Every other recommendation we are given has to do with arresting the *mental* dissipation of energy.

Mental Environment

The mind is our greatest spendthrift of vital energy; the more it fidgets, the more energy we waste. Bringing the wandering mind under gradual control can be a difficult, tricky business, and in this endeavor Yoga advises that our most powerful support lies in the practice of *ritual*.

A yogic ritual is any action repeatedly performed for the explicit purpose of directing our awareness toward the Self. Daily meditation is of course our most important ritual, and the more ritualistically our meditation is performed each day, the more benefit we can derive. Ideally, meditation should be performed each day at the same time and place, in the same way, because ritual becomes second nature through constant repetition. Just as athletes develop their own unique rituals of thoughts and actions which they run through before every event in order to bring themselves to peak performance level, so each of us should develop our own personal ritual to focus all our energy on meditation.

Though the rituals recommended by Yoga are also employed by many religions, the rituals themselves are not religious; they are simply known to be the most effective techniques in helping us to focus both our mind and senses on the inner Self. Religions use them for the same reason meditators do—because they work.

One such ritual is kneeling and bowing. Though the current religious connotation of this ritual act is that of "groveling" or placing one's self in a submissive relationship to some external will, the true meaning of this ritual is quite different. Kneeling and bowing are meant as gestures of Self-affirmation, not Self-denial. Kneeling is a gesture of humility, which is traditionally recognized as one of the finest qualities a human being can possess. Today humility is thought to be synonymous with self-abasement, but in reality it is a sign of enormous strength. The king who abdicates his throne and becomes a beggar is practicing self-abasement, not humility, showing that he is incapable or unwilling to fulfill his responsibilities as sovereign. However, the king who, as a dinner guest, chooses to seat himself at the foot of the table rather than at its head, is still a king, but in displaying humility he shows us that his power is so great that he need not rely on external signs of status for support.

Bowing is the simple act of placing the head below the heart. Meditators bow before and after meditation with the understanding that they are bowing to their own inner Self, and when they bow to some external thing they only do so with the understanding that the object they are bowing to is symbolic of their own Self.

Traditionally, meditators light a candle and incense before meditation; often they ring a small bell and chant certain mantras. Again, these rituals are not utilized because religions use them, but because they effectively enthrall the senses and focus the mind on our inner Self. The flame represents the light of the Self, as actually perceived in meditation; similarly the incense, bell and mantras are all employed because of the resemblance they bear to things we experience inside us during meditation.

Many people will find these traditional rituals to be valuable assets, but in the event that some of us do not, it is far better to simply set them aside for the time being rather than use our resistance to them as an excuse to suspend our meditation practice. The purpose of ritual is to help, not hinder us in meditation, and a ritual is only effective if it truly reminds us of the inner Self; otherwise it is an empty ritual, a waste of time. Mental ritual is much more potent than that which is merely an outward show. Kneeling is meaningless unless it is performed through a desire to learn humility; bowing is meaningless unless performed with an attitude of Self-reverence, or at least a desire to acquire such an attitude.

Within the framework of each individual's ethics and philosophy, some set of rituals should be evolved to systematically lead our mind away from agitation and toward the stillness of the Self.

5. The Need for Self-Discipline

Spiritual scientists remind us that one of the hardest lessons for most of us to learn is the fact that getting something for nothing in this world is simply an impossible dream. Though we are willing to put in long hours of hard work each day just to earn the material things we want in life, when it comes to spiritual growth many of us expect to find some magic formula that will bring us great rewards with little or no effort. Thus, we become suckers for every new fad which promises that miracle we seek, and in the end the only ones who profit are the conmen who hoodwink us into believing they can give us what they themselves don't have.

Common sense tells us that self-improvement can never be achieved without expert guidance and personal effort. Just think how long we all must attend school merely to learn how to function in society, or how much guidance, effort and discipline are required in order for us to become adept at any human skill or profession. Is it reasonable, then, for any of us to expect something as valuable as Self-realization to be handed to us on a silver platter?

Meditation is the simple act of setting aside a small portion of our day just to be alone with ourself, to increase Self-awareness so that we can function in life with more authority and satisfaction. It requires self-discipline to learn, just as when we were young it took parental discipline to get us into bed at night, to make us eat at mealtime, and to teach us to bathe and clothe ourself properly. Now these disciplines are second nature to us and we can clearly see that the little bit of discipline we endured in the beginning was well worth the effort. Meditation is even more essential to our day than the disciplines of body maintenance, only now we no longer have our parents to urge us on, so unless we have tremendous will-power, we need a meditation teacher to guide us in our practice.

Even though it does require discipline, however, we should remember that meditation is meant to make life easier for us, not more of a chore. It is up to each of us to make our meditation practice something we genuinely look forward to, even when it's inconvenient (just as we always manage to eat, even when it's inconvenient). As more and more of the rewards become apparent in our life, our motivation will automatically increase.

Once a great spiritual teacher was walking down a country road with a group of his students and they passed a field in which a farmer was digging for water. Having already dug four dry wells, each fifty feet deep, the farmer was now wearily digging his fifth well, with tears of frustration streaming down his face. The master said to his students, "Behold what a great fool this man is! He has dug four wells of fifty feet without success; now he begins another and the only water he has to show for his labor is that which flows from his eyes. If he had dug just one well, 100 feet deep, he would not only have saved a lot of space, time and effort, he would also have tapped the underground spring by now."

The students understood that their master was using the frus-trated farmer to teach them all an important lesson about life. Chances are, each one of us has left some dry wells lying aban-doned in our past, too. How many times have we begun a certain discipline which promises to yield us happiness, digging with great enthusiasm through the soft topsoil; but then, when the going gets a little tough, when our shovel gets stuck in clay, roots or stones, we suddenly have second thoughts, asking ourself, "Is this really the right place to dig?" At this point some kibbitzer always comes along, peers down the hole at us and scoffs, "What are you digging *there* for? Everyone knows there's no happiness down *there!* You should be digging over where I'm digging!" So we climb out of the hole, rest a bit and begin a new hole somewhere else, this time certain that we're right. If we're not careful, one day our life will be over and when we look back across the years to see what we have left to show for all our efforts, all we'll see is an endless trail of empty holes.

Each of us knows that sooner or later we must pick some system of self-fulfillment and resolve to keep digging away at it until we strike pay dirt. The yogic prospectors who have already mined the Land of Meditation assure us that we could not select a richer place to dig. In reading this book we are examining the merits of a specific self-improvement system, and should we decide that this discipline is worthy of our efforts, it is hoped that we will also resolve to keep digging until it yields its guaranteed bonanza.

Now that we understand the mechanics of meditation, it's time to examine the very heart of Yoga itself—the philosophy upon which the entire science is based. The yogic doctrine of Reality forms a unique philosophical system because it is not a dry theoretical product of the human intellect; rather it can be best described as "experiential philosophy," since the truth of its postulates may be personally experienced by each of us through the practice of meditation. No part of yogic philosophy demands belief with blind faith and there are no "unexplainable mysteries"; it is therefore a perfect philosophical system which leaves no room for argumentation because it is accompanied by a science which provides step-by-step instructions on how to verify the accuracy of its pronouncements. In the section which follows we will examine this remarkable ancient doctrine in the light of modern scientific thought, discovering exactly how and why the process of Self-realization through Yoga works inside us.

Part Three

The Philosophy
and Theory of Yoga

1. True Philosophy

The word *philosophy* means "love of knowledge." Most of us think of knowledge as the stockpile of information and ideas stored in the human brain, but truly speaking this is not real knowledge at all—it's merely "learning." The difference between knowledge and learning is like the difference between knowing someone personally and just knowing *about* that person. In other words, knowledge is learning which has been personally experienced.

True philosophy is a science which strives to know, rather than just know about, such things as the essential nature of Creation and the meaning of life. Nowadays, we generally don't think of philosophy as a science because most modern-day philosophers are idea-organizers rather than researchers; instead of embarking upon paths designed to lead them to a direct perception of universal truth, they prefer to create ingenious systems of thought which merely theorize about reality and life. Yogic philosophers, on the other hand, have no interest in intellectual theories; their only concern is with Truth they can personally experience. The Eastern Rishis were all "knowers," while most modern philosophers are merely "thinkers," and this is why in ancient times most people were in agreement about the basic nature of things, while nowadays most people are in disagreement.

The bottom line of Yoga's message to the world is this: In matters of philosophy, no one need take anyone else's word for anything, because each of us is capable of knowing the highest universal truths firsthand, by direct perception. To achieve this knowledge, we need only look inside our own being through the practice of meditation. This is not just intellectual theory drummed up in some author's mind; it's the documented accomplishment of countless meditators over thousands of years. In libraries throughout the world there are many detailed accounts by meditators from every period of history. These accounts offer firsthand descriptions of meditation experiences, and they also describe in detail the profound truths which become revealed in the course of one's inner research.

When we first begin to study these accounts, we find that many of their descriptions seem to clash with one another, suggesting that perhaps each meditator's experience of universal truth varies dramatically depending upon the era, culture, background and tradition from which he or she comes. For example, even though all of our great religions have been inspired by beings who have attained Self-realization through meditation, the basic scriptures of each religion seem to present Truth in terms and images which differ greatly from the way other religions describe it. In meditation, Hindus tend to see Hindu gods and goddesses, Christians see Christian saints, Buddhists experience the Great Void, etc. The ancient Greeks, Aztecs, Egyptians, Polynesians, etc. each perceived a completely different hierarchy of gods and goddesses.

Many people wrongly conclude from this that only the great beings from their own particular tradition have seen the "real" truth, while all the others throughout history have been deluded. Such a position is unsound, but at first glance the only other possibility seems to be that each religion must be connected to its own unique system of Truth, and that somehow all the different truths of all the world's religions are equally supreme. This possibility, however, is denied by virtually all religions, every one of which maintains that a single reality is the basis for all of Creation.

Most modern religions make no attempt to resolve this dilemma, so perhaps spiritual science can shed some light on it for us. According to yogic philosophy, all meditators experience exactly the same system of universal truth; however, the form in which that Truth presents itself can vary depending upon our personal beliefs and special needs. Yoga tells us that the face of God (meaning supreme truth or supreme reality) changes from one religion to another because each creed is specifically designed to fill the needs of certain select people, so it characterizes Truth in a manner compatible with those needs.

Truth itself is formless but it can present itself to us in many forms. Those who seek Truth through a Christian discipline may experience it in a Christian form; Buddhists may find Truth cloaked in Buddhist garb; spiritual scientists may see Truth revealed to them in non-religious form. Yogic science transcends the limited scope of all religions and presents its model of Truth in a timeless idiom, using imagery understandable to people of any era, culture, background or tradition; and in so doing it reveals the common ground out of which all the world's diverse descriptions of Truth have grown.

Should we decide to start our own meditation practice, we will probably be interested in comparing our own discoveries with what the ancient Rishis and other meditators have discovered to be the essence of universal truth. Though the *form* of this Truth as we experience it will probably reflect our personal beliefs, the *essence* should be precisely as Yoga describes it.

At this point in our investigation, some important questions have undoubtedly arisen, and these now deserve our full attention. Such questions are: If the very core of our being is this all-powerful, all-knowing, all-blissful Self, how and why did we ever lose contact with it and set ourself up for endless pain and misery? If we decide to practice Yoga meditation in order to re-establish union with our inner Self, what is the exact process of Self-realization we can expect to experience? How does this process begin; what stages will we go through along the way; and what will it be like when we reach the final goal? What are these "universal truths" which Yoga guarantees us we will personally perceive through meditation, and exactly how can we come to know the essential nature of the entire cosmos just by looking inside our own body?

To find answers to such questions, yogic scientists have systematically examined the whole of Creation to determine just what makes it "tick." Yoga philosophy is not dry theory, it's the detailed findings of ancient psychic explorers who were the very first human beings to probe the farthest reaches of Creation as well as the primal depths of their own being. The following six chapters present the barest outline of what those pioneers learned.

As we go along, in order to illustrate how effectively Yoga's language captures the essence of even the most subtle realities, we'll compare each yogic concept with corresponding ones from modern science and religion whenever possible. Through such comparisons, perhaps we will discover that the Truth of ancient spiritual science, the Truth of modern physical science, and the Truth of all religions is the exact same Truth approached from different angles.

In order to fully appreciate how and why meditation works inside us, Yoga tells us we must understand some things about the human body which are not commonly known nowadays. But before we can fully comprehend the nature and purpose of these little-known inner mechanisms, we must first become familiar with some basic information about the cosmic environment in which each human lives. If we were to study fish, for example, it would be best to begin with a thorough understanding of water, and in the same way our study of human beings would be incomplete without some appreciation of the intimate relationship which exists between our individual being and the vast cosmos of which we are a part.

Both modern and ancient science assure us that we are all made of exactly the same material as everything else in Creation, and ancient science adds that there is a remarkable relationship between our mysterious inner world and the equally mysterious universe which contains us. In order to detail this remarkable relationship, let's begin by examining the cosmos, first as modern science sees it, and then as it's perceived by yogic science.

2. The Universe of Modern Science

Newton's World

For thousands of years Oriental philosophers have been telling us that the world we live in is an illusion. It is statements such as this that have earned for Eastern sages the label ''inscrutable,'' for most modern people simply cannot understand how any responsible human being could assert that this quite obviously real and solid world does not in fact exist. If we are among those who share a firm belief that modern science will prove the ancient sages to be wrong, we will be surprised to learn that things are not working out that way at all.

The everyday world with which we are all familiar—the world which we perceive with our physical senses and interpret through our mind—is governed by the laws of classical physics laid down for the most part by Sir Isaac Newton in the sixteenth century. These natural laws were arrived at through reason, logic, and careful firsthand observation of the world around us, and our own day-to-day experience consistently seems to prove them to be true.

This Newtonian world of the mind and senses is very real to us. It is a world of solid objects separated by empty space; a world in which a mysterious force called gravity reaches across this empty space and pulls all things of substance earthward. In this world, all material objects have just three dimensions—length, width and thickness—each of which can be precisely measured, and such objects cannot just spring into existence out of nowhere; instead, they must be built up out of certain already existing basic elements. Every event in this world has a distinct beginning and end—it lasts for a specific period which again can be precisely measured—for here, time is a sequence of fixed units of duration, flowing at a constant rate no matter where we go, like identical, successive footprints marching out of a beginningless past and pacing off into an endless future.

Newton's universe is a system of perfect, clearly definable order; it runs like a gigantic, well-oiled machine with quite distinct parts, each of which serves a specific function and interacts with the other parts in a completely predictable fashion. In this universe, any event can be traced back to some initial cause, and any object can be broken down into progressively smaller constituent elements until at some point we will arrive at certain basic building blocks of substantial, indestructible "stuff" which cannot possibly be further decomposed.

Just how real is this world which is so familiar to us all?

Until this century, physicists thought that the main goals of their science were to accurately measure the objects and events of the universe and to find out just how these relate to one another. All that they needed in order to accomplish these objectives, they believed, were precision instruments capable of disclosing the exact detail of whatever they wished to observe. As scientific technology advanced, however, nature began to present her observers with some unexpected and annoying paradoxes. With every passing year, physicists have developed instruments of increasing sophistication, yet in spite of this their observations of nature still remain as imprecise as ever. No matter what level of reality they become able to look at more closely, instead of getting sharper it actually appears to be more vague the more closely they look, until gradually another, deeper, level comes into focus, revealing the previous one to have been illusory.

It seems that any attempt we make to clarify some aspect of Creation only results in introducing us to new dimensions which in turn present us with the same vagueness of resolution. To illustrate this, let's attempt to take a really close look at an object which we have already spent a great deal of time examining throughout our life: our own face. Now what could be more *real* than that thoroughly familiar countenance which greets us every morning in the bathroom mirror and looks back at us from every reflective surface throughout our day? Over the years that it's been with us, think of the many hours we have spent in careful scrutiny of its every detail—peering at a bloodshot eye, a new blemish or wrinkle, etc. How many hours have we invested washing it, moisturizing it, medicating it, shaving or cosmetizing it? But despite all this, how well do we really know our face? Have we ever actually seen the essence of it—the basic elements which make it a face instead of something else, and which make this particular face different from every other one?

Our unaided physical senses permit us a reasonably good experience of "faceness" at its most superficial level—a collection of various features such as eyes, ears, nose, mouth, cheeks, chin, etc; but if we wish to look deeper, we will have to take the assistance of scientific instrumentation, which serves to extend the normal range of our senses. Now, with the help of scientific technology, we are able to take a closer and closer look at this object we call our face, but the closer we look, the less we see of a face and the more we begin to see a vast terrain of skin cells.

The nearer we get to these, the less we see of skin cells and the more we begin to see their molecular structure. The face which we set out to observe more closely has dissolved into a landscape of skin cells, which in turn has dissolved into an orderly array of variously shaped, continually oscillating molecules. Now, as we carefully approach this vibrating network of diverse structural patterns, the less we see of it and the more we begin to see the precise arrangement of atoms which are bonded together to form each molecule.

Here, according to Newtonian physics, our excursion is expected to end, for the word *atom* means "that which is indivisible." Until the beginning of this century, atoms were thought to be the basic building blocks of our material world—solid spheres of indestructible substance which rebound off one another in a completely predictable way, like tiny billiard balls. Indeed, what could possibly be more elementary than these miniscule particles of matter, so small that one-hundred-million of them, placed side by side, would make a row only this long: _____ (one centimeter).

Sure enough, as we observe these shadowy spheres from a

distance, they do indeed appear to be solid balls of some material substance, a substance which must therefore be the very essence of not just our own face, but the entire objective universe as well. To discover the nature of this essential substance, all we need do now is take a closer look at one of these quivering atoms.

As we draw nearer, however, we note with amazement that the atom, too, becomes more vague instead of clearer. Its "solid" surface begins to appear more and more hazy, like a fog-bank which becomes less substantial the closer we approach it. Finally, we simply pass right through this misty outer shell, and as we do we hear an eerie, high-pitched musical tone, some thirty-four octaves above our normal hearing. Then, inside the atom we discover what appears to be nothing but a vast void of empty space!

At first it seems as if our atom has simply dissolved into pure nothingness, but upon closer examination we discover that this space we're in is not entirely empty after all; in fact, it contains new particles which are so much smaller than the atom that half a million of them laid side by side would barely stretch across the width of single atom! The atom, then, is not the very bottom rung of the material ladder, for it is also made up of smaller elements, infinitesimal spheres of substance arranged in much the same way as our own solar system. In the center of the atom is its nucleus, composed of particles called protons and neutrons, and spinning around this nucleus, like planets rotating around a sun, are a third type of particle called electrons.

Like our solar system, the atom consists almost entirely of empty space. The electrons are separated from one another and from the nucleus by distances which are comparatively greater than the distances between heavenly bodies in our own solar system. If we could enlarge a single atom to a diameter of fifty yards, its nucleus would be no bigger than a grain of salt, and its electrons would be like a few specks of dust circling the nucleus at a distance of twenty-five yards.

Now, let's go back to our bathroom mirror a moment and try to comprehend the significance of this discovery in terms of that face we see reflected before us. If our human body is made of cells, which are made of molecules, which are made of atoms, which are made of a little bit of "stuff" and a lot of empty space—just how substantial is our body and all the objects in the world around us?

The nucleus of an atom accounts for almost 100% of the atom's solidity, yet this same nucleus occupies only one-million-millionth of the atom's total volume; the rest is empty space. This means that if all the actual substance in our entire body could be plucked from all that empty space and packed into a compact mass, the resultant speck would be barely visible under a high-powered microscope. In fact, if we were to extract just the substantial part from every human being on earth, then pack it all together into a single mass, we would end up with a lump no bigger than a pea!

The planet we live on is a sphere of "solid" matter 8,000 miles (13,000 km) in diameter; yet, if we could remove the empty space from all its atoms and compress only the real substance into a solid chunk, the entire earth would fit quite comfortably into any major football stadium. Imagine a stadium full of dust being hit by a cosmic hurricane which lifts the dust particles into the air and disburses them throughout an area of space 1.5 trillion cubic miles in size. That's how *solid* our world really is.

How does this reality compare with what our senses tell us? As we stare at ourself in the bathroom mirror, can we really fathom the fact that we are looking at almost completely empty space? Despite what we seem to see, only $\frac{1}{1,000,000,000,000}$ of our body is solid substance, which means that 99.9999999999% of it is empty space.

But no matter how often such information forces us to realize the awesome difference between the true nature of the world and the way we all perceive it to be, our right understanding soon erodes away under the steady stream of false testimony furnished by our own eyes, which constantly assure us there is dense substance filling matter, when in fact there is almost none. As Plato aptly put it, "Our prison house is the world of sight."[1]

How can matter be so airy, yet look and feel so solid? As we observe our sample atom through more advanced instrumentation, we discover that it's the movement of atomic particles which accounts for the solid appearance of matter, and it's the electrical forces acting upon these particles which give matter its solid feel.

Each electron circles its nucleus at an enormous speed of about 600 miles per second, constantly veering this way and that, like string wound around a ball, moving so fast that the atom appears to be a solid sphere, in the same way that a spinning propeller appears to be a solid disk. Our face, as well as every other material object in Creation, appears solid to us because our visual response is too slow to detect such rapid movement. Atomic particles move so fast in the vast space around them, they appear to us to be everywhere at once, seeming to fill space with solidity by virtue of their ability to occupy an enormous number of different places in the wink of an eye. Because of the dizzying speeds with which particles move within each atom, atoms themselves oscillate at a frequency of about a quadrillion times per second, and this makes them appear to be even bigger. Atoms combine to form molecules which vibrate a million times per second, and these in turn combine to form cells which vibrate a thousand times per second. When any object vibrates, in effect it moves from point A to point B and back to point A again; and if it repeats this movement fast enough, it will appear to us to be one solid object whose length stretches from A to B. How can we expect to detect between a thousand and a quadrillion different images in a single second if our eyes cannot even register the separate images delivered by a movie projector, which flash upon the screen at the rate of only twenty-four per second?

Although the rapid oscillation of material particles explains matter's solid *appearance*, it still does not explain the *opaqueness* of material objects. After all, while a spinning propeller may indeed present us with the impression of a solid disc, the disc we see is quite transparent; why then can't we also see through all material objects? The answer, science tells us, rests in the fact that human eyesight functions only within a particular range of sensitivity. It seems that atoms and molecules are about a thousand times smaller than the wavelengths of light to which our vision responds; therefore, since none of these light-waves are small enough to pass through dense aggregates of atoms, they can give us no indication of such objects' porous structure. If, on the other hand, our eyes were sensitive to smaller wavelengths—X-rays, for example—much of what now appears opaque to us would seem transparent.

In addition to the solidity that we *see* being an illusion, so too is the solidity that we *feel*. Just as planets are kept in constant orbits by a balance between the attractive force of their sun's gravity and the repulsive centrifugal force exerted by the planet itself as it circles, there are also electrical forces of attraction and repulsion which keep an atom's electrons at a certain distance from the nucleus. Therefore, when we touch any material object, whatever solidity we feel is a result of the forces within the atom, which greatly resist its being further compacted. What we feel pushing back at us is not some solid "stuff" at all, but the same force which makes it difficult for us to push together the alike poles of two magnets.

That face which gazes back at us from our bathroom mirror looks and feels solid because the two properties just described are inherent in every atom, and each material object is made up of a staggering number of these miniscule illusionists. If just our head could be enlarged to the size of the entire earth, the atoms which comprise it would be only as big as peppercorns. Imagine how many peppercorns it would take to fill a sphere the size of this planet; that's how many of these minute electrical entities have united in harmony to form the incomparable information processor we call "my head."

At our present level of observation we now see that there is really nothing of actual substance in the objects of our material world, except for three solid particles called electrons, protons and neutrons. As continued scientific progress permits us to approach these elementary particles, however, Mother Nature once again unveils before us some unsettling phenomena.

As we close in upon an electron, for example, while we are still some distance away from the speeding nuclear satellite, we suddenly spot another type of particle moving through the void toward us. It turns out to be a photon, an elementary particle of light energy traveling at an awesome 186,000 miles per second, which makes the electron's velocity of only 600 mps seem snail-like by comparison. The two particles seem to be on a collision course, and we watch excitedly, fully expecting that in accordance with

Newton's laws, the massless photon will simply bounce off the solid electron, for this is the way we have been taught that light reflects off of material objects.

We hold our ears as the two speeding objects meet, but to our amazement there is no resounding crash at all, and the ball of energy is not deflected from its course; instead, the photon seems to become *absorbed* by the electron. Infused with this additional energy, our electron now becomes extremely excited—so much so, in fact, that it leaps into a completely new orbit and races about even faster than before. This lasts for only a short while, then suddenly, the photon seems to spring back out of the excited electron and dart away into space at the speed of light, after which our electron calmly returns to its original orbit as if nothing at all has happened!

Was the ejected photon really the same one which was absorbed earlier, we wonder, or did the electron *create* a new one out of the energy it absorbed from the other? For that matter, we cannot even be certain that the electron we are now observing is the same one that was there before the collision. In fact, a quantum physicist would tell us that when the original electron and photon met they were both annihilated and a new electron of higher energy was created from their united forces; this new electron lived a very brief existence and then spontaneously transformed itself into yet another electron and photon! Undeniably, something very strange is going on here. Despite the atom's seeming similarity to a miniature solar system, it certainly is not behaving like one at all.

Shifting our attention to the more massive particles which make up the atom's nucleus, we draw nearer and observe that the nucleus is in a state of terrific agitation. The protons and neutrons seem to be held in close proximity by some very powerful force, strong enough to override the repulsive force which particles of similar charge exert upon one another; and these particles react to their close confinement by racing about the nucleus at speeds of about 40,000 miles per second! This causes the nucleus as a whole to quiver at an enormous rate of about ten sextillion (that's a one followed by twenty-two zeroes) vibrations per second.

Then, as we look more closely at this seething maelstrom, we are struck by a series of staggering discoveries. First, we see that protons and neutrons are not irreducible entities after all; it is now clear that they are composed of smaller particles called *quarks,* which are bound together by still other particles called *gluons*. We also see that the protons and neutrons themselves are prevented from leaving the nucleus by other basic particles called *mesons*.

As such bewildering observations continue, we also discover that the so-called empty space around us is not as empty as it once looked, but instead is populated by a vast array of distinctive subatomic particles. In fact, working at this level of observation, modern physicists have enlarged their list of elementary particles from three to *more than two-hundred separate types,* none of which seems to be much more elementary than any other. What has happened to our classical notion of matter being made of basic building blocks?

Still another amazing phenomenon comes to light at this level of observation. With disbelief we watch as two supposedly solid material particles collide head-on at high speed, and instead of bouncing off of one another or breaking into smaller pieces, they somehow become transformed into *four* different particles, *none of which is smaller than the two which collided*. As if this were not enough of a puzzlement, we then see two of the newly created particles leap together and merge, *causing one of the recently annihilated particles to become reborn*. (This is comparable to watching a red crystal ball crash into a blue one, and instead of shattering or rebounding, they both simply vanish, leaving in their places four new crystal balls of the same size, none of which is either red or blue; then, as these "spheres from out of nowhere" roll away from the scene of the accident, two of them suddenly come together and flow into one another, transforming themselves into the red crystal ball once more!) The inescapable conclusion seems to be that *subatomic particles are both destructible and indestructible at the very same time*.

If a basic particle of matter is a solid sphere of some substantial "stuff," then how could two of them merge, and how could one of them break up into two solid particles the same size as the original? By this time we are dying to get a closer look at these mysterious entities, and the moment scientific progress presents us with further extensions for our senses, we eagerly begin to zero in on an electron, whose behavior accounts for most of the major properties of matter.

As we approach this orbiting particle, we notice that it appears to be surrounded by clouds, much like the earth, but it is traveling so fast that the cloud layer seems to trail off behind it, stretching all the way around its orbit; in fact, the electron looks like a comet that is orbiting the sun so fast it's catching up with its own tail.

Soon we are at the surface of this shadowy smear; then, taking a deep breath, we plunge inside. To our amazement, *there is nothing of substance in here at all*—that is, nothing solid that we can see or feel. And yet, there is a presence here, a power which can be felt all around us, and there is an incredible, ethereal music as well, as if we are standing in the center of a vibrant energy field. In vain we search its limits for some trace of solid substance, but there is none. Leaving its confines, we back away into empty space and note that the farther we recede from it the more solid it appears; then we approach again and move inside it, where once more we find nothing but a field of singing energy.

In desperation we rush to the nucleus and examine every type of particle we come across, but each time the result is the same. The nucleus of our atom seems to have dissolved into nothing but a vortex of singing energy patterns. The elementary particles which make up our material world have proven in essence to be nothing but minute packets of vibration—quantities of energy which display the special property of appearing solid!

As we sit here in the middle of our atom, watching "solid" particles which have absolutely no solid substance in them, we are suddenly reminded of a cryptic statement penned nine-hundred years ago by the Christian saint, Paul, who wrote, "The world was created by the word of God so that what is seen was made out of things which do not appear."[2]

Though it may well seem that somehow we have slipped away from physical reality and entered a realm of mystical theology, the world which we have entered is, in fact, the universe of modern science.

Einstein's World

Twentieth century physics has discovered that the universe is capable of presenting a vastly different appearance depending upon the way we view it. Newton's model of reality makes sense to us because it accurately explains the world we normally perceive around us every day; but Newton's laws, it now turns out, are valid only for large aggregates of atoms and for objects which move at velocities far below the speed of light. When we descend to the more basic realm of atomic and subatomic particles, however, these laws no longer work and must be replaced by more appropriate ones such as those of quantum mechanics. And, when we begin to contemplate things which move at speeds approaching that of light, the universe then seems to run according to the rules laid down in Einstein's model of relativity.

The universe as seen by contemporary physicists is not a world which we would recognize as our own at all, for it is not a realm that is normally accessible to our limited mind and physical senses. This world cannot be broken down into basic building blocks of solid, indestructible substance; here, each material particle walks a razor's edge between existence and nonexistence; we cannot say that such a particle is present at any particular point in space at a particular time, nor can we say it is absent. In the world of modern physics, it is just as accurate to say that matter is made of vibration as it is to say it is made of particles.

In this world, space and time do not remain constant throughout the cosmos, for modern science has found that matter exerts a strong influence upon both; it "bends" the space around it and slows down time nearby it. There are no straight lines in the modern world of physics, because the universe itself is curved by the matter it contains. In fact, space is structured differently in different parts of the universe, and time flows at different rates throughout the cosmos. Space and time, it seems, are not even separate entities in this new world-view; instead, they are sort of laminated together to form a four-dimensional reality in which material particles can move forward and backward through time just as easily as they can move left and right through space. In a 4-D reality, time can be viewed in any direction just as space can; therefore, there is no before or after in such a world; events are not caused by anything—they just *are*.

The size of an object cannot be measured accurately in this reality, either, because no matter how "solid" it is, its length changes when it begins to move; the faster it moves, the more its length contracts. Events also cannot be timed accurately, because time is not a fixed measure of duration any longer; a clock in motion runs slower than when it is standing still, and the faster it moves, the slower the time it keeps. If, for example, we were to put one twin brother in a rocket ship and send him on a very speedy trip through outer space, he would return *younger* than his earthbound brother.

One of the most intriguing discoveries of modern physics has concerned the essential property of matter known as *mass*. An elementary particle is not considered material unless it has mass; the more mass a thing possesses, the more matter it contains. For centuries the mass of an object was believed to be connected with some solid, basic susbstance; then along came Albert Einstein, who destroyed such notions with a simple but world-shattering equation: $E=mc^2$. This famous mathematical statement showed that mass was in fact nothing but an extremely compacted form of energy; it indicated that even an object with a tiny amount of mass—say a feather—contained a vast amount of locked-up power, called rest energy.

Nuclear fission has been one method devised by science to unleash some of this rest energy from material particles, and even though this method is not a very efficient one, we all know what effect it had during World War II on the cities of Hiroshima and Nagasaki. As yet, no method has been found to release *all* the energy contained in an object's mass, but if and when this is accomplished, the world's energy problems will be solved forever. For example, if all the rest energy could be liberated from a single quart or liter of gasoline, it would run a 200-horsepower automobile 24 hours a day for 10,000 years!

Einstein's theory revealed that mass and energy are so closely related that either one can be converted into the other; in short, material particles can be transformed into pure energy and, even more spectacularly, such particles can actually be *created* if enough energy is available. This accounts for the puzzling occurrence we observed earlier when we witnessed a pair of material particles collide and become transformed into four completely different particles the same size as the originals. Since each particle is essentially nothing but a bundle of energy, when one collides with another the involved energy may simply become rearranged into a different pattern, in effect causing the annihilation of the original particles and the creation of new particles of different types. If one or both of the original particles were traveling fast enough, the kinetic energy of their motion could be converted into new mass at the collision point, causing additional particles to come into being. In this way, every elementary particle can be transformed into other particles, so it is impossible to designate any of these as the fundamental elements of matter.

The fact that the mass of any material entity is nothing but a specific quantity of energy indicates that we can no longer look at the world around us as a collection of static objects, for matter is not composed of solid substance, it is in fact made up of dancing patterns of energy. Every material object, be it our own body, a tree, or a mountain, is essentially just a temporary phase in a dynamic process involving a certain amount of energy. At an earlier point in this process, some pure energy slowed down to a speed below that of light, at which point it congealed into mass; and at some point in the future, should the equilibrium of this stable form of energy be disturbed in any way, it can shed its temporary property called mass and become pure energy once more. The manifestation we know as "matter" is simply one of the attendant effects of this energy's transformation into mass; thus, an object is really more of an event than it is a thing of substance. The moment its mass disappears, an energy pattern no longer projects a material appearance.

Material particles may look and feel solid, but they are not; in fact, modern science no longer views subatomic entities as objects at all; now they are looked upon as dynamic patterns or processes.

Movement is not just one of their properties, it is their essential nature. The atom is now seen as a system of comingling waves, a pattern of interacting energy vibrations.

Matter, then, is made of energy, and energy is something dynamic, something associated with activity and not with some sort of solid "stuff." Thus, the existence of matter cannot be separated from its activity, which is the very essence of its being. The world which we perceive around us may seem to be a vast empty space containing independent, solid objects, but in reality that space contains nothing but vibrating fields of energy.

In the light of our conflicting daily experience, such a reality is difficult to comprehend; yet, the findings of modern science do not stop here. Physicists have also made a revolutionary discovery about the way these fields of energy interact with one another.

In Newton's world, material objects affect each other by exerting various types of force which have the mysterious ability to reach out across empty space to attract or repel solid things. Such forces hold atomic nuclei together, give the atom its stability, and even keep our solar system and galaxy from either flying apart or collapsing.

As we began to discover during our exploration of the atom, however, forces do not in fact work the way Newton described them. The protons and neutrons of an atomic nucleus, for example, are not held together by some ephemeral power, but through the exchange of still other types of particles, called mesons. Similarly, electrons are held in their orbits through the exchange of photon particles, and it is now believed that even the force of gravity does its work through the agency of still another type of particle which science has dubbed the *gravitron*. Since photons and gravitrons are considered to be massless particles, this means that their range is virtually unlimited; once they are ejected from a source, they will travel to the very ends of the universe—or until they are absorbed by other particles.

All particles, then, interact through forces which are nothing but an exchange of other particles; thus, force and matter are simply different aspects of the very same phenomenon. At this point, our picture of the universe becomes completely devoid of any isolated entities—even isolated energy fields—because if all material objects are made of particles which are patterns of energy, and if the forces which act between such objects are also made of particles which are patterns of energy, then the whole of Creation must be but a single, enormously intricate web of interconnected vibrational patterns.

The world we live in is like a brilliant and intricate tapestry depicting a myriad of diverse images which are so realistic and eye-catching that they completely obscure the fact that they are all woven of the same silk, and that this silk also binds them all together into a single, resplendent whole. This universal tapestry is engaged in ceaseless motion, like an energy kaleidoscope; and yet, despite the fact that transformation is its primary characteristic and that these changes involve an infinite variety of patterns, these patterns can all be quite neatly categorized into just a few distinct types of manifestations, thus disclosing an undeniable presence of universal order.

At this point in our investigation, the material universe of modern science has dwindled in essence to just two primary ingredients—a vast vacuum of space and the vibrant energy patterns that fill this vacuum. Exactly how, we may now wonder, does one relate to the other? What is this powerful, singing void that we discover at the heart of every subatomic particle in Creation, and how does it differ from the void *out*side each particle? What is the nature of the energy which forms each particle? How does this energy suddenly make a particle appear out of nowhere, and what happens to it when the particle vanishes? For answers to such questions, we must now turn our attention to the vessel which contains the universal contents—the vacuum of space itself.

Modern Physics Enters The Void

The first observation that we make the moment we set out to study the phenomenon called "space" is that the adjective "empty" can never accurately be applied to it. Since we have already found that the energy fields we call "matter" are all interconnected by other fields which we call "forces," there cannot be even the tiniest area of space anywhere in the cosmos in which at least one of these field-types is not present.

According to relativity theory, however, an energy field does not just *fill* the area of space which contains it—the field actually *is* the space itself. An energy field determines the actual structure of the space it inhabits; therefore, modern physics has abandoned all distinctions between fields and space. The consequences of this discovery become far-reaching indeed when we remember that matter is nothing but a particular type of energy field, for this means that matter and space must now be considered inseparable and interdependent. *Modern physics considers matter and space to be two different aspects of a single phenomenon.*

This explains why the closer we look at a material particle, the more all distinctions between it and the space around it become lost. It also accounts for the astounding fact that such particles can be observed actually springing into existence directly from the void, as well as vanishing suddenly back into nothingness. What we are seeing are simply two different sides of the same coin.

The reigning model of the universe upheld by physicists today is that of quantum field theory, which effectively combines the laws of classical physics with those of quantum theory and relativity. This view of the cosmos erases all distinctions between matter, energy and space, encompassing them all within a single physical reality called the *quantum field*. This field is present everywhere, and its most distinctive characteristic is that there are two apparent aspects to its basic nature: (1) it has a continuous structure which we know as "space" and "time" because this aspect seems to exist constantly and changelessly throughout the cosmos and also throughout the past, present and future; and (2) it also has a granular or particle aspect which we know as "matter" and "force" because in this aspect the quantum field appears in the form of discontinuous, localized particles which enjoy only temporary existence. The field continually oscillates between these two apparently dissimilar states, incessantly transforming itself from one to the other.

Now we can no longer consider space to be simply a static background for events or a passive container of objects, for it does in fact possess a vital, self-governing structure of its own. If we want to really understand the nature of a subatomic particle, therefore, we must observe it in *connection* with the space around it, instead of trying to draw distinctions between the particle and that space.

Observed in this light, for example, an electron reveals itself to be a kind of "energy knot," a blemish on the face of its underlying field; it does not in fact revolve around its nucleus as does our earth around its sun; instead, it propagates through space like a water wave, and clearly does not consist of any selfsame substance at all times. A material particle, it turns out, is simply a local condensation of the quantum field, a temporary concentration of energy which appears solid to our sight and touch. In the words of Albert Einstein: "We may therefore regard matter as being constituted by the regions of space in which the field is extremely intense. . . . There is no place in this kind of physics both for the field and matter, for the field is the only reality."[3]

The physical vacuum, as the void is called in quantum field theory, is far from empty nothingness, for it contains an infinite number of every type of particle in potential form, which also indirectly means that it contains *all material objects* in potential form as well. Every object in the world around us is a transient particle manifestation of the quantum field, and every interaction among these objects, as well as between us and them, is also carried by this field in the form of vibrational waves. If it were not for this living, moving void, if it did not continually vibrate in an endless dance of creation and destruction, there would be no physical universe, no perceptible reality at all, anywhere. The discovery that the physical vacuum or void is alive and active is one of the outstanding revelations of modern physics.

As yet, science does not know what the quantum field is made of, but it is now considered the fundamental substance of all material phenomena in Creation. It is not, however, viewed as the basis of all *non*material phenomena, most notably the force of gravity. Convinced that there must exist an even more fundamental ground field which would prove to be the basis of both the quantum and gravitational fields, Einstein spent twenty years of his life in pursuit of such a unified field theory. Finally, in 1949, he presented a mathematical solution which brings these apparently diverse phenomena under the same set of equations, but three decades later his theory remains unverified, since no practicable way has yet been found to confirm the results of his mathematics with experimental evidence.

Nevertheless, in what is perhaps the most astounding example of "East meets West," today's physicists have completely verified the ancient Oriental assertion that the material world is an illusion, and in addition have come within a hair's breadth of confirming another famous Eastern postulate as well—the one proclaiming that "All is One."

Now that we have examined the world-view held by modern physicists, the view put forth by yogic scientists may not seem as bizarre as it once did to Westerners, for as we shall see, the two views are strikingly similar. The major difference between them, in fact, may be that most of us will likely find the yogic model of reality, with its dramatic use of metaphor, to be a great deal more comprehensible than the abstract mathematical concepts presented by contemporary physics. Let's compare the two and decide for ourselves.

3. The Universe of Yoga

Despite the endless diversity that we perceive around us, the universe consists of only one ingredient—a single, all-pervasive substance which is the common source of each and every property that defines the world in which we live. Space, time, force, matter—virtually all objects and events are manifestations of this fundamental ground field of unceasing, indestructible vitality.

Such statements, expressing the unity of all Creation, describe a world-view which is commonly shared by both the vanguard physical scientists of today and the venerated yogic sages of antiquity. While modern science has brought this aspect of reality to light through an in-depth examination of the outer world, yogic science has arrived at the same discovery by delving into the world within. Thus, we now have further confirmation of the ancient yogic teaching that the internal reality (the inner Self) is identical in nature to the external reality (the cosmic Self).

The similarities between modern science's description of basic reality and that put forth by Yoga do not stop here, however. In the course of this chapter, as well as elsewhere in this book, we will find that recent scientific discoveries are corroborating, with amazing frequency, the world-view outlined by the philosophies of many spiritual sciences. Of course, compared with the spiritual scientist who has been investigating the true nature of things for thousands of years, today's physical scientist must be considered a neophyte in the quest for the essence of reality.

One of the most important similarities between the physical and spiritual sciences is that in both these disciplines, all true knowledge must be supported by scientific experimentation and not just creative intuition or intellectual reasoning.

In any scientific field, two main types of experimental research are performed. In the first type, experiments attempt to solve one or more of the baffling riddles with which nature constantly confounds the human intellect; and in the second type, previous experiments are repeated in order to verify the original results. Modern physical science is, of course, actively engaged in both types. Yogic science, on the other hand, is no longer involved in experimentation aimed at breaking new ground, for this ancient spiritual discipline no longer needs to contend with any unsolved riddles; its blueprint of reality has been totally complete for countless generations, so the only type of experimental research being performed in this field nowadays is the second type. Any one of us may repeat the ancient Rishis' experiments and personally verify their findings *by experiencing the essential nature of reality for ourself*. Accordingly, we should expect yogic science to be capable of presenting us with a truly comprehensive picture of Creation's real structure, unlike the limited models of modern science, which still contain many important, unfilled gaps.

Glaringly absent from the findings of modern science, for example, is the exact nature of the universal, organic substratum that forms the ground field from which all manifest reality springs forth. What exactly is this fundamental, nonmaterial, ever-active, all-pervasive, indestructible "stuff" that unifies Creation? What is this power it possesses which enables it to assume or relinquish material form apparently at will? And exactly who or what decides when these manifestations shall occur or vanish?

To answer such questions, Yoga presents us with a concept called "the universal mind." Since most Western readers will undoubtedly decide that this concept sounds suspiciously like the one they refer to as "God," before we go any further perhaps we'd better attempt to establish some common understanding about the concept of divinity as it applies to the field of spiritual science.

Is God Dead?

The modern concept of God is a highly ambiguous one, meaning many different things to many different people. Some of us are uplifted by it, while others find it offensive; some of us believe that God is the force of Truth or Love, while others insist that He has a humanlike form. Members of organized religions generally view God as sectarian; they feel that their sect alone has access to supreme divinity. Nonreligious people either question His existence or deny it altogether, proclaiming Him to be a fabrication of the human mind.

Most modern scientists argue that there is no place for the concept of divinity in its models of Creation, but there are many notable exceptions and their number is increasing rapidly. This may be surprising to many of us who have grown up in an era of violent conflict between science and religion, but the fact is that this centuries-old feud is well on its way to becoming resolved amicably, thanks to the coming-of-age of modern physics.

The battle began back in the Middle Ages, when physical science was still naive and steeped in ignorance, and so the Church unwisely took upon itself the responsibility for explaining things which were really not in the province of religion. Thus, every natural phenomenon was explained to the masses in a theological or miraculous context, a move which the Church would later look back upon with much regret, for as the discoveries of a rapidly maturing field of physical science began to prove such church pronouncements wrong one by one, people became increasingly skeptical about the validity of religious dogma altogether.

The climax came when Newton presented his model of a creation constructed like a vast precision machine, quite capable of running itself without divine supervision. Western philosophers then used this model of a mechanical, impersonal cosmos as an excuse to banish all notion of spiritual purpose from Creation. Throughout this conflict, theology was further handicapped by the fact that its countless sects were found to be in constant contradiction with one another, while science the world over spoke out with a single, authoritative voice.

Nevertheless, though modern science had set out to utterly demolish the concept of God, scientists soon began to learn that they were hopelessly mismatched with an adversary who was far more powerful than expected. Instead of annihilating God, physical science has only managed to taint His reputation for a mere few hundred years; in the end it has been science which has been humbled and compelled to retreat, confining itself once and for all to the material aspect of reality and leaving spiritual matters to the sphere of religion where they belong.

The Newtonian universe has proved to be illusory, and physical science has been forced to forever give up any hope of isolating and observing ultimate reality, that formless, fundamental ground field from which spring forth all manifest phenomena. Despite its systematic debunking of church pronouncements regarding mundane physical objects and events, science has never been able to disprove the real heart of religious belief, the common essence which all religions share, which is the conviction that ultimate reality can be experienced only by mystical means and never by intellectual endeavors.

Thanks to our modern scientific revolution, then, physical science has ceased to compete with religion; the two fields are complementary rather than contradictory, the purpose of religion being to explore and chart that level of reality at which physical science becomes ineffective. This reconciliation was foreseen by the great physicist Wolfgang Pauli, who in 1927 made the following statement to his fellow scientist Warner Heisenberg: ". . . it was precisely the idea of an objective world running its course in time and space according to strict causal laws that produced a sharp clash between science and the spiritual formulations of the various religions. If science goes beyond this strict view—and it has done just that with relativity theory and is likely to go even further with quantum theory—then the relationship between science and the contents which religions try to express must change once again."[4]

By and large, an understanding of this amazing reconciliation has not yet filtered down to the average person, for our modern literature, art and philosophy are all still steeped in the now-archaic belief that Creation is meaningless and purposeless. This being the case, let's now take a more up-to-date look at the cosmos to see if we can once again find a place for God among all our scientific discoveries.

The Universal Mind

"My religion," wrote Albert Einstein, "consists of a humble admiration for the illimitable superior spirit who reveals Himself in the slight details we are able to perceive with our frail and feeble minds. That deeply emotional conviction of the presence of a superior reasoning power, which is revealed in the incomprehensible universe, forms my idea of God."[5]

This "superior reasoning power" described by Einstein reveals itself to modern physicists in a few important ways which indicate that there is some form of actual *intelligence* working at the most basic level of reality. Since intelligence can be defined as the ability to create and maintain order for a specific purpose, the existence of some cosmic intelligence would be indicated scientifically if we could find some evidence that both *order* and *purpose* are fundamental elements of the universal structure.

During the infancy of quantum physics, when scientists saw the Newtonian model of Creation crumbling before their very eyes, theories of cosmic chaos came into vogue for a short time; but then, as deeper levels of reality began presenting themselves to the amazed observers, the universe once more proved to be a system of perfect order. In fact, it is just this cosmic harmony which enables theorists such as Einstein to predict and discover natural laws simply by solving mathematical equations.

Bell's Theorem is one result of modern research which effectively supports the existence of a harmonious universal order by showing that the behavior of subatomic particles is determined by what other particles are doing at that moment—*regardless of the distance that separates them*. Each particle seems to "know" at all times what every other particle is up to, and this implies that all the subatomic entities in Creation are in some way intimately interconnected.

Order, then, is unquestionably a basic ingredient of Creation, but what evidence is there to indicate that there is also some sort of *purpose* at work?

Well, thanks to modern physics' discovery of a law called "the principle of minimum action," it has now been shown that the interactions which take place at the subatomic level of reality are not simply the effects of previous interactions; rather, they happen spontaneously in order to bring about effects of their own: that is, they occur *with an intention to fulfill an explicit purpose!*

At the most elementary level of our physical world, then, things do not happen because they are caused by other things, but instead *all events take place as if there were a final cause in mind.* In the words of physicist Max Planck, the founder of quantum theory, "Theoretical physics has reached a kind of causality *with a definite theological character,* without in the least contradicting natural scientific laws." Then he adds that this principle of minimum action just mentioned above "cannot help but awaken in unbiased minds the feeling that nature is ruled by *a rational will aiming at a specific goal."*[6] (italics added)

Whoever or whatever it is, this cosmic intelligence must either be separate from its creation or an integral part of it. Were it to remain aloof, running things from some remote place outside the universe, its nature would be forever inaccessible, and its laws completely unintelligible to us. But modern scientists are discovering over and over again that Creation is governed *from within* and not through external manipulation. In other words, *God must be somewhere in the universe,* and we have already determined that the universe seems to contain only one thing—that mysterious, vibrant "stuff" which we have not yet been able to define. Could this omnipresent substance have anything in common with the all-pervasive intelligence that most of us call God?

Yogic doctrine confirms what reason and logic lead us to propose at this point: that this omnipotent field, whose eternal dance of creation and destruction accounts for the entire cosmos, must also be the cosmic intelligence that establishes and maintains universal order with a specific purpose in mind. In short, God is not different from His Creation; the universe is God Himself.

According to Yoga, there is only one real ingredient in all of Creation, and that ingredient is Intelligence—"divine consciousness." The universe, then, is nothing less than a vast sea of vibrant consciousness, an intelligent mind-stuff which produces the characteristics we identify as matter, force, space and time. This means that everything in Creation is made entirely of this divine consciousness, which, of its own free will, becomes all objects and events. The totality of this cosmic mass of consciousness is referred to in Yoga as *the universal mind;* religion calls it *God;* and modern science labels it the *fundamental ground field*.

Forever hidden from the probing instruments of physical science is the metaphysical fact that the primal energy which vibrates in each subatomic particle is nothing less than a unit of pure awareness. Thus, to obtain an experience of the formless aspect of reality as well as its substantial one, we must invoke the essences of both science and religion, which of course is exactly what the field of spiritual science has done. In the words of Albert Einstein, "Science without religion is lame; religion without science is blind."[7]

The Terminology of Yoga

Modern physicists and yogic scientists alike derive their knowledge of reality by investigating realms which are not perceivable by the physical senses. Since the concepts and images of human language are designed to reflect and support only that level of reality which can be perceived by our senses, both physicist and Rishi find such language to be all but useless in describing their experience of more subtle realms.

Accordingly, physicists employ two different forms of communication in order to convey their ideas and discoveries to others. First, through the abstract language of mathematics, they construct models of reality which can become extremely powerful tools for humankind when applied through technological experimentation, but such models are generally meaningful only to their fellow scientists; the ordinary layperson finds this language all but incomprehensible, like some secret code that can only be deciphered by an expert. Therefore, in order to communicate with the rest of us, physicists try to devise accompanying models of verbal concepts which, though necessarily slightly vague and imprecise, at least convey the essence of their ideas or findings to the masses.

Yogic scientists also employ two different types of language to convey their discoveries and teachings. First, through abstract scriptural terminology, they encapsulate the full import and significance of reality's basic aspects and thereby make eternal wisdom preservable throughout the ages; but like the mathematical models of modern scientists, these scriptural aphorisms are often so inscrutable that much of their true significance becomes lost to us unless we hear them explained by an accomplished master. The profound caution that "Even the devil can quote scripture for his purpose" attests to the fact that without expert guidance the ordinary person can easily misinterpret the scriptural aphorisms passed down by the perfected masters of spiritual science.

Esoteric scripture, then, is often employed by perfected masters in order to communicate *with one another*. But, since they, like the modern physical scientists, also desire to make their discoveries available to virtually every person interested in learning about true reality, they also endeavor to express the inexpressible as clearly as possible through the simple and concrete symbology of metaphor. By encapsulating abstract metaphysical concepts in the form of familiar images, they make it possible for every one of us to grasp the essence of even the most subtle realities and apply this knowledge to our everyday life.

Of even greater significance is the demonstrable fact that the symbols employed by yogic science are not merely contrived representations of essential truths, but are also intimately connected to these truths in a mysterious way which will be made clearer when we examine the phenomenon of *mantra* in a later section. This connection empowers each yogic symbol to serve as a kind of spiritual transformer, a channel through which energy of transformation can be transmitted to us from perfected masters; thus, through repeated contemplation of these symbols we find that gradually, along with a steady refinement of our intellectual understanding, our everyday *experience* of reality becomes corrected as well.

Yoga's metaphoric models of reality date back far beyond the beginning of recorded history. For untold millenia such knowledge was imprinted solely upon the memories of specially gifted sages, passed on from mind to mind, generation by generation, only through spoken word and memorization. To provide spiritual seekers with all the necessities for a successful ascent to Self-realization, a number of complete philosophical systems have been passed down by the ancient Rishis, each providing a detailed road-map for the journey to the topmost peak of spiritual enlightenment. Though all of these philosophies lead their followers to the exact same goal, each outlines a slightly different route along the mountainside; and in addition, each employs its own unique set of images and concepts to explain the true nature of reality.

Our primary concern in this book will be that yogic philosophy known as *Trika,* more often referred to as *Kashmir Shaivism,* for this system of knowledge is the keystone philosophy of Siddha Yoga. Kashmir Shaivism is said to date back to the very beginning of time, born not through inspiration but through divine revelation, and the authenticity of this assertion has been affirmed countless times by beings who have attained cosmic consciousness through the experimental application of its teachings.

Shaivism is heralded as a perfect system of knowledge because it accurately outlines the exact nature of Creation, life, human psychology, and the process through which any person may achieve union with the supreme universal principle. In terms of its comprehensiveness in detailing the complete structure of reality, Kashmir Shaivism stands at the paramount position in the field of yogic philosophy, its sophistication exceeding even the great system of Vedanta.

The keystones of Shaivism are (1) its nondualism, showing the one unifying principle that underlies everything in Creation, and (2) its proclamation that every individual is inherently divine. As it is a minutely detailed and complex system of knowledge, it would be hopeless to accurately survey all its teachings in a single chapter of this book. What follows, then, is a highly simplified overview of this ancient yogic blueprint of reality, our intent being to capture the essence of this remarkable doctrine while sacrificing much of its subtlety.

Although Shaivism meticulously stratifies reality into thirty-six distinct levels, it also teaches that we can sustain a good general understanding of Creation's essential nature by examining just the topmost two, from which all the others emanate. In the language of Kashmir Shaivism, these two fundamental aspects of reality are called *Shiva* and *Shakti*.

The Shiva and Shakti of Kashmir Shaivism

Trika philosophy refers to ultimate reality as *Paramashiva*, a concept so abstract and nebulous that the only way any of us can ever really comprehend it is by personally experiencing it through meditation. But meanwhile, Shaivism tells us that the closest we can come to such an understanding intellectually is to think of this supreme reality as consisting of two essential aspects—a static one called Shiva and a dynamic one called Shakti. This philosophy presents Shiva and Shakti as abstract universal principles, but perhaps we can more easily gain a general understanding of their nature by employing a yogic artifice called deification: we will personify these cosmic principles and examine them in the form of Lord Shiva and his goddess consort, Shakti.

Many of us may feel put off by the endless parade of gods and goddesses described in Eastern philosophies, but such repulsion is usually due to our failure to understand that these deities merely represent universal principles which the Rishis have chosen to personify in order to make them easier for us to comprehend. The cosmic principles on which all of Creation rests are far too subtle and elusive for the human mind to grasp in their actual, formless state, so Yoga simply lends them substance to make their essence more accessible to us. The cosmic mates Shiva and Shakti are the supreme deities of Shaivism because they embody the highest cosmic principles.

Lord Shiva represents the most fundamental aspect of reality, and he is therefore depicted as the ultimate divinity. Being static in essence, Shiva does absolutely nothing, yet his mere existence makes it possible for everything else in Creation to exist. Though Shiva is a static entity, we mustn't get the idea that he's passive, dull, lazy or lifeless, for nothing could be further from the truth. He may not actually be *doing* anything, but that's only because he doesn't have to—he *is* everything.

Just as a spinning gyroscope appears to be at rest when in fact it is the extreme opposite of rest, so too does Shiva appear to be inactive when in fact he is the supreme opposite of inactivity. Shiva does not act, because he is Action itself; he does not exist, he is Existence itself; he is not wise, he is Wisdom itself; he does not love, he is Love itself; he does not become anything, but he is everything, and everything is he. Bristling with vitality, brimming with power, wisdom and bliss, Shiva is the ultimate potential energy, the cosmic lion eternally about to pounce, perfectly balanced and vibrantly alive in every fiber of his being.

If we think back billions of years to before the moment of Creation, before even time itself, and ask ourself, "From what did this Creation spring?"—the answer will be "Shiva." Without Shiva, nothing else could ever be; everything that is, exists because of him, and yet he remains completely unaffected by it all. Shiva is the supreme witness. Truly speaking, of course, pure, unmodified Shiva is not even a "he," "she," or "it"; Shiva is the very essence of gender itself. So difficult is the task of describing Shiva, the ancient Vedas can only state that he is "*neti, neti*"—"not this, not this"—meaning that Shiva cannot be described in any terms within the grasp of human knowledge.

The highest attainment in meditation is the merging of our limited, individual consciousness with Shiva's unlimited, absolute consciousness, the result being that we experience the state of Shivahood for ourself. The yogic Rishis, in attempting to describe this indescribable state, have called it *Sat-Chit-Ananda,* which in Sanskrit means that his essential nature is that of absolute existence, absolute consciousness, and absolute bliss.

As absolute existence, he is omnipresent; he alone exists everywhere at all times, remaining unchanged throughout eternity;

he is the vessel in which the whole of Creation exists, and he is also the entire contents of this vessel. Since he and he alone exists, all else being but forms of him, he is the supreme truth, the highest reality, and the ultimate universal power. As absolute conscious- ness, his awareness is unlimited; there is nothing which he does not know, and nothing which he does not witness. As absolute bliss, his joy is not dependent upon anything at all; it is unsurpassable, undiminishable, and unending.

By now we may have realized that if Shiva were the only aspect of supreme reality, we'd all be spared the fun of trying to discover the secrets of the universe, because the manifest uni- verse would not exist. (Remember, Shiva never *does* anything— including create universes—he just *is*.) Of course, countless universes exist *in* Shiva, but only in potential form, unmanifest. So how does the unmanifest become manifest?

This question brings us to a very tricky philosophical point, the kind for which the Orient is famous: *Since Shiva is everything, he is also his own opposite*. This means that Shiva can be both static and dynamic—motionless and active—*simultaneously*. Though it seems impossible to our rational 3-D mind that a single entity can display two such seemingly opposite characteristics at the same time, modern science has affirmed that such apparent paradoxes can indeed become resolved in higher dimensions of reality. In fact, in the previous chapter we saw how the quantum field of current physics exhibits two apparently opposite aspects which are almost identical to those of Shiva; this field is, at the same time, (1) formless, motionless and all-pervasive, and (2) substantial, active and localized.

One way in which the active aspect of Shiva is effectively por- trayed in the East is by depicting him in the form of *Nataraja*—the Cosmic Dancer. As such, Shiva is shown performing three of his most important actions—creation, sustenance and dissolution. The quantum field of modern physics, we will recall, also gives birth to an endless array of forms, which it sustains for a time, then absorbs back into itself. Acknowledging the aptness of Nataraja as a sym- bolic representation of manifest reality, the renowned physicist

Dr. Fritjof Capra has written:

> ... Shiva, the Cosmic Dancer, is perhaps the most per-
> fect personification of the dynamic universe. Through
> his dance, Shiva sustains the manifold phenomena in
> the world, unifying all things by making them partici-
> pate in the dance—a magnificent image of the dynamic
> unity of the universe. . . . The dance of Shiva *is the
> dancing universe;* the ceaseless flow of energy going
> through an infinite variety of patterns that melt into one
> another. . . . Modern physics has . . . revealed that
> every subatomic particle not only performs an energy
> dance, but also *is* an energy dance; a pulsating process
> of creation and destruction. . . . For the modern physi-
> cist, then, Shiva's dance is the dance of subatomic
> matter.[8]

Because it is so difficult for us to grasp the concept of Shiva
being both motionless and in action at the same time, Shaivism
takes pity on us and assigns a separate identity to each of these
cosmic attributes. Thus, we now find *two* deities presiding over the
supreme universal principle: Lord Shiva embodies the static
aspect, and the goddess Shakti, the dynamic aspect. Still, we must
always remember that the two, in reality, are one—like the two
faces of the same coin.

Shiva and Shakti are depicted as male and female—cosmic
mates—not because they unite in any sexual way but because they
are permanently, eternally married. The sacred bond of marriage
as we know it signifies a spiritual union between two human
beings; on a mundane level the mates continue to exist as two
separate individuals, but on a more subtle level they are one. The
marriage of Shiva and Shakti represents the supreme example of
such a mystical union.

In Shaivism, the term *Paramashiva* denotes both Shiva and
Shakti together; in Vedanta, the concept of *Brahman* is comparable; and in modern physics, as we have already seen, the quantum
field is a fair approximation, though Einstein's proposed unified
field is even closer. (Of course, such field concepts of physics

relate only to the physical universe which, as we will see shortly, Yoga categorizes as only one stratum of a multi-layered Creation consisting of numerous other levels of more subtle realities.)

According to Shaivism, it is out of the eternally perfect marriage of Shiva and Shakti that the universe is born. The word *shakti* means "power" in Sanskrit, and when capitalized it refers to the active attribute of Paramashiva. This Shakti, then, is Shiva's potential power turned kinetic; she is energy in action. While Shiva is static and quiescent throughout eternity, his Shakti aspect—which is dynamic and creative—manifests only periodically, and it is during such times that a material universe comes into existence.

Spanda-Shakti

Cosmic creation is said to begin when Paramashiva expresses a desire to this effect: "I am one; let me be many." It is at this moment that the universal mind is born. Though Shaivism does not employ this precise concept, it is being borrowed here from other yogic philosophies to enhance the clarity of our presentation.

A mind, according to many spiritual sciences, is nothing but pure consciousness contained and limited by desire. The universal mind, then, is simply boundless consciousness which has become enclosed within the confines of the desire to create a universe. (The limitations of this metaphor are obvious, of course, for in reality Shiva can never be contained or limited in any way; thus, it would be more accurate to say that his pure consciousness *appears* to become contained within the limits of a desire to create.) For the sake of simplicity, however, we can liken the universal mind to a gigantic glass bowl filled with water, the glass container being the creative desire, and the water being the Consciousness which has now become oriented toward fulfilling that desire. This, then, is the arena in which Creation will take place.

Now that the stage is set, it is time for Shakti to make her grand entrance. From deep within the mass of Consciousness which has become the universal mind, she bursts forth in the form of an initial creative impulse called *Spanda*—a cosmic throb or vibration. In the parlance of modern physics, we would say that a causal vibration issues from its ground field.

This Spanda-Shakti is akin to delivering a stiff jolt to our enormous bowl of water—only this jolt comes from the very water itself. When a container of still liquid is suddenly jarred, the first thing which happens is that a single shock wave passes through it, causing the entire volume of liquid to pulsate en masse. But then, as this initial vibration reverberates off all the sides of the container, a countless number of reflected waves are sent back through the liquid. When these reflected waves begin to interact, the liquid soon becomes filled with a vast array of interconnected, interrelated, constantly changing interference patterns of vibration, each of which is unique in that its precise form is unmatched by any of the other patterns; yet each is also identical to the others in that they are all made of exactly the same substance.

This, states Shaivism, is approximately analogous to the way Shakti's initial Spanda reverberates through Shiva's consciousness to form an intricate web of energy patterns which manifest as the universe of objects and events. If this emergent world-view sounds strangely familiar, it's because it exactly duplicates the one put forth by the quantum field theory of modern physics.

If, as both Yoga and modern science agree, the universe does indeed consist of interference patterns displayed against the static background of their ground field, then this would mean that the whole of Creation is one gigantic hologram, and the most amazing quality of a hologram is the fact that its entire contents are contained in each of its parts. If we were to use holographic equipment to make a hologram of an apple, for example, we could pass coherent light through the resultant photographic plate and cause a perfect three-dimensional image of the same apple to hover in midair before us; then, if we were to shatter this plate and project the same light through just one fragment of our broken hologram, *an image of the whole apple would still be produced*. Transposing this phenomenon to the level of a cosmic hologram, therefore, it would not be at all inaccurate to say that the whole of Creation is contained in each and every one of its constituents. Each vibrational

pattern in the universal mind is an information storehouse containing not only *unique* data, which make it stand out as an independent
manifestation, but also *general* data concerning the complete structure of the cosmos. In other words, the entire universe is contained
in every object and event—in every instant of time, every parcel of
space, every subatomic particle of force and matter.

Perhaps we can gain some idea of what the fundamental level
of reality must be like if we pretend that our bowlful of quivering
water is indeed the actual universal mind, and that we are now
inside it, completely immersed in its mass of vibrant Consciousness. All around us the teeming reflected waves, which have
evolved from the initial Spanda, are interacting to form a myriad of
vibrational patterns in the water—*and one of these patterns is us.*
The only thing which sets us apart from the mass of Consciousness
around us is our unique pattern of vibration.

Let's ponder this a moment. When a vibration moves through
water, it is not made of the same water throughout its journey, any
more than a wave on the surface of a lake is made of the same water
particles as it moves toward the shore. A vibration is merely an
energy impulse that causes the substance in its path to pulsate in a
certain pattern as it passes through.

This fact takes on serious implications when extended to the
phenomenon we call matter. In the previous chapter we found that
even a material particle, being essentially a packet of vibration
moving through the substance of the quantum field, is not made of
the selfsame ''stuff'' as it moves along; it, too, propagates through
its ground substance just as a water wave does.

Since our own physical body consists of these same particles,
does this then mean that as we walk along the street, *the Consciousness of which we are made constantly changes?* Let's explore this
intriguing possibility further.

Figure 6 depicts a packet of vibration which gives the appearance of a material particle moving from right to left. (This is, of
course, only a two-dimensional representation of what is really a
very complex, 4-D phenomenon.)

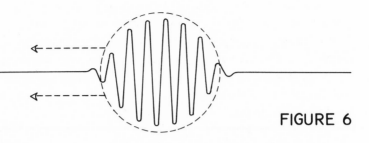

FIGURE 6

Now let's consider the way this vibrational packet effects the ground substance through which it passes. In Figure 7 we see a row of water particles in the direct path of a vibration packet traveling from right to left. As it moves along, the particles of substance in its path become agitated by its vibratory power, which causes them to oscillate in the exact same configuration as the packet's vibrational pattern. After it passes, the particles settle down in approximately the same place as they were before; certainly they do not travel along with the vibrational pattern.

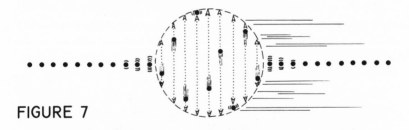

FIGURE 7

Yoga tells us that if we now transpose this phenomenon to the level of subatomic particles we can simply substitute units of Consciousness for our row of water particles; the result will be the same. Therefore, it seems that we are not, in fact, made of the selfsame substance from moment to moment throughout our physical existence; our body is merely a complex pattern of vibration which causes the sea of Consciousness to adopt a compatible configuration as we pass through it!

Supreme consciousness is all-pervasive; there is just as much of it *between* two objects as there is *inside* them. What we perceive as an object is determined solely by the intensity of activity in a particular area of the quantum field, activity induced by the presence of a strong vibratory pattern. It is not Shiva's all-pervasive consciousness that we perceive as the world of objects and events, then; what we perceive is Shakti's activity.

When we experience the material reality around us, therefore, it is not its basic substance which we perceive, but merely the *movement* of that substance. Shiva's pure, transcendent being is forever imperceptible, for his state is that of total oneness, far beyond the duality of the seer and the seen; the only way we can ever know him is by becoming him through the attainment of Self-realization.

Shakti, however, is easy to perceive; in fact, it is impossible for us *not* to perceive her throughout every waking moment of our life. The Sanskrit word for our physical world is *jagat*—"that which moves"—and Shakti is movement personified. She is everything we see, everything we touch, everything we hear, taste and smell; she is even our own body, the instrument through which we perceive the world. Indeed, she is a perceptible form of Shiva himself, and Yoga tells us that if we really learn to see her in ourself and in the world around us, if we become her intimate friend through meditation, someday she will surely introduce us to her mate.

Meanwhile, we might as well face up to reality. Both modern science and ancient Yoga agree that from a material standpoint we are all nothing more than infinitesimal vibratory patterns in a cosmic bowlful of quivering Consciousness, never made of the same "stuff" from one moment to the next. We're incapable of perceiving the basic substance of reality, even though it's everywhere. Like an ocean fish which frantically combs the sea in search of water, we look high and low for the ultimate truth, the supreme reality, despite the fact that the object of our quest is all around us and inside us all the while.

Creation's Basic Building Blocks

As we have already seen, modern physics has abandoned the notion of matter being reducible to elementary units of solid, indestructible substance, for the subatomic particles which make up all material objects have proved to consist of nothing more than vibrant energy. Physicists know that whatever the quantum field is made of, its substance is nonmaterial, and when the field assumes its granular aspect, it is not that substance which appears to us as solid material particles, but merely the *movement* of it. In other words, the ground substance which pervades the cosmos is eternally imperceptible, regardless of whether it is in its formless aspect or its particle aspect, and what we identify as our physical reality is simply a network of patterns created by interacting vibrations propagating through this all-pervasive substance. Our physical senses do not respond to things of substance, but to particular patterns of movement; thus, if there were no movement occurring in the quantum field, there would be no perceptible reality.

Movement, then, must be considered a basic ingredient of manifest Creation; but is it the only ingredient? What about the ground field itself? Does the fact that we cannot perceive its basic substance mean that it plays no essential part in the drama of Creation?

Shaivism, of course, states that Shiva's stillness and Shakti's activity are both essential and inseparable aspects of reality. First of all, Shiva is the ultimate source of all movement; if the potential for movement did not exist in him, it could never become actualized in the form of Shakti. And secondly, though we cannot perceive Shiva, if he did not exist it would be equally impossible for us to perceive Shakti's movement, for Einstein showed that movement is undetectable unless it occurs against a background of relative stillness. In the total blackness of outer space, for example, we could be speeding along at a million miles per hour and yet we would have no sensation of movement whatsoever unless we passed some relatively fixed object. In the same way, then, Shakti's movement is perceptible only because it occurs against the background of Shiva's perfect stillness.

Though explanations of this sort are useful in giving us at

least some vague idea of what the world is like at its most basic level, we must constantly remind ourself that the true essence of reality is beyond the ken of the normal human intellect. Such concepts as "movement" and "stillness" as we know them are but very gross approximations of their extremely subtle counterparts which function at the highest level of reality. From the viewpoint of Paramashiva, movement and rest are not irreconcilable opposites; he is fully capable of engaging in both simultaneously. At the level of the physical universe, however, such apparent dualities seem to be eternally antagonistic; they cannot exist simultaneously at precisely the same place and time.

But even so, modern science still agrees that our material reality is founded solely upon these same two phenomena, only instead of occurring simultaneously, in the physical universe these two essential elements seem to alternate perpetually, in the form of vibration.

As we have already seen, our entire peceivable reality is based upon the phenomenon we call "vibration," and vibration is essentially nothing more than the rapid alternation between movement and stillness. When anything vibrates, it oscillates rapidly back and forth between two points, as does a pendulum or a child on a swing. The figure below depicts one complete cycle of vibration, which science measures from the center point (A), to the outwardmost point of swing on one side (B), across to the outwardmost point of swing on the opposite side (C), and back to the center point (A) again.

FIGURE 8

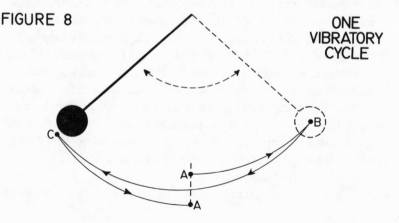

ONE
VIBRATORY
CYCLE

When anything oscillates, it repeatedly reverses the direction of its movement; but in order to do this, at the outwardmost point of each cycle (points B and C) it must slow down and completely stop for just the tiniest fraction of an instant before it continues on its journey in the opposite direction. Thus, what we call vibration is a rapid and repeated alternation between movement and rest; it is the way in which Shiva and Shakti manifest at the level of the physical world.

The entire universe, from the moment of Creation to the moment of its ultimate dissolution, may be viewed as single cosmic cycle of movement which has sprung forth from a state of absolute rest, and which will eventually return to that same quiescent state. Within this master cycle of vibration, everything which exists can also be viewed in terms of progressively smaller types of cycles, from the existence-cycle of galaxies to that of solar systems, planets, individual beings and objects, all the way down to the most elementary subatomic particle, which consists of nothing more substantial than a unit of pure consciousness in rapid oscillation. Everything in Creation, big or small, gross or subtle, is not only vibrating, it is also made of vibration; and this vibration, at its fundamental level, is nothing less than supreme consciousness in motion.

When we spin a coin on a table, both sides of it are always present before us simultaneously, yet we are able to perceive only one side at a time as it spins. If the coin is spinning fast enough, in fact, we don't seem to see either side at all; instead, we see a solid-looking, transparent sphere which, like a subatomic particle, really isn't what it appears to be at all. In this way, supreme consciousness (Paramashiva) appears to alternate perpetually between two phases—Shakti's movement and Shiva's stillness— and it is these two aspects of reality which function as the basic building blocks of manifest Creation. They are not just important properties of reality; they are its very essence.

In the Beginning . . .

Once we discover that the whole of Creation can be defined in terms of vibration, it then becomes possible for us to interpret even the poetic language of religious scripture in a way that makes it quite compatible with the views of modern science and Yoga. Vibration affects the human senses in many different ways; the eyes interpret it as form and color, the skin as texture and density, the nose and mouth as aroma and flavor, and the ears experience vibration as sound, such as music or words.

If we accept "music" as being a poetical equivalent of vibration, for example, then this fifteenth century quote from the Eastern poet-saint Kabir begins to take on added meaning:

> The heart of the sky, wherein the Spirit dwelleth,
>   is radiant with the music of light.
> There, where the pure, white music blossoms,
>   my Lord takes His delight.[9]

According to Shaivism, Creation begins when Shakti issues from Shiva in the form of a causal vibration, Spanda. At first glance this concept seems to have little in common with the following biblical statement: "In the beginning was the word, and the word was with God, and the word was God." But if we interpret "word" here as a poetical rendering for the vibration of Spanda-Shakti, we can just as accurately state that "In the beginning was the Shakti, and the Shakti was with Shiva, and the Shakti was Shiva." Interestingly, the world's oldest scripture, the Vedas, contains language strikingly similar to that of the Bible:

> *Praajapatir vai idam aaseet*
> *Tasya vaag dviteeya aaseet*
> *Vaag vai paramam Brahma*

"In the beginning was the Creator, within whom was the word, and the word was the Lord Himself."

Actually, when we combine the metaphors employed by Yoga, religion and modern physics, we can paint an even clearer picture of the principles involved in Creation. Beginning with this poetic rendering from Genesis, for example: "And the earth was without form and was void; and darkness was upon the face of the waters." Here, the Bible states that pre-Creation was a void without form. We may imagine this void to be Shiva in yogic terms, or in scientific terms the quiescent ground field, completely devoid of activity. Then, our biblical quote adds that "darkness was upon the face of the deep." Again, "the deep" may be seen as but another metaphor for Shiva, the void. Since there is as yet no motion in the fundamental ground field, there is only "darkness," which science defines as the absence of light, a type of vibration.

Finally, the Old Testament quote states that "the Spirit of God moved upon the face of the waters." Here, "the Spirit of God" is, in yogic terms, the polar opposite of Shiva, meaning Shakti or vibration. The image of Shakti moving upon the surface of water is a wonderfully accurate way of illustrating how vibration moves through a substance or medium. If we think of Shiva as a vast ocean, Shakti may then be likened to the waves moving across its surface. A wave is a vibration. When we stand on the ocean shore and watch the waves roll in, we know that the particles of water in any particular spot are not moving toward us, they are merely being undulated up and down—they are vibrating. Yet, it appears as if each wave has a continuous identity; we can watch one begin far out at sea and follow it all the way in to where it crashes on the beach. Each wave appears to be an existent thing, but in reality it is just vibration moving across the face of the water, causing the illusion of a separate entity leading a temporary existence upon the water's surface.

This, Yoga tells us, is what the universe is like. Shiva is a big ocean of Consciousness, and Shakti is all the bubbles, foam, ripples and waves upon its surface, patterns of movement which appear to us as people, planets, stars and galaxies. Everything we see around us is like a wave in the ocean of pure Being; the water takes on certain forms for a while, then merges with the depths again. Some of these vibrational entities exist for extremely brief periods (most elementary particles, for example, remain cohesive for just the tiniest fraction of a second), while others remain manifest much longer (the human body takes about a century to disintegrate, and a galaxy maintains its individuality for billions of years); in any case, none of the manifestations of the universe are permanent—all eventually must return to the ground field from which they have arisen.

Everything which has ever existed or will ever exist, be it short- or long-lived, animate or inanimate, mental or physical, as small as an elementary particle or as vast as an entire world system, is essentially just a partial experience of the entire cosmic field of interrelating forces. Like all the unique forms on the surface of agitated water, everything in Creation is made of exactly the same basic ''stuff''; each entity is just a particular portion of a single mass of Consciousness—a portion which is temporarily vibrating in a special way.

The Christian mystic Angela of Foligno probably had no knowledge of Kashmir Shaivism, yet in the thirteenth century she wrote an essay describing her moment of Self-realization, explaining that two supreme principles were revealed to her in turn, and these principles sound suspiciously like Shakti and Shiva:

> The eyes of my soul were opened and I beheld the plentitude of God, by which I understood the whole world both here and beyond the sea, the abyss, and all other things. . . . And in this I beheld nothing save the Divine *Power,* in a way that is utterly indescribable, so that through the greatness of this wonder the soul cried with a loud voice, saying, "The whole world is full of God." Wherefore I understood that the world is but a little thing; and I saw that the power of God was above all things and the whole world was filled with it. . . .
>
> After I had seen the power of God, His will and His justice, I was lifted higher still; and then I no longer beheld the power and will as before. But I beheld a *Thing,* as fixed and stable as it was indescribable; and more than this I cannot say, save that it was good. And although my soul beheld not love, yet when it saw that indescribable *Thing* it was filled with indescribable joy,

so that it was taken out of the state it was in before and placed in this great and ineffable state. . . . But if thou seekest to know that which I beheld, I can tell thee nothing save that I beheld a Fullness and a Clearness. . . . Thus I beheld a beauty so great that I can say nothing of it save that I saw the Supreme Beauty which contains in itself all goodness.[10]

Shakti's Multi-Layered Creation

When we consider how little we know about our own universe, the possibility of other universes existing simultaneously should hardly surprise us. Such notions were common throughout the world during the heyday of ancient metaphysics, but now that metaphysics has been exiled by modern science, speculations about the existence of other dimensions of reality have pretty much become limited to the fields of spiritualism and science fiction. Most modern people assume that the claims of ancient occultists will eventually be proved false by Western science, but in this area as in others we've examined earlier, science seems to be moving toward supporting the ancient "myths" rather than debunking them.

With the discovery of so-called black holes in the universe, holes which seem to be sucking in matter like cosmic vacuum cleaners, astronomers have begun to speculate about the possible existence of another universe of "anti-matter" at the other end of those holes. Scientists further speculate that we may actually be exchanging substance with this other universe, losing matter through "black holes" and getting new matter through "white holes" situated possibly at the center of each galaxy. With such mind-bending concepts occupying the thoughts of our best Western scientists, perhaps we should not deal too lightly with the yogic view of a Creation structured in multi-layered realms.

According to the ancient texts, Shakti issues forth as Spanda and then oscillates at every frequency from infinity down to zero, bringing many stratified levels of Creation into being. The slower she vibrates, the more she makes Consciousness become congealed so that in the first realm the forms which she creates are extremely subtle, while in the latter ones, which include our own universe, they are very dense indeed. The grosser the forms which Shakti manifests, the more they obscure the true reality and take on an appearance of reality themselves instead. These realms are like a series of veils obscuring the formless Shiva; the deeper the realm in density, the greater the obscuration. For this reason they are called the realms of increasingly modified reality; the grosser the realm, the more true reality fades and illusion becomes clearer. Thus, Creation represents an awakening of Shakti as the manifest world, but a falling asleep of Shiva as far as pure consciousness is concerned.

Each realm is made of increasingly gross elements. The easiest way to conceive of these realms is to think of them as independent universes of which ours is the densest. Figure 9 illustrates the six major realms which Shakti manifests during her descent into matter. The Bible characterizes them as the six days of Creation.

The words Mind, Ether, Air, Fire, Water and Earth represent archetypal elements or universal principles and should not be confused with the substances we know by those names. For example, in the Earth Realm—our physical universe—everything that has substance is made of the Earth Element, so this element is comparable to what we call "matter." In the same way, what we know as "mind," "ether," "air," "fire" and "earth" are only very gross manifestations of the cosmic principles with the same names.

Just as the Earth Realm is inhabited by beings (us) with bodies made of Earth (matter), each of the other five realms contains beings with bodies more subtle than our own. In our realm, Consciousness is so veiled by the extreme density of the forms it assumes that we humans are completely imprisoned in the illusion of reality it creates, unable to even glimpse the real fabric of Creation beneath the bright "solid" patterns of the physical universe. Beings in the higher realms are bound in varying lesser degrees, and those at the opposite end of the spectrum from us are in no way bound by the world they live in.

According to Yoga, there are many more realms in Creation than just the six major ones indicated in Figure 9. One ancient text, the *Maha Nirvana Tantra*, outlines fourteen levels of manifest reality, while Kashmir Shaivism, which dissects Creation with far

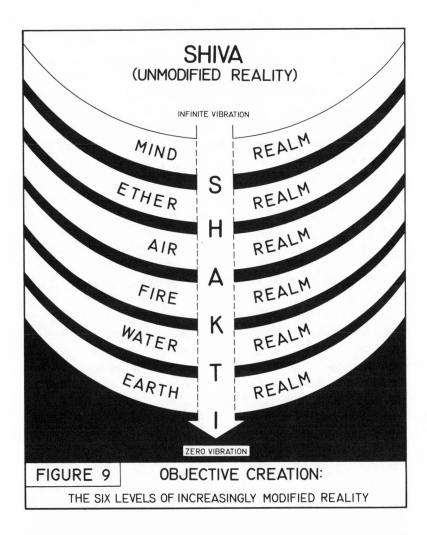

FIGURE 9 | OBJECTIVE CREATION:
THE SIX LEVELS OF INCREASINGLY MODIFIED REALITY

greater precision than any other philosophy, delineates a full thirty-six separate planes of existence, among which are distributed some 224 inhabited worlds.

If all this sounds preposterous, we must remember that the purpose of this book is not to convince us that such things exist, but simply to describe what Yoga tells us we can each experience for ourself through meditation. Yoga calls the different inhabited worlds of these realms *lokas* or *bhuvanas,* and much has been written about them by meditators who have personally observed them throughout the centuries. If any of us is interested in testing the authenticity of these lokas we may compare the numerous eyewitness accounts of them which have been written, or better still, we may choose to meditate and find out for ourself.

Now that we've examined the unfolding of Creation and its structure upon completion, all that now remains to be covered is the end of Creation, or Dissolution.

Dissolution

Vibration is movement that occurs in cycles. Since everything in Creation is vibration, then Creation itself must also be cyclical—a gigantic cycle of evolution and dissolution which begins when Shakti moves within Shiva and ends when she returns to her potential state again. As soon as each cycle ends, a new one begins. According to Yoga, our present universe is just one in an endless chain of universes which have previously been created and destroyed, and there will be countless universes after ours.

Until recently, astrophysicists could neither confirm nor deny this yogic view of cyclical Creation, but discoveries made in just the past few decades have begun to shift the weight of scientific evidence quite clearly toward the position upheld by the ancient sages.

For the past fifty years astronomers have known that all the galaxies in the universe are rapidly flying away from a common center, and the speed with which they are receding from one another suggests the possibility that at one time, billions of years ago, all the matter in Creation suddenly exploded outward from a single point, a blast which marked the exact moment that Creation began. Despite the fact that this "big bang" theory was supported by the discovery that the universe is expanding, most scientists doggedly refused to accept the possibility that the cosmos had a definite beginning, for then they would have been forced to attend themselves to the question of who or what began it. Thus, for decades the big bang theory played second fiddle to the more comforting "steady-state" theory, which held that the universe is exactly the same as it has always been and will always be the same as it is now.

The steady-state theory continued to hold sway right up until 1965, when two researchers from the Bell Laboratories discovered that our planet is enveloped in a faint glow of radiation which is coming at us uniformly from every direction in the universe. If indeed the cosmos had begun with a "bang," followed by a gigantic, white-hot fireball, this mass of intense heat and brilliant light would never entirely vanish from Creation; instead, as the universe continued to expand, the glow from the initial explosion would simply grow more and more faint. The all-pervasive radiation discovered in 1965 consists of the exact pattern of wavelengths expected for the aftermath of just such an ancient cosmic explosion. In yogic terms, the vibrational pattern that these researchers discovered is nothing less than the remains of the initial Spanda of Creation, the first creative impulse which caused the universe to become manifest, which now sustains it, and which, when it finally returns to its ground state, will effect the dissolution of the cosmos.

As a result of this monumental find, the steady-state theory has finally, though reluctantly, fallen by the wayside, leaving the big-bang concept the only plausible explanation for the history of the universe. Now, astrophysicists must live with this imposing question: What existed *before* the moment of Genesis?

If the universe was *created*, as the world's scriptures have insisted all along, then it follows that someone or something had to create it. Whatever hard evidence there might have been to give science clues to these mysteries was certainly burned up in the intensity of that awesome primal explosion. In the words of Robert Jastrow, Director of NASA's Goddard Institute for Space Studies, "At this moment it seems as though science will never be able to raise the curtain on the mystery of Creation. For the scientist who has lived by his faith in the power of reason, the story ends like a bad dream. He has scaled the mountains of ignorance; he is about to conquer the highest peak; as he pulls himself over the final rock, he is greeted by a band of theologians who have been sitting there for centuries."[11]

Having proved beyond a reasonable doubt that Creation did indeed have a beginning, modern scientists have now been made to ponder whether or not the cosmos will also have a distinct end. Two possibilities are now being explored with regard to the future of the universe: (1) it may continue to expand forever, or (2) it may eventually stop expanding and begin to contract. In order to determine which of these two possibilities will become reality, it is essential for astronomers to know how much matter exists in the universe. Matter's mass exerts gravitational pull, so if there is enough of it present in the expanding arena of Creation, it will eventually drag the receding galaxies to a halt and begin pulling them back toward their original center.

As recently as 1978, astronomers had estimated that the universe contained only about one-tenth the amount of matter required to "close the universe"—to prove that Creation is indeed a complete cycle with a beginning, middle and end. Since then, however, they have discovered the existence of previously unsuspected cosmic gas clouds between two galaxies, and since such clouds are material in that they contain great amounts of mass, the presence of such phenomena throughout the cosmos could increase the amount of known mass to a level which would close the universe. In addition, more recent findings have indicated the possibility that a subatomic particle called the *neutrino*, which was previously believed to be massless, may indeed contain a small amount of mass. If true, this discovery alone could more than double the known mass of the universe.

Thus, science is coming closer and closer to confirming the yogic model of a cyclical Creation. Furthermore, astronomers expect that if the universe does indeed prove to be closed, its contraction phase will end when all matter in Creation comes together at a single point, a collision which theorists expect will eventually produce another big bang—meaning that a new universe will then emerge, made out of the melted-down stuff of our present world—and this cyclical process could well repeat itself into eternity. Such speculations, prompted by recent findings, have led Dr. Fritjof Capra, theoretical physicist at Stanford and The University of California, to state that ". . . modern physics leads us to a view of the world which is very similar to the views held by mystics of all ages and traditions."[12]

The thought of our present universe being just a single throb in an endless oscillation between creation and destruction may overwhelm us with the apparent meaninglessness of it all; but there is no use fretting about such things, for our finite reasoning power is useless when it comes to fathoming the infinite. Yoga tells us that the closest we can come to comprehending the eternal cycles of Creation is to think of them all as simply the play of Consciousness —Shiva and Shakti having fun. If, from our present point of view, we can't fully appreciate the entertainment value of such Divine Sport, so what? Other people probably don't understand why *we* have fun doing some of the things we like to do, either. The Rishis advise us that there is only one way to appreciate the merits of this sport, and that's to become one of the players—which means expanding our awareness until it becomes the cosmic kind.

This, then, is the environment in which we live. Whether we examine it from the viewpoint of Yoga, modern physics or religion, it always proves to be an astounding, mystifying, paradoxical experience. But what, we may now inquire, is the role of humankind in this incredible Creation? To find out, we must now focus our investigation upon the investigators themselves.

4. The Part that Makes Creation Complete

Up to now, our examination of the universe has focused upon *objective* Creation—all the things and happenings which we perceive throughout the world around us. What we have not yet investigated is the *subjective* aspect of the cosmos—namely, that part of us which perceives the objective universe from within the confines of our human body.

Inside our body there dwells a nonmaterial instrument of awareness which we refer to as our "mind," and beyond that lies a presence which is more subtle still: the inner Self—the essence of our being. Nowhere in our perusal of the objective cosmos was there any mention of the human mind or inner Self being created. How, then, did they originate? What is their place in the Grand Design, and what specific function has been assigned to them? It is to these important questions that we now direct our full attention.

Observer or Participator?

From somewhere behind those probing eyes which greet us in the mirror each morning, *the real us* gazes out upon Creation. Our mind, brain and senses are the instruments through which we view the world around us, and invariably what these instruments tell us is that the universe is filled with diversity and duality, despite the fact that both modern physics and ancient spiritual science assure us there are no isolated objects in the cosmos, that everything in manifest Creation is intimately interconnected and interrelated— even apparent opposites—and that all phenomena arise from and eventually subside back into a single, all-pervasive ground substance, which, though imperceptible, is the only true reality.

Our mind, brain and senses also tell us that we, as the perceiver of the external world, are forever separate and removed from everything around us. Since our normal perception of the outer world has already proved to be defective, how reliable, then, is this notion that we are completely disconnected from the rest of Creation?

The modern physicist has found that, although this feeling of separateness appears to be valid at the level of reality that our senses perceive, at a more basic level it, too, proves to be erroneous. When making observations in the realm of subatomic particles, physicists have learned that it becomes impossible for them to keep themselves clearly segregated from the objects they are attempting to observe. It seems that the very act of observation entails an interaction between the observer and the object of observation, and this interaction automatically alters the nature of the object.

If the universe is in essence nothing but a vast network of intermingling vibratory patterns, then both we and the object we wish to observe are simply two such patterns which have begun to interact, each having some effect upon the nature of the other. After all, the act of observation cannot take place across empty space because, as we have already seen, there is no such thing as empty space. All objects are intense, temporarily stable energy patterns, and all interactions among them take place in the form of more subtle, less stable energy patterns. This second type of pattern overlaps and joins all those of the first type into a single web of interconnected patterns. Thus, we become faced with another interesting paradox of modern physics: In order to observe an object accurately we must completely isolate it and remove it from any external influences; and yet, in order to observe said object we ourself must interact with it!

All our definitions and measurements of the external world, then, are nothing more than the effects of interactions which create certain sensations in our consciousness. All the properties and propensities which we assign to things cannot be relied upon to exist when we are not observing them. The closer physicists look at one property of a subatomic particle, such as its velocity, the more uncertain another property, such as its location, becomes. Since it is impossible to separate themselves from the objects of their observation, today's particle physicists now consider it inappropriate to think of themselves as "observers"; they now consider themselves "participants" who alter the very structure of nature by the act of perceiving it.

Max Born, the renowned German physicist who was one of the founding fathers of quantum physics, commented extensively upon this unexpected discovery of modern science, as evidenced in the following excerpt from one of his published papers:

> [We have all been] taught that there exists an objective physical world, which unfolds itself according to immutable laws independent of us; we are watching this process like the audience watches a play in a theatre. . . . Quantum mechanics, however, interprets the experience gained in atomic physics in a different way. We may compare the observer of a physical phenomenon not with the audience of a theatrical performance, but with that of a football game where the act of watching, accompanied by applauding or hissing, has a marked influence on the speed and concentration of the players, and thus on what is watched. In fact, a better simile is life itself, where audience [observers] and actors [observed objects] are the same persons. It is the action of the experimentalist who designs the apparatus which determines essential features of the observations. Hence, there is no objectively existing situation, as was supposed to exist in classical physics.[13]

If, as modern physics insists, *there is no objectively existing situation* to be perceived by us, then what are we to make of this very real and solid world of beings, objects and events which we seem to experience all around us? If the material world is not "out there," then where is it?

It's All in Our Mind

Both Yoga and modern science assure us that the only things which really exist in the universe around us are (1) an all-pervasive, organic ground substance which, though everywhere, cannot be perceived, and (2) a vast array of interconnected, constantly changing patterns of vibration, some of which are capable of interaction with our physical senses. This, we are told, is all that exists "out there" at this very moment; it's all that has ever existed "out there," and it's all that will ever exist "out there" until the end of time.

But somehow, whenever *we* enter the scene, suddenly "out there" seems to take on a completely different appearance. We look around us and see a multitude of independent objects and events, forms and colors; we listen and hear a multitude of sounds; we sniff and smell a multitude of aromas; we touch and feel a multitude of densities, textures and temperatures; we taste and savor a multitude of flavors. How, then, is it possible that true reality consists only of interacting vibratory patterns, when all our personal experience tells us that there are solid *things* out there?

Despite the convincing testimony of our mind, brain and senses, there still remains an annoying fact which must be reckoned with: *Solid matter does not exist.* As we saw in the previous chapter, modern physics has discovered that what we experience as matter is in reality nothing more than a particular pattern of energy vibration which displays the amazing property of *appearing* to be solid when in fact it is not. This leads to an interesting conjecture: *What if there is no observer present to perceive that appearance of solidity?* The inescapable conclusion seems to be that the world assumes a substantial appearance only when it is being perceived!

According to Kashmir Shaivism, the universe cannot exist unless it contains both an *objective* side (all the objects and events in all the many realms of manifest Creation) and a *subjective* side—some sort of witness capable of perceiving the objective world. Translating this into our physical reality, it means that *no material object as we know it can exist unless there is a perceiving subject present to experience its existence.*

Most of us will find this rather hard to swallow, because common sense tells us that even though no one may be on hand to witness an object's existence, the object could still be there all by itself. For example, we might argue that even if there were no living creatures here to perceive this world, the world would still be here, wouldn't it?

Ah, but would it? And this is where we begin to slide into a very creepy "Twilight Zone," for despite the obvious fact that each and every one of us experiences that there is a very real and solid world outside of us, both modern and ancient science inform us that this material world does not exist "out there" at all—it exists only in our mind. In short: *No mind, no world.*

Modern physicists view the universe as a teeming sea of energy patterns, and they know that matter is really nothing more than a cohesive mass of vibrational packets which appear to us as particles, and which in themselves contain no such properties as color, solidity, aroma, flavor, texture, density, etc. If we then ask these physicists how they reconcile this scientific picture of reality with the world which they perceive through their physical senses, they will probably state that all the qualities of our everyday world of sights, sounds, smells, tastes and feelings are created and superimposed upon reality by the mind of the perceiver.

Perhaps the best way for us to achieve at least a general understanding of this astounding concept is through an example which combines images borrowed from both Yoga and modern science.

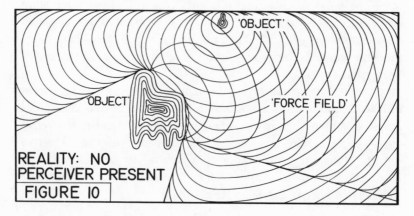

'OBJECT'

'OBJECT'

'FORCE FIELD'

REALITY: NO
PERCEIVER PRESENT

FIGURE 10

In Figure 10 we see represented a small field of interacting energy patterns. Let's assume that this field is just a minute section of the cosmic sea, though of course in reality it would be much more complex than this simple, two-dimensional rendering.

The white background represents Shiva, the static ground field, and the wavy lines symbolize Shakti, interacting waves of vibrational movement. In this particular field we find two "objects" —temporarily stable and intense energy patterns—and between them is a more subtle and unstable force pattern which joins the two objects together and mediates an interaction that is taking place between them. Since there is as yet no perceiver present on the scene, the only distinguishing characteristics among these patterns are that each displays a unique configuration, intensity, and range of influence. This represents reality in the absence of a perceiving mind; in no way does it resemble a scene that we would recognize as belonging to the material world.

This illustration is symbolic of what is really "out there" when no mind is tuned into objective Creation; it's what is really all around us when we close our eyes, for example, thereby ceasing to bestow such qualities as form and color upon these patterns.

The next illustration (Figure 11) outlines what begins to happen the moment a perceiver appears upon the scene. Suddenly, the smaller object-pattern becomes a source of light, and its surrounding field begins to behave as if it's made of photon particles radiating outward in every direction from the object's center.

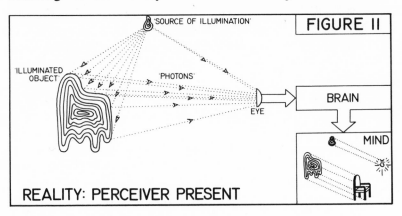

Some of these photons flow directly into the perceiver's eye, while others are absorbed by the pattern on the left, which now reveals itself to be some sort of perceivable object. This pattern, too, now begins to behave as if it were made of particles instead of vibratory waves; its electrons absorb photons from the light source, become excited for a split second, and then eject new photons, in effect reflecting the light back into space. Many of these "reflected photons" enter the perceiver's eye, which precisely records the pattern of arriving photons and relays it to the brain.

Though it seems as if our eyesight actually "reaches out" across empty space and lights upon an object before us, this is not the case at all. We never really *see* any external object, for our eyes are sensitive only to the photons which such an object emits. Even if there were really a solid object before us, we would still be able to see only the photons reflected from its surface, not the object itself. Then, this photon pattern interacts with the retina of our eye, producing chemical changes in particular cells which in turn relay a pattern of electrical impulses to our brain. Once again, this electrical pattern does not even vaguely resemble the object we are supposedly "seeing."

At this point, according to Yoga, our mind now deciphers this pattern of electrical impulses and uses it to faithfully recreate, out of its own "mind-stuff," an exact duplicate of the external energy pattern from which the photons have just arrived. Thus, we see in Figure 11 that in the perceiver's mind there now appear internal patterns which are like mirror images of the ones outside: the mind assumes the shape of whatever it perceives in the outside world.

Now the mind is ready to work its most amazing miracle. These newly created internal patterns interact with that part of the mind concerned with the sense of sight, and immediately there is evoked within us sensations of form, color and space. Our intellect then tells us that the objects before us are a chair and a burning light bulb, and our ego adds that we, the perceiver, are distinctly separate from both. Then, as Figure 12 illustrates, our mind combines all these newly bestowed qualities into a multi-dimensional mental hologram, which we then project into the outer world, interpreting the objects as we now see them in our mind to exist

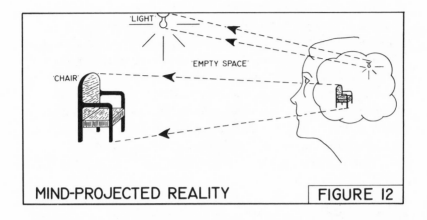

MIND-PROJECTED REALITY   FIGURE 12

before us in that same form. This entire process, from the moment we open our eyes to the time we perceive a chair and burning bulb before us, takes no more than a few billionths of a second!

Of course, though it is perfectly true that the physical world *as we know it* exists only in our mind, this does not imply that there is nothing objective at all ''out there.'' The universe around us is indeed filled with ''objects,'' but these do not possess any of the definitive qualities which we normally apply to ''objectness.'' For example, in the exact spot where we perceive a chair to be, something is really there—a unique pattern of energy which will remain intact as long as the object we know as a ''chair'' exists. However, the only time that particular pattern will ever take on the characteristics of ''chairness'' will be when it is being perceived by someone, at which time the properties of a chair as we know it will be projected into that pattern by the perceiver's mind.

If we were to now move forward until the pattern of our body came into contact with that of the chair, that same vibrational pattern would then begin to interact with the part of our mind connected with the sense of touch, causing within us sensations such as density, texture and temperature. Thus, each energy pattern we perceive manifests itself in a particular way to one or more of our senses; some, though imperceptible to our sense of sight, interact instead with our hearing, smell, taste or touch.

One way for us to imagine the real world of vibrational patterns in space is to compare them to the air around us, which is presently filled with invisible television signals. In the very place where we are now reading this book, the space around us contains countless vibrating TV waves. If we were to record these waves on an oscilloscope, all we would see would be squiggly lines— patterns of vibration; but if we were to bring in a TV receiver and tune it to those signals, we would suddenly perceive a whole world of objects and events projected onto the TV screen.

Those vibrating TV waves in the air around us are actually *formless versions* of all the things we could perceive if a TV set were present. In the absence of a receiver, however, all those sporting events, quiz shows, newscasts, cowboys, landscapes, music, words, etc., are still in the air around us, but only in the form of vibrating waves; they cannot materialize until a receiver is present to tune them in, process and interpret them, then project them through its picture tube and loudspeaker in the form of images and sounds.

This is very much like the way Creation works. The objective world is there, all right, but only in the form of vibrational patterns. It has no substance until some perceiver comes along and tunes it in, interprets it, and then projects its appearance of substance into the perceiver's own mind. Just as the TV screen or loudspeaker can never see the actual vibrations that the receiver's tuner has picked up from "out there," so too the mind can never perceive the actual sea of Consciousness which it is constantly transmuting into substantial form.

When a being becomes Self-realized, however, and transcends the limited mind, he then becomes able to perceive not only the mental world of form and substance, but also the real world of vibrating Consciousness as well. According to Shaivism, such a being experiences all the objects and events of the material world as existing in a subtle sea of shimmering blue Consciousness, a perception which is said to be indescribably beautiful and a source of endless delight.

So, a Creation without a perceiver is like television signals without a TV set, and this is why Shaivism states that such a Creation could not be considered as having true existence.

Our TV analogy works fine in describing how the world of form, color and sound exists only in the mind, but what about the world of density and texture? Perhaps the strongest evidence supporting the existence of a material world "out there" comes from our own physical body, which constantly comes into direct contact with things which quite obviously have substance. After all, how can that stone wall not be there when our body crashes into it so convincingly? What we forget with such reasoning is that our physical body is made of matter, too, so it only *appears* to have substance. Our body is just a particular field of vibrating Consciousness which interacts with all the other fields around it, some of which can be passed right through without resistance, while others interact with ours in such a way that we cannot intermingle with them, so they feel solid to us. A cloud, for example, may look the same to us as a huge mound of cotton, but their vibrational patterns are such that we can pass right through one, while the other resists us and therefore we say it has more density.

It's also important to note here that by no means are our physical senses capable of perceiving *all* the vibrations around us. The physical body responds to an extremely limited range of vibrations, which means that there are actually not just one but many different worlds around us all the time, but their vibrations are so subtle we can pass right through them without having any awareness or perception of them whatsoever. The fact that some people can "see things" which others cannot is due to their having activated one or more subtle psychic senses which lie dormant in most people and which are made operational through the practice of Yoga.

Meanwhile, the next time we crash into a stone wall, we may console ourself with this true understanding: "In a place which appears to be 'out there,' what appears to be my physical body has appeared to crash into what appears to be a stone wall, causing what appears to be 'me' a lot of what appears to be pain!" In reality, of course, all that has happened is that there has been an interaction between two particular fields of vibrating Consciousness; everything else has occurred in our own mind.

Most of us are familiar with the classic philosophical riddle which asks, "If a tree falls in the forest and no one is there to hear it fall, does it make a noise?'' From our present level of understanding, not only would there be no noise, but with no perceiver present to witness the event, no tree would fall at all, because that tree can exist as a tree only in the mind of some perceiver. If we were there at the time, of course, we would witness the event of a tree falling, but in our absence the only event taking place would be a sequence of modulations in a particular field of vibrating Consciousness. Without an experiencing subject present, in fact, the entire forest would not exist in material form, nor would the earth or the sky, the solar system, the Milky Way galaxy or the entire universe. This is why Shaivism says, ''Because you exist, everything exists; without you, nothing is.''

Modern physicists now agree that the perceiver is a fundamental element of Creation. To quote the famous scientist, Dr. James Jeans: ''The complete closed world consists of three parts—substratum, phenomenal world and observer.''[14] Renowned physicist Arthur Eddington then adds, ''Recognizing that the physical world is entirely abstract and without 'actuality' apart from its linkage to consciousness, we restore consciousness to a fundamental position instead of representing it as an inessential complication occasionally found in the midst of inorganic nature at a late stage of evolutionary history.''[15]

Even when we attain an intellectual understanding that the objective world as we know it is not really ''out there,'' we will still experience great difficulty in maintaining this understanding in our daily life, because once we become used to looking at things in a certain way it's very hard to change that point of view. For example, in a recent scientific experiment subjects were fitted with eyeglasses designed to make everything appear upside down. Within just a few days of wearing these topsy-turvy glasses, however, everyone in the experiment had learned to correct the obvious misinformation their eyes were receiving, and they began to perceive everything right side up again in their minds; then, when the glasses were removed, they suddenly saw the world as upside down again until their minds made the desired adjustment once more!

So the mind greatly resists being made to view the world in a different way from the one to which it has become accustomed.

Even though we all know very well that the mind is quite capable of housing a complete multi-dimensional world including space, time, form, color, sound, taste, fragrance, density and texture— for it does this very convincingly each night in our dreams—still we find it extremely difficult to foster in ourself a constant awareness that our waking state is also just another state of mind, and that our waking world is not "out there" at all. In fact, how can there even *be* such a place as "out there" if, in reality, all there is in the entire Creation is just one single thing?

Most of us will readily accept the fact that our brain and senses are merely instruments which we employ in order to perceive the universe; they belong to us, but they are not the real us. Though our senses dutifully record and relay to our brain all the information they receive throughout the day, unless our mental awareness is also focused upon the information received by the brain, we will not experience its existence. For example, when we are lost in thought, our eyes may be wide open and yet we do not really see anything before us. Thus, unless the mind is actively connected to our senses, we do not perceive an external world. No object assumes any of its familiar qualities for us until its mental counterpart is created in our mind and is interpreted by those functions of mind which operate through the physical senses.

Thus, we now know that the function of mind in Creation is to make manifest the material world as we know it. This notion is not limited strictly to the field of spiritual science, either. A few progressive, contemporary physicists have recently postulated a holistic model of the cosmos which they call "the theory of the holonomic order of the mind/brain/universe." According to this theory, the mind, the brain, and the external universe are all parts of a single creative entity, the entirety of which is contained in any of its parts. Reality, speculate the holonomic physicists, is the perceived result of interactions among these three types of being, meaning that objective Creation is as much within the mind/brain as it is within the external universe.

To explain the function of the mind, however, still does not explain its origin. Is the mind a bona fide perceiver, or is it nothing more than another instrument of perception, like the brain and senses? Also, we still have not discovered the function and origin of the inner Self in God's Creation. What is the relationship between the Self and the mind? For these answers we will have to look to Shaivism—until, of course, we can find out for ourself, firsthand, through meditation.

Creation = Self + Mind/Matter

In describing earlier the process of Creation according to Kashmir Shaivism, it was explained metaphorically that Shakti issues from Shiva in the form of infinite vibration and, as she slows down, all the objective realms come into being. But we also know that Shiva and Shakti represent two eternally united aspects of a single cosmic principle, so it's clear that one could never really issue from the other. What actually happens, then, is that they only *appear* to become separated—a concept with which we should all feel quite comfortable by now. Truly speaking, Creation is not the work of just Shakti alone; Shiva also becomes an integral part of the manifest cosmos.

During the process of Creation, both aspects of the supreme principle voluntarily take on limitations, with Shiva appearing to become the subjective side and Shakti appearing to become the objective side. Paramashiva's pure consciousness becomes, in effect, divided into three basic types of manifestation: (1) Self—the Knower, (2) mind—the instrument of Knowing, and (3) matter—the Known. While the Self constitutes the subjective side of the universe, mind and matter together constitute the objective side, for Yoga considers "material" everything which is not pure transcendent consciousness.

Shakti takes on limitations by appearing to separate from Shiva and assume the form which Shaivism calls *prakriti* or nature, including our mind and all the objects and events of manifest Creation. At the same time, Shiva also takes on limitations by seeming to take the form of countless individual souls, called *purushas,* and these become the experiencing subjects of Creation. Actually, of course, both subjective and objective Creation are simply the opposite poles of a single, continuous spectrum of vibrating Consciousness, the highest, most subtle frequencies manifesting as the Self, and the lower, more gross frequencies manifesting as mind and matter. The vital difference between these two poles is that subjective Consciousness possesses powers of awareness and perception, while objective Consciousness does not.

The mind, being a manifestation of objective Consciousness, is therefore itself an inert object. Without the subjective awareness of a purusha flowing through it, the mind is like an unplugged television set, completely unable to receive, process, or convey information. On the other hand, a purusha without a mind through which to perceive is like an observer without eyes. Mind is the essential instrument through which subjective Consciousness perceives objective Creation.

Since Shiva is equally present throughout the universe, there must be a purusha in every manifest object, even every subatomic particle; hence, everything in Creation possesses some level of awareness, but unless there is also a mind therein, there can be no experience of the objective world as we perceive it. In this respect, then, it can be said that although everything in existence is made of Consciousness, only the subjective element is "conscious." We speak of ourself in the very same way, in fact, for when we are wide awake and perceptive of the objective world we describe ourself as "conscious," while when we're in deep sleep—insentient and unaware of anything—we're "unconscious." These two states differ only in the degree to which our mind is operational. When it is fully functioning, we're conscious, and when it's "unplugged," we lose conscious awareness. In the same way, we can think of the subjective purusha as Consciousness which is relatively awake, and the objective prakriti as Consciousness which is relatively asleep.

Just as the objects of Creation are infinite in number, so are the souls, each of which is like an individual cell in Shiva's cosmic body. Just as every one of countless drops of water is identical in essence to the ocean, each purusha is essentially identical to Shiva. When a purusha loses the awareness that it is Shiva, however, and instead begins to identify itself with the instruments through which it perceives—e.g. the mind, ego and body—it becomes a "bound soul"; and when it becomes re-established in its identity as Shiva, it becomes a liberated being. What we call the "Self" is simply that aspect of the purusha which is pure Shiva, without any false identification clouding its essential nature; thus, a soul is said to be "Self-realized" when it becomes free of false identification and regains its lost state of Shivahood.

Summing up the viewpoint of Shaivism, then, we can say that for Creation to exist in a substantial form, it must consist of both a subjective and an objective aspect. The universe as we know it comes into existence only when there is an interaction between the perceiving Self and perceivable matter, and this interaction is mediated through the instrument of perception called mind.

Entities with more sophisticated minds are called "higher life forms" because they have more perceptive powers than "lower life forms," and the most gifted of all perceivers are human beings; thus, we represent the capstone of Creation's subjective structure. To illustrate this in a clear and simple manner, Yoga employs a most effective instructional tool—the allegory.

When Yoga masters wish to share with us some subtle esoteric knowledge, they often choose to tell us a symbolic story which conveys the essence of their teaching in simple images. Such tales are called allegories—extended metaphors in which the inter-actions of cosmic principles are depicted in the form of humanlike relationships. In this way, very profound and complex concepts are reduced to fairy-tale-type narratives in which, though the characters and events may be contrived, the essential Truth is never sacrificed or sullied.

One such allegory is entitled "The Secret Key," which describes the subjective role of humankind in the great cosmic drama of Creation. Some of this narrative we may recognize as a further simplification of symbology covered in previous sections; the rest will be discussed in more detail afterward. Though this tale is ancient, it is also timeless, which means that it can always be related in very up-to-date language.

The Secret Key

Once upon a time, long, long ago, there was absolutely nothing anywhere. Imagine a total void stretching out forever in every direction, an infinite emptiness made of pure, unmanifest Existence, Consciousness, and Bliss—going nowhere and doing nothing.

This was Shiva.

To you and me, the condition described above may sound a bit too vague to be much fun, but Shiva didn't feel that way at all; to him, just "hanging out" was perfectly wonderful. That is, it was *almost* perfectly wonderful—all except for one tiny part of him which was slightly discontented.

How could anything possibly disturb Shiva's infinite repose? There could certainly be no restlessness in that part of him which was pure existence for that was completely content just *being*—it didn't have to be anything in particular. As for the aspect of eternal bliss, what possible complaint could it ever have? That leaves us with the part made of supreme consciousness, and therein lay the rub. To be sure, it was great fun to understand and be aware of everything everywhere, but at this point "everything" was only a potential, not a manifest reality. What's more, it's the nature of consciousness to seek some sort of self-expression. So it was this small part of Shiva's infinite consciousness which began to become a little edgy in the Void.

Shiva never does anything; therefore becoming restless is completely contrary to his nature. This caused the tiny part that was a malcontent to gently emanate from him and become his cosmic complement, the goddess Shakti. Now Shiva had a mate, and this was perfectly fine with him; everything was O.K. with Shiva—he was the ultimate Mr. Nice Guy. Shakti, however, was the ultimate agitator; she was not a bit happy with what she saw all around her, which was, in fact, nothing at all. Being Shiva's consort, she naturally shared his sterling qualities of Existence, Consciousness and Bliss, but in addition to these she boasted another characteristic uniquely her own: Boredom. If you can imagine boredom on a cosmic scale, you will undoubtedly sympathize with Shakti's predicament. Not satisfied with just hanging around all day like her languid mate, Shakti did what any other activist would do when feeling oppressed by the status quo: she began to agitate for change. (And agitation is vibration, remember, and vibration is kinetic force—energy in action.)

Being very bright and talented, Shakti decided to express herself by doing something creative with her consciousness. As we all know, being a Creator is very hard work; first you have to engineer your Creation, then supervise and maintain it, and finally when you're through with it you have to take it all apart and clean up the mess. This was not Shakti's idea of fun; she was only interested in the recreational aspect of self-expression and not in any administrative responsibilities. It would be far more playful and exciting, she decided, to become the Creation itself rather than its Creator. So the first way she expressed herself was by creating a supreme ''Boss,'' whom she called Ishwara, and instructed him thusly: ''Ishwara, see that something pretty is created out of me so I can play in it for a few billion years.''

Ishwara was the perfect Lord of Creation, a superb administrator as well as a creative genius. His initial act was the creation of a talented Board of Directors to serve under him. Brahma was Vice President in Charge of Creation, Vishnu was V.P. in Charge of Maintenance, and Rudra was V. P. in Charge of Demolition. At their first board meeting Ishwara gave them their assignments: ''Brahma, I want you to create a great universe out of Shakti's body, a universe so beautiful and intricate it will keep her happily occupied for billions of years. Vishnu, you are responsible for keeping this Creation running smoothly until she's finished with her play. Rudra, when the game is over, you put everything back where it came from and clean up the mess. Any questions?'' There were none; no questions were necessary. All the gods had played this game countless times before; the real challenge lay in making each universe even more breathtaking and sophisticated than the preceding ones.

Brahma then stood before the goddess Shakti, who by this time was so aquiver with excitement and anticipation that she was virtually invisible, and he wrapped a veil around her many times, each layer causing a grosser universal realm to spring into manifest existence. This rendered Shakti content at last, for now she had a vast cosmic playground in which she could express herself through countless forms. Shiva, too, was supremely happy, because Shiva was always supremely happy.

Now, however, it was Ishwara who was dissatisfied. Being the high and mighty, ephemeral intelligence that he was, he had no way of checking on the work of his subordinates. He had no eyes with which to see the universe, no nose with which to smell it, no ears with which to hear it, no mouth with which to taste it and no hands with which to touch it. Moreover, he had all the responsibilities of being the great Lord of the Universe, with neither the excitement of manipulating his domain (as his board members did), nor the fun of being a part of it (as Shakti was). "Why should everyone else have all the fun and excitement?" he fumed.

Determined to rectify the situation as soon as possible, he called Brahma into his office and said, "I want you to make me a very special creature. In addition to the usual physical senses, it should have the ability to understand and appreciate the wonders of Creation. It must also have the power of discrimination—an ability to recognize the difference between reality and illusion—and it must be able to manipulate its environment. Inside this creature there should be a place in which a fragment of my own pure being can be installed, so I can work with and enjoy the universe through its body and mind. Is all that clear?"

Brahma thought a moment. "Sounds as if you're asking me to make a human being," he finally said.

"Good thinking," agreed Ishwara. "Give it top priority."

Soon the very first human body was ready, and Brahma asked the Lord for a fragment of his own being (which he called a *purusha,* or "soul"), and placed it inside the human's heart. At once Ishwara became plugged into his cosmos, and the initial results seemed very promising. Now he could perceive and enjoy all the wonders in Creation; he could also modify his environment in different ways, and keep tabs on the work of his board members. The human being seemed to be having a really fine time, too, sampling all the sensual pleasures while secure in the knowledge of actually being the Lord himself experiencing his domain through a very sophisticated instrument called the human body.

Everything ran smoothly for a day or two, until suddenly the human got a taste of pain and suffering, the dark side of Brahma's Creation. To Ishwara, of course, everything experienced through the human being was pure bliss; pain and suffering were every bit as wonderful as pleasure and happiness; he loved every detail of Creation quite equally. But the human did not like pain and suffering at all because, quite frankly, they *hurt*. At the first experience of slight unpleasantness, the human cried, "Phooey on this nonsense! I'll take uninterrupted bliss any time!" and it immediately merged its soul back into Ishwara, leaving its body behind to die.

Ishwara was suddenly cut off from the universe again, so he called Brahma and complained. Brahma admitted that his first model of a human had developed a few bugs, which he promised to iron out when the bodies went into full production. Suspecting that the first experiment had failed because the human had lacked adequate companionship, Brahma now created two human beings, a male and a female, with a soul installed in each of them. This gave Ishwara two instruments through which to function, hence doubling his enjoyment of the universe and delighting him immensely. His enthusiasm was again short-lived, however, for as soon as the human couple encountered pain, they merged back with Ishwara and left their bodies behind to die.

"Back to the drawing board," sighed Brahma, and this time he decided to go all out and create a hundred human beings, each with a fragment of Ishwara inside. Again Ishwara enjoyed a few days of ecstatic enjoyment, but then the souls were flocking back to him by the score, and all of them were telling exactly the same story: "Experiencing Creation through human bodies is great fun from up here, but from down there it's the pits!"

In desperation Ishwara called a meeting of his Board of Directors and asked for their advice. Brahma said, "Listen, Boss, those human beings are the finest creatures ever created. If you ask me, we've got a maintenance problem, not a creative one, and maintenance is not my department."

Iswara turned to his maintenance V.P. "Any ideas?"

Vishnu nodded. "As I see it, so long as these humans know that they're each an extension of you, they'll keep running back to you as soon as the going gets a little rough for them down there. How about if we modify them a little, just so they'll forget their connection to you? That way they won't know how to get away from pain and suffering, so the souls will all stay in their bodies.''

"Good idea," agreed Ishwara. "Let's give it a try."

So Vishnu saw to it that the few remaining humans suddenly forgot that they were really extensions of the Lord, and they immediately stopped merging back with him in the face of pain and suffering. Their numbers began to multiply and soon there were thousands, then millions of them. Now Ishwara had millions of eyes, ears, noses, mouths and hands, and his enjoyment of Creation was millions of times greater than ever before. But gradually the experiment began to turn sour once again.

This time, as humans experienced more pain and suffering than they thought they could bear, they knew of nowhere they could go for relief. Thinking themselves to be all alone in the vast unfathomable universe, with no connection to divinity, they began to feel desperate, frustrated and terribly lost. Crime, violence and immorality reached epic proportions. Everywhere deluded, deranged people were abusing, torturing, even killing themselves and one another; it soon became apparent that if something wasn't done humanity would completely destroy itself again.

Exasperated, Ishwara called another board meeting and told its members that their jobs were on the line. "What's this world coming to anyway?" he exclaimed. "It's getting to the place where a poor god can't even enjoy a little universe once in a while without a lot of hassles!"

This time, Rudra the Destroyer spoke up. "Look, Chief, what say we just dismantle the entire works and call it quits?"

Ishwara peered at him. "And just what do we tell Shakti?"

Rudra shrugged, "Tell her we decided to end the game a bit early this time."

"Four billion years early?" fumed Ishwara. "Are you nuts? Why, she'd run my tail so far into the boondocks the Void would seem overpopulated in comparison!"

Vishnu, who had been in deep meditation, was aroused by Ishwara's shouting. "What we all seem to be forgetting here," he said, "is a little thing called Compassion. I mean, those poor people are really *suffering* down there. We need to find a happy medium between their being able to merge with you any time they get a little toothache, and their not being able to get back to you at all no matter how tough it gets for them."

"Good point," Ishwara nodded. "Any thoughts about how we strike this happy medium?"

"Well," Vishnu continued, "how about the old Secret Key routine?"

"I get your drift," Ishwara said. "We hide the knowledge of humankind's true nature—make it difficult but not impossible to find."

"Right. Only those people who want more than anything else to be free of pain and suffering will be able to discover the Secret Key that will help them find their way back to you."

"Okay," Ishwara agreed, "the Secret Key routine it is. Now we need to decide where to hide this key so that the humans will have a hard time finding it."

"How about at the bottom of the ocean?" Brahma suggested. "They'll never think of looking there."

Ishwara thought a bit. "No, I see them inventing submarines and diving bells. As soon as one of them finds it, everyone will start using it."

"How about the moon?" Rudra suggested.

"I see space ships," Ishwara said. "They'd all have the key again in no time."

"I know!" said Vishnu triumphantly. "Let's hide the key right inside the human body! That's the last place anyone would ever think of looking for it!"

"Brilliant!" agreed Ishwara. "Even when someone discovers it within his or her own body, other people will refuse to believe that the exact same key is inside them as well!"

And so, under Ishwara's orders, Vishnu caused a great flood to cover the earth, wiping out all but two members of the wicked, lost race of humans, and inside these remaining two he hid the Secret Key. The new race of humans survived and multiplied; Ishwara soon boasted billions of eyes, billions of ears, billions of noses, mouths and hands. The humans constantly strove to maximize pleasure and minimize pain; but no matter how frantically they all searched for the Secret Key which would end all their suffering forever, only a few ever thought to look within.

This allegory captures the essence of everything we've covered in the past two chapters, and much more. Despite all the various characters, settings and events it portrays, the tale really contains only one character, one setting, one event: Shiva. All gods and goddesses are merely different aspects of Shiva—cosmic principles isolated and assigned unique names for ease of comprehension. Truly speaking, in fact, *all* names (including our own) are only aliases of Shiva; all forms and events are really Shiva in disguise. Here is the story of the Secret Key in a nutshell: Shiva (in the form of a human being), forgetting that he is Shiva (the Supreme Lord), searches inside Shiva (the universe) trying to find Shiva (the Self), all for the entertainment of Shiva (in the form of Shakti).

As all of us have undoubtedly guessed by now, our Secret Key is none other than the inner Self—every human being's direct link to the universal mind. The use of a key to symbolize the hidden Self inside us is a wonderfully appropriate analogy. A locked door can be opened by just one special key; no other key will work the latch, and yet there could be countless duplicates of this unique key— enough identical copies for every person on earth to carry one in his or her pocket. In the same way, the inner Self is our only key to the source of all Creation, and this key is identical in every human being: the exact same Self is shared by all of us.

On the surface, each one of us is independent and unique, but underneath we are all united—joined to one another by a common core of being—as illustrated in Figure 13 on the following page.

The figure shows the cross-section of a group of islands jutting up from the ocean floor. Each island is like an individual human being. The air above the surface of the sea represents the realm of conscious awareness—our normal waking state—what we call the outside world. In this realm everyone's independent ego functions and we appear as separate entities to one another. The underwater area represents the unconscious realm, the inner world of which

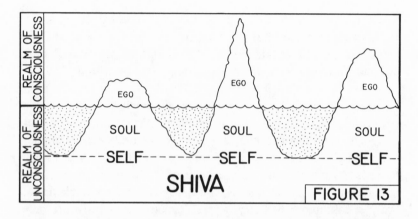

FIGURE 13

few of us are ever aware. The earth of the sea floor is Shiva, the source of all Creation. What we call an island is really just a projection of the ocean floor, and similarly, what we call a human being is really just a projection of Shiva. The deepest part of our being, which we call the Self, is simply the point at which Shiva begins to take the form of a human being. As the illustration clearly indicates, we could explore the outer world till doomsday and never discover the underlying unity existent in all of Creation. Only through meditation, the exploration of the inner depths, can we ever hope to see things as they really are.

How the Key Got Lost

What fateful quirk did the gods install in us to make us ''misplace'' the most essential aspect of our being? If we have always carried inside us this pure and perfect Self, our own private conduit to the very source of infinite power, love and wisdom, how did we ever let ourself lose touch with it? What made us trade a priceless treasure for an almost worthless copy which causes us endless pain, suffering and frustration?

The quirk, Yoga tells us, is simply in the way our organism functions in its environment. Remember back in Part Two when we described how the constant fidgeting of the body and mind tends to lure our awareness away from the deeper aspect of our being?

Because of this quirk, our natural inclination is toward limiting our self-awareness to our most superficial aspects—our body and mind. Unless we are raised in a culture which provides us with guidance and encouragement in the development of inner awareness, our talent for perceiving and operating on the more subtle levels of our being tends to atrophy and become dormant.

The primary focus of our modern educational system is on conceptualization rather than feeling. Our reasoning power is cultivated, while our power of intuition is ignored. Both at home and at school, children are programmed to accept and respond to models of Truth contrived by their elders rather than being encouraged to sharpen their own instinctive abilities to distinguish between right and wrong, reality and illusion. In Western culture, the three R's are considered essential for a happy, productive and fulfilling life, while such things as self-exploration, self-expression and inner unfoldment are not. So much emphasis is placed upon mental gymnastics and learning how to manipulate our external environment, and so little emphasis is placed upon the realization of our psychic potential, it is little wonder that modern civilization has become, at the same time, both a material wonderland and a spiritual wasteland.

Once we become limited to experiencing everything through just our body and mind, we are doomed to perceive the rest of Creation as being decidedly separate from us; life becomes the defensive act of seeking personal survival at any cost in an alien environment whose obvious purpose is to destroy us at the first opportunity. An awareness imprisoned solely in the body and mind is doomed to operate entirely through the physical senses, which are designed to project awareness outward, not inward. Thus these senses perpetually send us the same message: *I am "here" and everything else is "out there," separate from me*. Yogic philosophy however, tells us that all our pain and suffering is a direct result of our failure to recognize and experience our intimate kinship with nature and our fellow human beings.

Up to this point we have dealt with the nature of humankind in general terms, and our goal is to eventually zero in on the individual human body itself, pinpointing the exact mechanisms which are activated inside us through the practice of meditation, and explaining precisely how this process of Yoga leads to Self-realization.

Before we can do that, however, we must first examine a few principles which may be vague or unknown to some of us at this time. First there's the yogic concept of evolution, which is decidedly different from most current notions about it; then we must briefly review the Eastern doctrines of reincarnation and karma, both of which hold prominent places in yogic philosophy.

5. Evolution, Reincarnation and Karma

Evolution

According to the current theories of modern science, evolution is thought to be a patient, inexorable law of nature which causes lower life-forms to gradually mutate into higher ones. In other words, the most popular modern view of evolution is that it is largely an automatic process which is simply happening to us, rather than something we are causing to happen. For example, in just the last hundred years the human brain seems to have developed a remarkable and unprecedented faculty for manipulating our environment, and as a result humankind is accomplishing astounding progress in the fields of physical science and technology. Most of us accept this as proof that humanity is automatically evolving en masse into a future race of superhumans with optimal intelligence, capable of completely dominating all the forces and resources of nature.

The science of Yoga, however, presents a picture of evolution which is dramatically different from the one most of us grew up with. The yogic Rishis advise us that nature has remained essentially the same since the beginning of time, and it will stay essentially the same until the cosmos is dissolved. There are, to be sure, incessant ebbs and flows which give Mother Nature an ever changing face, but ultimately she will end up exactly where she began; there can be no improvements in nature because it was already perfect to begin with.

Our entire recorded history covers only about 8,000 years, though the cosmos has existed for billions of years. What we know about the activities of nature up to now represents just an infinitesimal sliver of the entire universal cycle, and if we limit ourselves to examining only the events occurring in this tiny isolated section of the whole, we are bound to see patterns which seem to indicate that things are moving in certain specific directions. If we could view more of the entire cycle, however, perhaps we'd see that for the *next* 8,000 years things will flow in exactly the opposite direction and cancel out all the so-called "progress" of our recorded past.

It's the same as if we were to study the ocean only when the tide is coming in; if we did we might well conclude that the land is slowly and steadily being swallowed by the sea. We could watch the tide for six full hours and not see any indication that it ever intended to reverse its march upon the shore. Only if we witness the full cycle of the tide can we realize the perfect balance of its ebb and flow. The same is true for the tides of time. For all we know, there may easily have been thousands of civilizations on earth, as highly advanced or even more so than ours, only these may be so deeply buried in the distant past that the nearest one is nothing but mythology to us now (the fabled Atlantis, for example).

The human brain is currently displaying an evolutionary surge for the simple reason that at this time in history more of our vital energy is being diverted toward the conscious mind, while less is being used to fuel the deeper mechanisms of our being. Thus, it can hardly be called true evolution when the more important aspect of an organism must go undernourished in order to *over*develop one of lesser significance. Fortunately, however, the rising outcry of spiritual hunger that is now being heard throughout the world and particularly in the West suggests that perhaps this modern era of mind-worship is already on the wane.

According to yogic philosophy, during the course of each universal cycle there occurs a revolving sequence of ages or *yugas,* each characterized by a general upswing or downswing in the level of human consciousness. The present age, called Kali Yuga, is said to be one in which the average person has extremely limited use of his inner potential; and during the next yuga he will have access to much more psychic power. Thus, as this age passes to the next, though it may appear to a purely objective observer that humankind is actually evolving *en masse* into some sort of superhuman species, the fact is that for all the added knowledge and power this "new-age human" will exhibit, he will still be every bit as bound as people are today. As we will see in a later section, the unfolding of psychic powers is only an early phase of the approach to Self-realization, and those who are stuck at this high level will have far less motivation to strive for Self-realization than those of us bound at lower levels.

Yoga asserts that there is only one truly evolutionary process in all of nature, and that process is neither physical nor mental—it's spiritual—and this evolution is not something automatic which humankind can simply sit back and let happen, it's an inner unfolding which must be willfully instigated and sustained by each individual. Yoga defines evolution as *the voluntary reversion of individual souls to the supreme source through personal effort.* This is just another way of saying that evolution is the process of Self-realization.

Whenever any one of us attains Self-realization, this does not simply mean that we reach the highest possible advancement that we are *personally* capable of in this lifetime; it also constitutes the attainment of the highest state that can ever be reached by *any* human being. The evolution of human into superhuman is a process of transformation which any of us can instigate and complete in this very lifetime, with proper guidance. No human being has the potential to achieve a higher state than any other person. Each of us contains inside us at this very moment the full potential to attain the highest state that any human being ever has or ever will attain. Some of us, however, are capable of attaining this goal more quickly than others, because some of us desire it more fervently. Motivation inspires effort, and effort yields rewards.

Scientists will never find a missing link between the animal kingdom and humankind, for we ourselves are a missing link— between animal and god. Yoga states that Self-realization can only be attained in a human body; it is not possible for any other form of life to unite its consciousness with the source of all Creation. Every life-form does, however, play a very important part in the cosmic pattern of spiritual evolution, and to understand this we must now turn our attention to the doctrine of reincarnation.

Reincarnation

Regardless of whether or not lower life forms are in fact *physically* evolving into higher ones, Yoga asserts that there is something which does evolve *through* the various forms of life, beginning with mineral and passing through the vegetable and animal kingdoms before earning the capability of inhabiting a human form. This nonmaterial, evolving entity is called a ''soul'' in Western spiritual traditions, and in Yoga it is called *purusha*. As we saw earlier, the process of Creation involves the accepting of limitations by both of the supreme cosmic principles; Shakti becomes veiled and manifests as prakriti—all insentient objects—and Shiva becomes veiled and manifests as individual purushas—the sentient perceivers of all the objects in Creation.

We must always remember, however, that even though there appears to be purusha and prakriti, the perceiver and the perceived, in reality there is only one thing in Creation—Paramashiva—the two supreme principles of Shiva and Shakti eternally united. Therefore, both Shiva and Shakti must be present in every element of Creation, so when we speak of ''purusha'' we refer to those things in which the subjective (Shiva) principle predominates, and when we speak of ''prakriti'' we refer to those things in which the objective (Shakti) principle predominates. In other words, strictly speaking, there is a purusha in *everything*, but in insentient objects it is essentially dormant and in lower life-forms it is only slightly active. This is why Yoga states that subjective Consciousness is sleeping in minerals, dreaming in plants, stirring in animals, awakening in humans and fully aware in realized beings.

According to Yoga, the only way an individual purusha can become ''fully aware,'' meaning aware of its identity as Shiva, is through personal experience. This means that every object in Creation is a vehicle for awakening purushas, and some vehicles take a lot more experience to operate than others. For example, the difference between a rock and a human body is like the difference between a kiddy car and a rocketship; just as an Australian aborigine is incapable of flying a rocketship, a primitive purusha is incapable of inhabiting a vehicle as sophisticated as a human body.

A lowly evolved purusha has so little awareness it is capable only of inhabiting simple, insentient forms such as stone and earth. As it gains experience, however, it evolves into more complex vehicles. Once a purusha evolves into the realm of living organisms, its evolutionary journey is called "reincarnation." Every living thing, be it a plant, animal or human body, exists only temporarily; so each time such a vehicle dies, the purusha which has inhabited it moves on to a form more suitable to its present level of evolution.

After it evolves through the vegetable kingdom, each purusha then inhabits simple forms of animal life, gradually moving up to forms which are more mobile and sophisticated. When at last it becomes perceptive enough to merit the rudiments of an inner psychic apparatus (mind, ego, intellect and subconscious), it earns a human vehicle for itself. Each time its vehicle dies, the purusha recycles itself into a new vehicle, carrying with it all the awareness and experience it has gained throughout its existence; and each vehicle it incarnates into is exactly suited to its needs and capabilities. A human vehicle is Creation's finest instrument of perception because it is not only *physically* mobile, but it also has the potential for tremendous *psychic* mobility, and this gives the purusha access to all the subtle realms of Creation. (The exact mechanics of human psychic mobility will be detailed in our next chapter.)

As a purusha evolves, it not only gains wisdom, it also gains power—the ability to direct the power of its own Consciousness. Just as everything in Creation is Shiva, everything is also Shakti, so every object contains her awesome power. In insentient objects, however, this power is completely unavailable to the inhabiting purusha, while in living forms it can be utilized in varying degrees. Shakti which has become available for use by a purusha is called *prana*, or "life-force." Higher forms of life have more prana than lower ones, so as a purusha evolves it is able to command more and more of the Self's unlimited power. A Siddha-purusha (a fully realized being) attains sovereignty over all the power in Creation.

The highest goal of every purusha is to perceive its own Self by removing the veils of ignorance which obscure its eternally pure Light of Consciousness. As these veils are slowly dissolved by knowledge obtained through experience, each purusha becomes more and more able to perceive its own true nature and also the true nature of the rest of Creation as well. Just as a beam of light penetrates a veil of darkness and reveals the true identity of whatever the darkness obscures, pure subjective Consciousness pierces the veils which enshroud the imminent Consciousness in all things sentient and insentient; thus, true perception reveals the whole of Creation to be a single, cosmic being, completely alive and aware of itself. When all the purusha's veils are removed, what remains is just its own pure light, and with this ''Enlightenment'' comes the realization that both perceiver and perceived are one divine being—one omnipresent, omniscient, omnipotent, all-blissful Self.

Only when we ourself attain Self-realization will everything become completely clear to us, but meanwhile another short allegory might help us to have a better understanding about the hows and whys of reincarnation:

One day, after Shakti had emanated from Shiva and become the manifest universe, Shiva found himself all alone with just his thoughts. Having pondered various things, he finally came to the problem of his own identity. ''Who in the world am I, anyway?'' he wondered. (Of course, you and I realize that Shiva, knowing everything, could never be ignorant about his own true nature; and yet, it was a grand game to play—one that he had instigated countless times before, purely for his own amusement.)

The only one who would surely know the answer, he decided, was his cosmic mate, but how was he to ask her this important question now that she had gone off and become everything in Creation? There seemed to be only one alternative: to find out who he really was, Shiva had to ask everything in Creation. To do this as quickly and efficiently as possisble, he split himself up into a myriad of fragments, called souls, and he scattered them throughout the whole of Creation, each with but a single assignment—to find the answer to the question, ''Who am I?'' Since the Earth Realm was the ground floor of the entire cosmos, it became the main laboratory for the souls' research.

Only when a soul has developed enough sophistication to perceive and analyze Creation with intelligence and discrimination does it become capable of seeking a meaningful answer to the question "Who am I?" Answering this question, then, is the entire purpose of a human being. To solve the great cosmic riddle, each soul can only proceed by a process of elimination: in discovering all the things which we are *not,* we are eventually led to the place where we can learn who we really are. If we look around us right now we will see many souls (including our own) in the process of eliminating all the things which they are not. Some are currently examining the possibility that their basic nature is to be found in such things as money, power, or status; others are diligently researching areas such as sex, evil, violence or gluttony; still others explore the fields of science, art, philosophy, sports or business. There are so many possibilities to examine that the research takes a great many life-times, between which each soul spends varying amounts of time in the other realms, organizing and digesting its work to date, as well as investigating those more subtle realms.

Only after exhaustive research over innumerable lifetimes, after every aspect of worldly life has been experienced and examined in minute detail, is the soul finally willing to consider looking inward. Turning inward, this ancient soul is at last able to perceive its own nature directly, and then returns to the Lord in triumph, joyfully proclaiming the answer it has scoured all of Creation to discover and experience: "I am Shiva! I am Shiva! I am Shiva!" When all the souls finish their research and merge back with Shiva, the cycle is complete and the entire Creation is absorbed back into its source. Then, after a period of rest, the great cosmic cycle is ready to begin again.

The entire cosmos is an enormous circle of birth and death, and every detail of this magnificent Creation reflects its cyclical essence. Vibration is the basic nature of everything in existence, and since vibration is cyclical, this means that everything in existence is alternately dying and being reborn with astounding frequency. In a single second of time, for example, every atom in Creation dies and is reborn one quadrillion times!

Our own galaxy, the Milky Way, is cyclical; it revolves around some as yet undiscovered point in the universe. Our own star system revolves around a fixed point in the Milky Way. Our own sun revolves around a point in its star system. Our own planet revolves not only around its sun and around its own axis, but it and its moon also revolve around each other. All this movement is cyclical—it's vibration.

One year is a cycle of birth and death for the planet Earth. Each day dies at dusk and is reborn again at dawn. Cyclical recurrence is the very keystone which supports Creation. Is it possible then that the human spirit is the only cosmic component that's noncyclical?

The idea of reincarnation may well seem strange to those of us raised in a culture based upon the assumption that "You only go around once in life," but just because we were raised to believe otherwise does not mean that the doctrine of reincarnation is false. Had we grown up in the Eastern Hemisphere, chances are our beliefs would be quite different.

Many reliable people claim to recall past lifetimes, and countless cases have been researched and documented throughout the ages. In such spiritual disciplines as Yoga, Zen and Tibetan Buddhism, practitioners regularly reach a stage in their psychic development at which many of their past existences become revealed to them.

There is also a strong philosophical support for the validity of reincarnation. If we accept the contrary idea that each of us lives only one life, then we must either believe that we are placed here that single time by a divine overseer, or that we simply sort of "happen" as a result of some meaningless sequence of cosmic coincidences. In the light of all we've learned about the universe so far, even scientists agree that the random-chance theory is no longer defensible. The universe is a system of perfect order; if anything in it seems to occur at random, it's only because we have not yet discovered the underlying harmony from which that event has sprung.

On the other hand, to uphold the belief that a Creator puts us each here for but a single lifetime opens up a real philosophical can of worms. Firstly, it implies that God creates a new soul for every birth, putting Him in the unseemly position of servant to the carnal whims of humankind, forcing Him to stand dutifully by, ready to supply a new soul on demand every time a man and woman conceive a child either intentionally or by accident, through seduction or rape, for wise or foolish reasons. It seems highly unlikely that any Creator would cast himself in such a role. Secondly, every scripture on earth describes God as all-powerful, all-knowing, just, loving and compassionate. Why then, if He gives each of us only one turn at life, does He deal some of us such a rotten hand? Why are some of us born blind, crippled, destitute or demented? Why do so many of us die right in the cradle after only a few brief moments of life, having our one and only precious existence snuffed out for all eternity even before it ever really gets started?

Not only do there seem to be inequities at birth, but life itself is often filled with incomprehensible injustices. Why are there so many senseless tragedies all over the world each day? Why do good, innocent people get struck down, tortured, mutilated and destroyed, while ruthless criminals live in comfort and luxury to a ripe old age? In the eyes of Western religion, the only way this situation can be explained is by assuming that the scales of justice are balanced after death, when the quality of our life is judged by our Creator, who then sees to it that we get the rewards and punishments we earned on earth.

The problem with such a system, however, is that it again casts grave doubt upon the just, compassionate nature of God. If we are all to be punished or rewarded according to the way we live our lives, how then could a Creator be considered benevolent if he deals some of us a handful of aces right from the very beginning, while others get the deck stacked against them? Some of us are born with good looks, talent, intelligence, material wealth and other attributes conducive to living a righteous, fulfilling, productive, ideal life; little wonder then that such people earn entry into heaven after death. Others, however, are born with twisted bodies and minds, no aptitude for productive work, in an environment which all but forces them to live a life of degradation and evil; little wonder then that such people end up in hell for the rest of eternity.

Some get dealt a winning hand and then are rewarded for winning, while others are dealt a losing hand and are punished for losing. Is this the work of a benevolent God?

The fact is, one of the most appealing aspects of the single lifetime theory is that we can take all the credit for our successes in life, while blaming either God or rotten luck for all our failures. Those who believe in reincarnation, however, must accept full responsibility for everything that comes to them in life, good or bad. According to Yoga, our present situation is the direct result of things we did in previous lifetimes, and the things we are doing now are determining the exact nature of our future. The yogic doctrine of karma explains how this process works.

Karma

Do unto others as you would have done unto you. This biblical statement is considered to be the Golden Rule of human behavior. It appears almost verbatim in the scriptures of most other religions, and as commonly interpreted it seems to be a reasonable code of conduct for civilized humans. If we don't like being hurt, it tells us, don't hurt somebody else. But wait a minute. What if we *like* to be hurt? Upon closer examination, the Golden Rule quite clearly advises us to be more considerate of our own preferences than those of others; it does not enjoin us to treat others as *they* would like to be treated, but as we ourselves would like to be treated if we were they. What is the true significance of this cryptic advice?

According to Yoga, the Golden Rule is not based upon moral or ethical considerations; its advice is purely practical. The reason why we should only do to others what we would like to have done to us is that everything we do will someday be returned to us in kind. The Golden Rule may be looked upon as an interpolation of a universal law: *As you do to others, you shall have done unto you.* This, poetically stated, is what Yoga calls the law of karma.

Western religion holds that the fruits of our actions are enjoyed or suffered in some afterlife situation, but the law of karma maintains that what we do in life returns to us *in life*. Even the most superficial examination of life around us, however, seems to disprove this contention of Yoga's; many people do not seem to get their just desserts in life. In fact, the law of karma makes no sense at all until examined in the light of reincarnation. Since karma is a system of perfect justice, quite often our actions do not return to us for many lifetimes. The classic example of this principle is as follows:

Say you are a very highly evolved soul, living a lifetime as an extremely pure and holy human being. I, on the other hand, am a relatively primitive soul, having spent a lot of time in the other realms but not much time on earth, and I am now living a lifetime of evil—hardly better than a savage beast. I, the worthless wretch, ruthlessly murder you, the saint. Now, would it be perfect justice for me to pay for my crime by being myself murdered *in this lifetime?* Is the life of an evil wretch exactly equal in value to that of a saint? Of course it isn't, no more than an employee with twenty years' experience is equal in value to one with just a few days on the job. In order for perfect justice to be achieved in such a situation, the law of karma demands that the primitive soul defer the payment of this karmic debt until that soul has become evolved to the exact same level of the one whose vehicle it once destroyed. When I, who was once a worthless wretch, have become myself a saint, then the saintly life I once took can be repaid; some primitive soul will come and murder me, and even though perfect justice will prevail, those around me at the time, not able to see all the way back to the root of the debt which has just come due, will look upon my death as a senseless tragedy.

All the unexplainable mysteries which flaw the dogmas of Western religion become solved when looked at from the viewpoint of karma and reincarnation. Even people who do not believe in these doctrines or in the existence of heaven and hell still seem to intuitively understand that somehow or other everything we do comes back to us; thus they try to lead a life of goodness, despite the apparent fact that being bad is often easier and more rewarding. Viewed with the law of karma in mind, acts of heroism, charity, compassion, tolerance or humility yield at least as much concrete benefit to the one who performs them as for those at whom such actions are directed.

Each of us is completely responsible for the situation in which we find ourself at every moment. Yesterday's actions become today's destiny, and today's actions become our future life. This is the law of karma.

Some spiritual sciences assert that only human beings are subject to karmic law. How can a universal law apply to only those souls which inhabit human bodies? To answer this question we must first understand the basic difference between a human and a subhuman purusha.

At some point in its evolution, each purusha attains sufficient qualities to merit human birth. As stated earlier, the fundamental difference between a human being and an animal is that a human possesses the inner psychic instrument called "mind," including the ego, intellect and subconscious. Of course, in the case of the higher animals this distinction becomes a bit hazy, for in such creatures the rudiments of mind are already in development; even so, it can generally be stated that the human being is the only organism in Creation with an "I" awareness—an awareness of itself as a distinct entity clearly delineated from the rest of the cosmos.

Because humans alone have this "I" awareness, we are also the only creatures with an awareness "not I"—meaning that there are things which we perceive to be distinctly separate from us. As soon as this I/not-I duality is conceived by an evolving purusha, its subjective consciousness, which considers itself to be "I," seeks to manipulate the objective consciousness considered to be "not I." This activity represents the birth of the individual *will*.

Karma is often called "the law of action and reaction" because it works in an identical way to that same law of physics. For every action sent out, an exactly equal reaction comes back. If there is no willful action, there can be no karmic reaction. In order for a soul to *act*, it must have an "I" to perform the action and there must be a "not I" upon which the action is directed. Since subhuman life-forms have no concept of "I-ness," they do not perceive themselves as in any way separate from the rest of Creation, so they cannot act.

If we are having trouble with the idea that only humans can act, we are probably thinking of action in the rather general way in which we refer to it daily. Usually we consider any physical movement an action, but technically speaking a movement can be either an action or a reaction. For example, if we have no desire for food, yet we force ourself to eat by an act of will, that's an action; if, however, hunger compels us to eat, that's *re*action. If we kill someone willfully, it's an action, but the same deed performed in self-defense would be a reaction. Human beings both act and react; subhuman life forms only react instinctively.

Action, as it applies to the law of karma, is the movement of the will, not of the body. Whether or not a particular activity produces karma depends upon whether or not will plays any part in it, and the part which will plays determines the type of karma incurred. A well-meaning surgeon whose patient dies on the operating table does not incur the same kind of karma as the robber who murders his victim to avoid identification.

The instrument through which the soul discriminates between what it considers to be "I" and "not I" is called the ego. Ego comes into being as soon as "I" comes into being, and the first action which ego performs is the creation of what it calls "not I." This duality of self and non-self is the essence of ego, and it is upon this foundation that the ego, as it matures through many lifetimes, builds an entire spectrum of dualities which do not exist for any subhuman soul. Qualities such as good and bad, right and wrong, pleasure and pain, perfection and imperfection, do not exist in the real universe; the real world just *is,* and nothing in it is inherently good or bad, beautiful or ugly, etc. Such qualities are merely projections of the human mind, and in the mind of each of us these qualities mean very different things. In effect, each mind is the creator of its own private universe, no two of which are exactly alike in either structure or character.

Most of our individual universes have certain things in common, of course; things such as $2+2=4$, red means *stop* and green means *go,* the earth is round, etc.—but in other respects they are often remarkably different. My universe may include karma and reincarnation, while yours may not; in my universe, John Doe might be a swell guy, while in yours he's a jerk, and in John Doe's universe he's God Himself. When we try to communicate with one another, we often find that we seem to be from different worlds, speaking different languages; the same words mean different things to different people.

All the mental anguish, insecurity, frustration and anxiety we experience in life result from dualities which only exist because our mind has created them. The more dualities we create, the more we suffer. As our awareness of self continues to grow over many lifetimes, however, our fantasy universe of self-imposed qualities begins to fade beneath an ever sharpening perception of the way things really are, until at last we achieve total Self-awareness and change our outmoded, phony reality for the Real McCoy.

Meanwhile, each of us is a miniature Ishwara, the big boss of a little universe, and through our Board of Directors (the various aspects of our mind) we create, modify, protect or destroy portions of our domain completely at will each time we are presented with a new piece of information. We are omnipotent within our own little kingdom; if we choose not to believe in something it simply does not exist for us.

Everything would be fine if ours was the only universe in existence, but unfortunately ours too often clashes painfully with rival universes or with the Real McCoy. The problem is that every thought we entertain not only takes form in our own private universe, but in the real one as well.

Thoughts are little bursts of energy projected from the mind, and energy is vibration. Just as Shakti's vibration modifies Consciousness into creating all the forms in the cosmos, so too the vibrations of the human mind modify Consciousness and give it form. Thought is an act of creation; in other words, *thoughts are things,* like little entities of energy launched from the human mind. When these little projectiles get launched, they have to land somewhere eventually; they can't just cease to exist because they're made of energy and energy can't just cease to exist.

The most powerful karmic missiles that the human mind can launch are those thoughts which project our emotions and desires. When we project an emotion or desire into some activity, this projection is called a motive, and it is the motive which puts a warhead on our karmic missile, not the activity itself. Physical activity is the expenditure of energy, not the production of it; in itself it cannot cause karma. Only the projection of emotion or desire through motive or thought can cause a karmic reaction. If the thought or motive is a positive one, the karmic reaction will be pleasant; if negative, someday we will be the unhappy recipient of "bad" karma.

The form which a karmic reaction takes depends upon how often and how hard we desire something, and upon the intensity of the emotions we project. As a soul becomes more highly evolved, gaining more awareness of self, it becomes capable of projecting more conscious energy, and this means that its emotions and desires bring quicker, more intense and more concrete karmic reactions. A powerful yogi, for example, can willfully manipulate objects, people or events in practically any way he wishes. If, on the other hand, the will is weak as in most people, permitting our emotions and desires to vacillate constantly, our present and our future both become a hopeless tangle of conflicting events, moods, relationships and goals.

For example, say we desire something—fame, perhaps— more than anything in the world, but our past karma is such that our present desire for fame cannot bear fruit for us right away. When we want something very badly and can't have it, we experience much pain and frustration, and this in turn leads us to wish we didn't want the thing, since the wanting causes so much suffering. Thus, we are now projecting conflicting desires: On the one hand we desire fame, and on the other we wish not to want fame. Eventually, perhaps in some future lifetime, *both* desires pay off for us; we become famous and at the same time we do not want to be famous! More misery follows, leading to more conflicting desires, which in turn result in more chaotic future karma. A knowledge of how karma works can help us to avoid building such painful traps into our future lives.

Vedantic philosophy delineates three basic categories of karma: *sanchita, prarabdha* and *agami* (also called *kriyamana*). Sanchita karma is the huge stockpile of accumulated actions we've projected in the past, actions from which we have not yet experienced reactions. Prarabdha karma is that portion of the main stockpile which circumstances permit us to experience in this lifetime; this present karma is what we refer to as "destiny"—that which must come to us in life no matter what. Agami karma is the karma we are presently creating by our current actions in this lifetime; these karmas get added to the sanchita stockpile for payoff in the future.

The chain of karma begins when the soul identifies with the ego, and is broken when the soul identifies completely with the Self. The Self is a purusha with total self-awareness; only the "I" remains—nothing is perceived to be "not I." A person is said to be Self-realized when the individual will becomes identical to the cosmic will, when the individual mind has expanded beyond its limits into the universal mind. At this point, all concepts of duality cease, all action ceases and the law of karma is transcended. Only one who is completely free of the binding chain of karma can truly be called a liberated being.

Even the most powerful worldly life is but a shadow of the ecstasy of becoming immersed in Sat-Chit-Ananda (the unmodified Existence, Consciousness and Bliss of Shiva), so even good desires are a trap; they keep us tied to the wheel of reincarnation until they all bear fruit. The only nonentrapping desire is the desire for Self-realization, because when it bears fruit the chain becomes broken.

Meanwhile, Yoga advises us to learn to use the law of karma to our best advantage. If we try to project only positive, non-conflicting desires and emotions, someday only pleasant things will come to us. In this universe of perfect order, not even the smallest effort goes to waste. If we meditate just once, then lose the discipline for ten years or even ten lifetimes, the next time we meditate will be our second attempt, and the benefits will compound accordingly. Child prodigies who exhibit remarkable talent early in life have earned their gifts through extensive effort in previous lifetimes. People who display occult powers in a lifetime devoid of psychic training are reaping the fruits of spiritual discipline during other incarnations.

Every emotion, every desire, and every motive that our mind entertains is a fragment of our own being cast out into the sea of time. Sooner or later we'll have to reel in each one of those baited hooks and swallow whatever we've caught. Just as Shiva's universe cannot end until all the fragments of his being (souls) come home to roost, so too our little bogus universe of limitation, duality and illusion cannot end until all our karmas have been balanced out, as Jesus put it, "to the last jot and tittle."

Now that we've completed our brief examination of evolution, reincarnation and karma, our background in Yoga is now broad enough for us to survey the little-known psychic mechanisms of the human body, as perceived by the ancient Rishis. In the next two chapters we will outline the exact nature of a human being; we'll pinpoint the subtle mechanisms activated by the practice of Yoga, and we'll detail the precise manner in which the process of Self-realization unfolds within our own being.

6. The Human Body: Temple or Factory?

Once upon a time a great Guru had two very accomplished disciples whom he decided to test for worthiness. Summoning the first, the Guru tells him, "Go out into the world and bring back the most precious thing in all Creation." After many arduous ordeals, the disciple finally decides that the most precious thing in Creation is the Lord Himself, without whom nothing else could exist. He prays for the Lord to appear to him so he can take Him back to his Guru as instructed, and finally, after much meditation, the Lord appears to the disciple and inexplicably bows at the disciple's feet. The amazed disciple says, "Why do you, the supreme Lord, bow to me, a mere mortal?"

"O noble one!" the Lord exclaims. "I bow to the human body that you inhabit. Without a human body, a seeker could never experience God, nor could God experience His own Creation."

The disciple then returns to his Guru all alone, and the Guru asks him sternly, "So, have you returned empty-handed?"

"No, Baba," the disciple replies. "I bring you this human body, which is the most precious thing in all Creation."

Delighted, the Guru applauds him for his successful quest.

Next, the second disciple is summoned, and the Guru instructs him thusly: "Go out into the world and bring back the most *worthless* thing in all Creation."

After many ordeals, the second disciple ends up trudging toward his Guru's ashram, having failed to discover the thing whose worth is lower than all others. Suddenly he steps in something quite repulsive: a pile of human defecation. "Ugh!" he exclaims, disgustedly wiping his bare feet in a clump of grass. "I'll take *this* back to my master, for it is surely the most worthless thing in Creation!"

As he bends over to scoop it up, the disciple hears a tiny whining sound, like a cry from a small animal; meanwhile, the feces slips from his fingers each time he tries to pick it up, and the tiny whining sound continues until finally he realizes that the cries are coming from the excrement itself! He kneels down, puts his ear close to the loathsome pile and hears it moaning, "Ohh, Ohh! Leave me alone! Oh, I'm so miserable!"

The disciple commiserates with it, saying, "I know how terrible you must feel, little pile of filth, being the most worthless thing in all Creation."

"*Me*?!" the feces exclaims. "*You're* the worthless one, not me! You and your miserable human body! Look at me! Part of me was once a sweet, delicious piece of fruit, beautiful to behold. Another part was golden grain, swaying gently in the summer breeze. A third part was a lovely vegetable, luxuriating in the fertile earth. And look at what the human body has reduced me to! You are nothing but a shit factory! You take beautiful things and turn them into shit! Oh, Ohh! Go away and let me be!"

The disciple returns all alone to his Guru, who asks him sternly, "So, you have returned empty-handed?"

"No, Baba," the disciple replies. "I bring you this human body, which is surely the most worthless thing in all Creation."

Delighted, the Guru applauds him for his successful quest.

The human body: is it a temple or merely a "shit factory?" Is it the most valuable thing in Creation or the most worthless? As this story effectively indicates, Yoga tells us it is both. Our physical body is of no value to us if we identify with it—if our awareness of self is limited to just the body—because this false identification limits the scope of our being by truly tragic proportions. If, however, we identify not with the body but with the Self which dwells within it, our body becomes a divine temple and a vehicle which carries us to Liberation; as such it is of inestimable value.

According to yogic science, a human being is the most perfect vehicle for subjective Consciousness in all of Creation, for only in a human body can a soul come to know every level of reality and attain Liberation. To achieve total union with the universal mind, even celestial beings must come down to earth and inhabit a human form, say the yogic texts. Let's now look at the total structure of a human being and find out why this being alone is capable of plugging into every level of Creation, even into Shiva himself.

Man as Microcosm

It may sound arrogant to say this, but the universe seems to have been built with human beings in mind. In terms of physical magnitude alone, the human body is the exact mean between the largest and smallest material entities in Creation. A super-red-giant star (the largest object in the physical universe) is just as much bigger than the human body as an electron (one of the tiniest of material entities) is smaller.

More importantly, spiritual scientists assure us that the relationship between human beings and the whole of Creation is exactly the same as that between acorns and the oak tree from which they spring: in other words, each of us contains the entire macrocosm in seed form. According to Yoga, then, Creation is like a great circle with its center in every human being, and each time a human is created the cosmos becomes re-created in perfect miniature, as illustrated in Figure 14.

A human being is, according to Yoga, a highly complex system of consciousness consisting of four interlocking bodies of graduated density. Our most subtle vehicle, the supracausal body of the Self, is said to be the size of a lentil seed; next comes the causal body, which is the size of a fingertip, followed in density by the subtle (or astral) body, which is thumb-sized, but because of the aura it produces, it appears to be even larger than the gross physical body. As Figure 14 illustrates, in each of us Shiva's abode is situated slightly external to the top of the physical skull. During the process of human creation, Shakti issues from Shiva and descends through what will eventually become the physical head and spine, and within the subtle body she installs a series of *chakras*, each corresponding to a separate realm of the macrocosm. The primary chakras are six in number and, since these figure prominently in the process of Yoga, it's important to understand their nature.

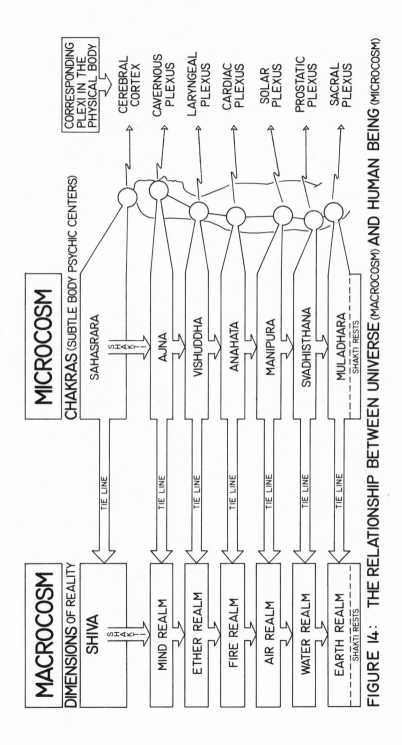

FIGURE 14: THE RELATIONSHIP BETWEEN UNIVERSE (MACROCOSM) AND HUMAN BEING (MICROCOSM)

A chakra is a focal point of psychic energy, something like a command post for the regulation of vital force at each of the various levels of our being, in much the same way that the nerve centers (plexi) function in our physical body. As Shakti creates the last and lowest chakra (muladhara) our physical body comes into being and then, for all practical purposes, Shakti becomes dormant at this point. Each chakra she installs during her descent is like a psychic tie-line containing special circuitry to connect us to its corresponding realm of the macrocosm. Just as our physical senses connect us to the physical universe, so too we have more subtle psychic senses which can function through each of the ascending chakras, permitting us to perceive and ''know'' every realm in Creation.

Yoga tells us that the human body (meaning all four bodies working in concert) is the only instrument in Creation that contains a connecting link to each and every level of reality. For this reason, the human body is considered the highest vehicle for evolving consciousness in all Creation. In it, the cosmic axis (macrocosm) has been duplicated as the spinal axis (human being). If we remember back to the section about Shiva and Shakti, we'll recall that Shiva represents unmanifest existence and Shakti is manifest existence—everything in Creation. Shiva and Shakti together constitute the universal mind, or God. Another way of saying it is that Shiva is the mind of God and Shakti is God's body because all of manifest Creation is quite literally the physical form of God. With this understanding, we can now fully appreciate the biblical contention that each human being is made ''in the image of God,'' for the entire macrocosm is God's body, and each of us is a miniature version of the macrocosm.

For reasons discussed earlier (and others which follow in the next chapter), ordinary human beings do not enjoy spontaneous access to the more subtle command centers within us. Conscious only of our physical bodies and limited minds, most of us are restricted to perceiving just a tiny portion of the Earth Realm alone, while imprisoned in individual bogus universes made of one percent experience and ninety-nine percent imagination. Most human beings are oblivious to the other levels of reality and completely unaware that each of us is Shiva himself, cloaked in a complex of sheaths or veils.

The average person is like a gigantic computer in whose memory banks is stored all the knowledge in Creation, yet through lack of proper maintenance most of its circuitry has become jammed. Getting these dormant circuits activated once again is the purpose of Yoga.

The word "yoga" means "union"—union among all the various levels of our being—and this word is used to designate the goal of total union each practitioner is reaching for. The actual process through which this union can be achieved is also called Yoga, as is the system of specific techniques used to activate and sustain the process all the way to completion.

The key to how it all happens inside us is a mysterious energy known as *Kundalini*. The word may sound Italian, but it's really Sanskrit, and it's one of the most important words we will ever meet.

7. Kundalini

Yoga tells us that upon conception of a human fetus, as the cosmic Shakti makes her creative descent through the subtle-body chakras as described in the preceding chapter, she deposits in each of these centers a vital energy or life-force called *prana*.

Prana, then, is a psychic substance which inhabits our subtle or astral body. Though it does not reside in the physical body, it is the energy which activates this body, vitalizing and coordinating all the countless functions we perform in life, such as walking, talking, eating, sleeping, working, playing, etc. Prana also powers the mind. It activates our physical senses, conveys their impressions to the brain, and it even processes those impressions; moreover it provides the energy which runs our ego, intellect and will, and every thought we generate is made of it. In short, every function, process and event associated with the term "human life" is illuminated, instigated, sustained, directed and executed by this conscious vital essence of human existence. Prana puts our body together before birth, holds it together and gives it life, then departs to let it decompose in death.

As indicated in Figure 14 on page 161, after Shakti creates the chakras and infuses them with prana, she then comes to rest just below the muladhara, which corresponds to the base of the spine in the physical body. At this point, Yoga tells us, she becomes essentially dormant within us and will remain so for our entire life unless she is deliberately reactivated, in which case she will then proceed to make her way back up through the chakras by the same route employed in her descent, and when she reunites with her cosmic mate, Shiva, the effect upon us is known as Self-realization.

The evolution of each purusha is mirrored by this cycle of creative Shakti: her descent represents our swing away from Shiva into perception of duality and ignorance of our essential nature, while her reactivation and ascent symbolize the swing back to Shiva, toward perception of cosmic unity and Self-knowledge. According to Yoga, then, spiritual evolution is a journey of only about three feet, the ascent to Enlightenment corresponding to the awakened Kundalini's ascent from the base of the spine to the top of the head.

Though all this may sound like a fairy tale to most Westerners, the existence of Kundalini has been supported by Western science for many decades. As early as 1932, C.G. Jung, who ranks with Freud as one of the greatest psychologists in history, held a seminar on the subject of Kundalini, at which he and his distinguished colleagues estimated that it would take a thousand years of depth psychoanalysis to accomplish the awakening of Kundalini in the average human being. Later, Jung wrote, "When you succeed in awakening the Kundalini so that it starts to move out of its mere potentiality, you necessarily start a world which is totally different from our [usual] world. It is a world of eternity."[16]

Through the use of a modified ballistocardiograph, the late Itzhak Bentov produced fascinating research to support the fact that Kundalini awakening leads to many physiological changes in the meditator, among which is a change in the mode of functioning of the nervous system.

Dr. Lee Sannella, who has studied Kundalini for years, has published his findings in a book entitled *Kundalini—Psychosis or Transcendence?*, in which he sums up his research as follows:

A new clinical entity, the rebirth process, [has now been] defined and documented. It is a dynamic, self-directed, self-limited process of mental and physiological purification, leading to a healthier and more developed state than what we usually consider normal. It has many characteristic features which may be objectively demonstrated. A cross-cultural survey reveals that this process is essentially similar in a wide variety of spiritual traditions. Although it was rare in the West as recently as a few decades ago, it now appears with increasing frequency.[17]

Here, the awakening of Kundalini is clinically described by Dr. Sannella as a "rebirth process" because it represents a 180-degree switch in the direction of our spiritual evolution. Human birth—the creation of the chakras in descending order from the most subtle to the most dense—represents the half of the evolutionary cycle leading away from Shiva and into entanglement in the illusion of the limited self; it represents the transformation of God into human being. Spiritual rebirth instigated by Kundalini awakening, on the other hand, represents the retransformation of human being back into God.

The Nadis

Spiritual scientists assert that our chakras are interconnected by a complex network of minute astral tubes called *nadis,* through which our prana flows. As we continue to remain ignorant of our true nature over many lifetimes, these nadis become increasingly clogged with impurities which prevent the flow of prana and cause us to lose almost all access to our higher chakras. The impurities which block these nadis consist of energy forms which we ourself have created with our own will. Self-limiting thoughts and motives constitute the bulk of such energy forms, but there are others as well. For example, so close is the relationship between our subtle and physical bodies that virtually anything that affects one automatically affects the other; thus, physical impurities such as body toxins caused by unhealthful diet, drugs, tobacco, alcohol, nervous tension, etc., cause corresponding obstructions in the subtle body as well.

Since the Kundalini must move upward through these nadis after activation, it is essential that all impurities be removed in order to permit her unobstructed ascent. Should the Kundalini become fully awakened before these impurities are removed, the effect upon our organism could be cataclysmic—like trying to run a million watts of electricity through a one-hundred-watt light bulb. For this reason various precise disciplines have been devised in order to purify our instrument adequately and then to awaken

Kundalini from its dormant state by degrees, thus preventing a possibly dangerous overload of our psychic circuitry.

The only way these subtle impurities can be removed from the nadis is through combustion; they must be burned away by what is called "the fire of Yoga." Most spiritual sciences accomplish this combustion by taking advantage of the close relationship that exists between the subtle and physical bodies. By the use of certain difficult techniques designed to produce heat in the physical body, a corresponding heat occurs in the subtle body, thus burning away the impurities in the nadis. These techniques rely upon extensive individual effort, and include such practices as the increased oxygenation of the blood through rapid breathing, intensified digestive fire induced by special diet or fasting, generation of muscular heat through physical exercises, etc.

In a few Yogas, however, a much easier course is elected. By far the hottest and most effective fire in the human body is the Kundalini-Shakti herself, and if she can be awakened very gently and kept active at a level perfectly suited to the capacity of our particular instrument, she herself will systematically consume the impurities which stand between her and her cosmic mate. In these special Yogas, all difficult techniques are bypassed in favor of giving the Shakti primary responsibility for the job of house-cleaning inside us. Such a path is Siddha Yoga, which will be examined extensively in the last sections of this book.

Kriyas

In Yogas which are powered mainly by self-effort, we must work on ourself from the outside inward, while Yogas powered mainly by awakened Shakti *work on us* from the inside outward. Meditators practicing these latter Yogas often experience a wide range of events taking place inside them automatically, without any instigation on their part whatsover. Any such spontaneous activity of the physical body, mind or emotions, resulting from a therapeutic movement of Shakti in the nadis, is called a *kriya*.

As the Shakti performs her daily work of inner cleansing and strengthening, a meditator may experience physical kriyas such as altered breathing, muscular spasm, change of body position, shaking limbs, head gyrations, vocal sounds, rushes of energy, chills or fever, etc.; occasionally a mild illness may manifest temporarily, as a latent infirmity is rooted out and eliminated from the system forever. As mental or emotional blockages are burned away, they often intensify briefly before becoming consumed in Shakti's fire. If the obstacle is mental in nature, the mind may suddenly begin racing wildly or it may become perfectly still; memories, desires and other thoughts may suddenly grip the mind and prove impossible to banish willfully. If the impurities are emotional, their release may cause weeping for no apparent reason, uproarious laughter or perhaps an overwhelming feeling of joy, love or inexplicable sadness.

As the Shakti reaches a dormant chakra and pierces it, we may feel pain, and as she vitalizes that particular psychic center our meditation may become graced by such delights as fantastic visions, divine music, ambrosial scents, rapturous intoxication and enchanting physical dance-movements, called *mudras*. As our instrument becomes more and more pure through meditation, we will also find changes occurring spontaneously in our daily life. A hot temper may gradually come under control, for example, or we may find our diet changing without any effort on our part, as the Shakti gently gives us a taste for those foods which best suit our special needs and takes away our desire for dishes that do us harm. The closer the process of Yoga leads us to a realization of our inner perfection, the more we find our daily life becoming a reflection of this perfection.

The Three-Foot Journey to Self-Realization

Of the more than 72,000 nadis in our subtle body, three are of paramount importance to our spiritual evolution. Their names are *ida, pingala* and *sushumna,* and they are the nadis which link the main chakras to one another. Ida and pingala spiral around the spine, intersecting at each of the six main chakras but not extending all the way up to Shiva's abode, the *sahasrara*. Sushumna is the only channel to the sahasrara, and it is like a superhighway running right up the center of our spinal cord from the lowest chakra all the way to the top. The Greek caduceus used as a symbol for modern medicine is a perfect representation of the chakras and the three main nadis, as illustrated below:

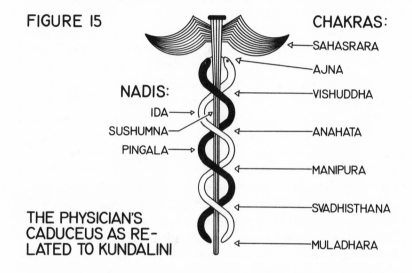

FIGURE 15

CHAKRAS:

SAHASRARA
AJNA
VISHUDDHA
ANAHATA
MANIPURA
SVADHISTHANA
MULADHARA

NADIS:
IDA
SUSHUMNA
PINGALA

THE PHYSICIAN'S
CADUCEUS AS RE-
LATED TO KUNDALINI

Ida is said to carry lunar prana and pingala, solar prana. These aspects of prana are roughly equivalent to the negative and positive poles of electricity, or the yin and yang of Chinese philosophy. Solar prana controls those inner processes which are warming, active and progressive, while lunar prana controls processes which are cooling, passive and retrogressive. Everything that goes on inside us is a product of the counteraction of these two forces. Only when the solar and lunar pranas become perfectly stabilized and united can the Shakti move into the sushumna, the actual pathway to Liberation, and eventually reach the sahasrara. Though there are many techniques designed to stabilize and merge the pranas, the safest course is the one which lets the Shakti do it for us.

In our illustration of a caduceus above we will notice that snakes are used to represent ida and pingala. The symbolic use of serpents in connection with Kundalini is common in many traditions, for two primary reasons: (1) When the Kundalini awakens, she often feels and sounds like a snake inside us, and dreams or visions of serpents are commonly experienced by meditators and are considered to be very auspicious. (2) In her dormant state, Kundalini is described by Yoga as lying coiled like a snake at the base of the spine, and her name is derived from the Sanskrit root *kundala,* meaning "coil."

Kundalini is like a wound-up spring waiting to unleash its awesome energy. The process of Yoga begins when this sleeping power is activated and begins to move upward through the chakras, piercing and revitalizing each one along the way. As she enters a chakra, its circuitry becomes operational again and the plane of existence to which it is connected becomes known to the meditator. To say that the planes become "known" to us means that we actually begin to function in those realms and even control the elements of which they are made. One result of this is that we gradually develop a host of phenomenal psychic powers, called *siddhis.* By learning to operate on all levels of reality with much more ease and effectiveness than most people can manage in just the Earth Realm alone, we soon find it quite natural to perform feats which seem fantastic or superhuman to the average person. For an accomplished practitioner of Yoga, moving from one plane of existence to another is as simple as it is for us to move from one room to another in our own home.

Usually, the very first indication that our meditation practice is starting to bring us extraordinary powers of perception is when we become aware of and begin to experience our own prana. As soon as we can unmistakably feel the tingle or flow of our own life-force—even briefly, in any part of our body—we can be sure that our Yoga has begun to bear important fruit. Then, in due course, if the Kundalini has been awakened within us, as soon as she can squeeze through even a partially cleared course all the way to the sahasrara, the Shakti will suddenly ascend to the top of the head for a brief time. This temporary reunion with Shiva gives us an experience of the state called *samadhi*—immersion in the Self. At this point it becomes absolutely clear to us that our own soul is an eternal, deathless entity. Once this state is reached even for an instant, we have attained the first level of Realization. Having touched the core of all Creation, we can never be the same again; we are permanently transformed.

At first, the samadhi state cannot be sustained for prolonged periods, since the impurities which still partially clog our instrument make it unfit to handle unmodified cosmic power indefinitely. As the purification and strengthening process continues, however, we become able to experience more frequent and prolonged samadhi states, each one reaching deeper and deeper into the Self until the center is finally reached, at which point we become fully and permanently Self-realized.

Meanwhile, each time the Shakti separates from Shiva and returns to the muladhara chakra, she deposits increased vitality in all the chakras along the way, causing them to function with more and more efficiency. As our practice continues, we become increasingly aware of the various levels of our own being as well as those of the entire cosmos, and this super-consciousness functions in us all the time, both in meditation and amid all the activities of our daily life.

What Will We Be Like
When We're Self-Realized?

Because the same Self resides in everyone, many people wrongly conclude that each of us must lose our individuality the moment we attain complete Enlightenment. To understand why such a notion is erroneous, we need only look at what happens to our karma when we become Self-realized.

The yogic Rishis state that at the moment of complete spiritual Enlightenment, all the seeds of both our past (sanchita) and future (agami) karma become "roasted" in the fire of Yoga; and, as we all know, a cooked seed can never sprout. What this means is that Self-realization not only destroys our huge stockpile of past actions which are still waiting to bear fruit, but it also absolves us from incurring any new karmic debts as a result of our future actions. As an Enlightened being, we automatically become liberated from all culpability under the law of karma—with one important exception: we still remain responsible for working out our prarabdha karma—those karmas which were intended to be resolved during the course of our present lifetime.

The human body which we now inhabit is actually held together by this prarabdha karma, and it is this karma which keeps our prana or life-force contained within our physical instrument. When our prarabdha karma is exhausted, Yoga tells us, our current incarnation ends; thus, if Self-realization were to destroy this karma along with our sanchita and agami, we would immediately leave the earth plane the moment we attained complete Enlightenment. Were this the case, humanity would be in a real fix, for if no one ever remained in the physical body after reaching full perfection, then humankind would be forever deprived of having Realized beings on earth long enough for them to share their wisdom with us and instruct us as to how we, too, can attain the same state of Liberation. Of course, this also means that such beings may have to undergo what normal people would consider to be tragic experiences—serious illness, personal injury, persecution, etc.—but the fact that they have transcended all pain and suffering makes it possible for them to endure any hardship without faltering from their unshakable state of supreme tranquility and bliss.

If we bear in mind the notion of our prarabdha karma, then, we will easily avoid the common misconception that Self-realization necessitates the loss of individuality. This, of course, is impossible, since all our distinctive character traits are a product of our prarabdha karma; thus, after full Enlightenment we are certain to retain our unique personality, right on through to the end of our physical existence.

To illustrate this, we need only examine the behavior of those perfected beings who have lived before us. Trying to pin down and label such a being is like trying to lasso the wind. Some have lived like kings, while others have resided upon garbage dumps; some have dressed in royal robes, while others have gone naked or even smeared their bodies with filth. Some were constantly surrounded with material wealth and yet they begged for crumbs in the streets, while others who had no possessions at all would throw away anything offered to them in charity. Some were great rulers over vast domains, while others were humble tradesmen; some delivered profound philosophical discourses, while others behaved as if they were idiots or madmen. Some gave their blessings with a caress, while others did it by throwing stones. Some never stopped traveling all their lives, while others hardly ever moved at all, lying around on stone slabs like great pythons. The life-styles of such beings are often quite eccentric and bizarre; thus, the yogic scriptures advise us that it is extremely difficult to recognize a perfected being simply by the way he looks or acts.

Why would any such being ever choose to live in filth and squalor instead of in a palace eating from gold plates? The answer to this seeming paradox touches upon the very essence of Self-realization itself. An Enlightened being, we must remember, represents the highest evolutionary attainment in all Creation; a human has become one with Shiva himself. According to some ancient texts, between the state of non-Realized humans and the exalted state of perfect Enlightenment, there are no less than 330 million divine positions, each higher than that of a human being but inferior to Shivahood, for each is but a temporary manifestation of the supreme Shakti, lasting no longer than the duration of one cosmic cycle. All the gods and goddesses in the lexicon of every spiritual science and religion may be viewed as representations of certain power offices in this cosmic hierarchy, offices which are filled successively by various evolving souls, none of which has attained complete perfection. This is why ancient texts state that even the gods and goddesses honor fully Enlightened beings who have transcended every power office to become one with the very source of all power.

Since perfected beings are living embodiments of the supreme cosmic principle, what could any of them possibly consider to be imperfect or profane? Perceiving the cosmos from the viewpoint of Shiva, they experience everything in Creation to be nothing less than their very own Self; thus, it makes little difference to them where they lay their heads or how their bodies are adorned. To such exalted beings, all things have become equally blissful and divine.

We all know exactly what life is like without the Self; we've been living it for ages. Even during the best of times we are operating with dismal inefficiency, like an auto with a weak battery, four flat tires, one good spark plug, dirty oil, watered gasoline and a leaky radiator.

Still, in many of us there is a stubborn resistance toward change, even when we know that a change is desperately needed. It's hard to trade in a life that we are at least familiar with—even if it isn't all that great—for one which seems mysterious and full of unknowns, even if it's purported to be far better than what we now have. "What will happen to me," we wonder anxiously, "as I begin to change from a mere human into what Yoga calls a superhuman? Will I suddenly turn my back on all my friends and loved ones because they're no longer 'good enough' for me? Will I throw away my entire wardrobe, shave my head and don a saffron robe? Will people call me a weirdo? Will I get fired from my job, divorced by my mate, and chased down the street by the neighbor's dog?"

Instead of reveling in the opportunity to realize more of ourself than ever before, we invent the absurd possibility that getting in touch with our very own Self will turn us into someone else! As long as we do not know the Self, Yoga advises us, we are suffering from the most miserable affliction ever visited upon humankind. The disease is called Ignorance—ignorance of the true nature of our own being and the true nature of everything around us.

Self-realization makes the perceiving consciousness within us become completely unveiled. The pure light of Consciousness projected by such a being is powerful enough to pierce all the veils in Creation, penetrating right to the essence of everything. If it's really growth we're looking for, spiritual science advises us to forget all our "self-improvement" courses and start meditating. The Self cannot be improved; it's already perfect. All we have to do is go inside and find it.

Part Four

The Path of
the Perfected Masters

1. To Climb or Not to Climb?

Before proceeding further, let's review some of the major points we have covered thus far. At the very outset of our excursion, we were confronted with a startling analogy sent down to us by the ancient pioneers who blazed all the trails which lead to Self-realization. These sages advised us that, compared to what each of us could be if we were to realize all our hidden potential, even the wealthiest, happiest and most powerful people among us are no better off than miserable beggars who spend each day scrounging for crumbs, never suspecting that right beneath the spot where they sleep each night lies a buried treasure of inconceivable proportions.

This hidden treasure-trove, we learned, is in the form of an inexhaustible wellspring of supreme bliss, peace, love, wisdom and power, and it's buried right inside us at the very core of our being. Yogic scientists call this core the Self, and they tell us that this inner Self is the "real us," our essential nature, from which we have become alienated due to the influence of certain natural forces that make us tend to direct our awareness away from the Self instead of toward it. Because of this tendency to look outside rather than within, we have developed a habit of trying to find such things as happiness and contentment in the outer world, when in fact the real source of everything we seek in life lies only in the inner world. This single factor, Yoga maintains, is the underlying cause of all our pain and suffering.

An earlier chapter illustrated the yogic contention that the only way we can ever regain access to our inner Self and all its treasures is by making a deliberate effort to overcome our tragic tendency to seek fulfillment through external things, and learn instead to look within. We discovered that the main technique which must be employed in this cultivation of self-awareness is known as "meditation," which simply means the turning of awareness inward. Thus, spiritual meditation leads us to Self-realization, the elimination of all pain and suffering from our life forever, and the enjoyment of permanent, boundless happiness.

We then examined the various general techniques which spiritual science recommends—techniques which have been proved through exhaustive research to be of great value in making our meditation practice as effective and efficient as possible. We saw that yogic techniques are based on practicality, and we became familiar with the primary aspects of meditation practice, including body posture, mind control, and a supportive environment.

Next, we took a brief look at yogic philosophy and saw how modern scientific findings are substantiating many ancient assertions concerning the true nature of Creation. We found that modern physicists agree with the venerable Vedantic philosophers who accurately proclaimed the material world to be illusory; and we also saw how current scientific research is well on its way to corroborating Kashmir Shaivism's description of the entire cosmos as a single, living, intelligent being—an indivisible universal Self which is identified in that tradition as Paramashiva.

Finally, we turned our attention to the role of human beings in the cosmic scheme of things, first examining the ancient contention that no Creation is even possible without a subjective as well as an objective side—that is, without a perceiver as well as a perceivable cosmos. We studied yogic science's discovery that each human being is a complex instrument through which a subjective purusha or soul perceives objective Creation; we saw that when, because of ignorance, a purusha identifies with the human instrument through which it perceives, it becomes limited and bound; and we also saw that when it realizes its essential nature, which is pure and divine consciousness, it is said to be "Self-realized" and immediately becomes unlimited, completely liberated.

We found that, according to yogic science, each human being is a complex, multi-dimensional entity, about which the following important assertions could be made:

1. Each individual Self is qualitatively identical to the cosmic Self.

2. Each human being is a miniature model of the universe, a microcosmic version of the entire Creation, just as each tiny sequoia seed contains an entire giant redwood tree.

3. Just as modern science has found that every material object in Creation contains tremendous locked-up nuclear energy, yogic science has found that there is an enormous reservoir of dormant psychic energy, called Kundalini, locked up within each human body, and when activated this energy can elevate any one of us to superhuman status through an organic process of psychic transformation known as Self-realization.

4. A Self-realized individual is one who is firmly established in total union with the cosmic Self, a human embodiment of Shiva.

The final chapter of the preceding section outlined the entire process of human psychic transformation in some detail, tracing its route through the chakras and sketching in the effects we might expect to observe as it unfolds within us. At this point, then, we should now be familiar enough with the general geography of Self-realization to at least decide whether or not the rewards which await us at the top of the mountain seem valuable enough to merit the climb. If much of what has been covered so far makes sense to us, chances are we will now be eager to press on and endeavor to discover the very best route to take for our ascent toward spiritual enlightenment.

Since this particular presentation is designed to focus primarily upon the path of Siddha Yoga, our scope does not permit a detailed exposition of every valid spiritual science and its relative merits; our purpose here is simply to expound the merits of Siddha Yoga, and hopefully to do so without seeming to imply that any other valid path is inferior. Many valid paths are presently in use by serious aspirants, and though they are all equally effective in that each one leads to the exact same goal, they all approach this goal by different routes; thus, each of these paths will appear to be superior in the eyes of those seekers who find its route most compatible with their particular tastes and talents. The important thing is not that each of us who aspires to Self-realization achieves it by practicing the same spiritual science, but that each of us finds the path which is most appropriate for us.

Dead-End Paths

As we have already seen earlier, a spiritual science can be considered valid and complete only if it provides a comprehensive system of practical techniques guaranteed to properly prepare an aspirant, then safely activate and direct the entire process of Self-realization until the state of Enlightenment is attained—not just partially or temporarily, but completely and permanently. According to the yogic sages, no spiritual science can lead us to perfect Self-realization unless it includes the awakening of Kundalini and permanent reunion with Shiva. Of course, in traditions other than yogic ones this energy may be referred to in other terms, and in some valid sciences it is not overtly mentioned at all; in any case, it may be taken for granted that the dormant Shakti becomes active during the course of every complete science, and if Kundalini awakening is not expressly stated as a goal on such a path, it may be assumed to be an automatic effect of the prescribed techniques. But regardless of the terminology employed by any science, we should easily be able to determine whether or not it includes the unfolding of the inner Shakti simply by researching the type of Liberation it produces.

For example, on some paths it is possible to achieve partial Self-realization without the activation of Kundalini, but any discipline which does not proceed beyond this point cannot be considered a complete spiritual science; it is a ''dead-end path'' which stops short of the highest pinnacle of Enlightenment.

Consider the classic example of the somber ascetic who has little regard for worldly life, humanity, his own body, and perhaps even God Himself. Through prolonged and intense practice of willful self-discipline, austerities and detachment from the world, this type of spiritual practitioner can forcibly subjugate his mind, along with all worldly desires, so that the veil produced by mental functioning is removed and universal truth stands revealed. But unless his Kundalini becomes fully activated at some point, he will become stuck somewhere short of the ultimate goal; thus, the state he identifies as "liberation" will be subject to severe restrictions.

Even though some lower states of samadhi may be attained while the Kundalini still lies asleep in the muladhara chakra, such a meditator can never experience any of the physical or psychic blessings which an awakened Shakti bestows—blessings such as automatic body purification and strengthening through spontaneous yogic kriyas, firsthand perception of all the realms in Creation, the boundless bliss that wells up as she awakens and unfolds, and the awesome psychic powers (siddhis) which attend her activation of the subtle-body chakras.

In an incomplete science which does not include Kundalini awakening, the practitioner's liberation is restricted only to periods of formal meditation, during which he completely loses all awareness. Such a state is known in Yoga as *jada* (inert) *samadhi*. Since it takes a fully active Kundalini to transform our entire being, burn up all our karmas, make us into superhumans, fill us with permanent bliss and reveal the essence of our being to be divine, adepts in a deficient science enjoy none of these benefits; instead, when they come out of their "jada swoons" they are still bound just like the rest of us—subject to the same pain, suffering and limitation. They do, of course, have one advantage over us in that they can periodically escape to jada samadhi, but they cannot bring that carefree state back with them when they return from meditation to the mundane workaday world.

In every complete spiritual science, both the inner Self and the universal Self are eventually perceived to constitute a single divine entity, and a perfected practitioner experiences a kind of natural samadhi all the time, maintaining a continual awareness of union with the source of all Creation, whether awake or asleep, during transcendental states and throughout all the activities of worldly life as well.

2. Kundalini Paths

In order to clearly delineate the relative merits of Siddha Yoga, let's first compare it to just the specific group of spiritual sciences which share with it the explicit goal of awakening Kundalini. Anyone willing to expend some time surveying this particular class of Kundalini-oriented disciplines would quickly discover that in almost every one of them we as new aspirants would be required to invest a great amount of personal effort in preliminary practices designed to make us fit to command the Shakti's awesome power safely and judiciously.

Toward this end, apprentices on such paths are usually expected to spend many years in the diligent performance of rigorous exercises aimed at bringing body, mind and senses under complete, willful control. Such preparatory practices generally include physical exercise, mental focusing techniques, and the practice of self-denial and austerities, as well as strict moral and ethical observances which demand the virtual elimination of such behavioral characteristics as violence, falsehood, covetousness, sexuality, impatience, ambivalence, anger, envy, sloth, etc., and the cultivation of such qualities as compassion, simplicity, dietary moderation, cleanliness, contentment, studiousness, faith, devotion, charity, modesty, humility, dedication and self-sacrifice. Such strengthening, purifying and character-building practices are considered essential preliminaries to involvement in any science in which practitioners awaken and direct the unfolding of Kundalini through the willful expenditure of their own self-effort, for unless such aspirants have first acquired both the strength to house the Shakti's boundless power and the ability to wield it righteously, neither they nor humanity at large could ever hope to benefit from her awakening in them.

During this preliminary preparation period, because it generally requires prolonged observance of self-discipline, self-control and self-denial, aspirants often find the outside world to be distracting and, like athletes in training, must choose to withdraw from worldly life for extended periods of time until the requisite skills have been mastered. The more an ardent aspirant is willing to sacrifice worldly enjoyments in order to intensify this process, the less time will be required to complete the apprenticeship phase. Then, once the main body of the science is entered into, each practitioner is usually required to put forth extensive additional self-effort in order to force the awakening of Kundalini and direct its unfolding. Since activation and unfolding of the dormant Shakti is reliant mainly upon an individual's willpower, there is always a certain amount of risk involved in the pursuance of most Kundalini paths, for without proper guidance or flawless personal discrimination, aspirants may inadvertently activate more of the Shakti's infinite power than they are currently capable of handling.

Among all spiritual sciences in which the awakening of Kundalini is an overt goal, however, Siddha Yoga is the only one which requires no preparatory practices and no personal effort for the activation of Kundalini; moreover, its practice presents no danger whatsoever to its practitioners.

In our last chapter, mention was made of a type of science in which the dormant Shakti could be awakened very gradually and in such a way that she herself would then go about performing all the necessary strengthening, purifying and character-building renovations for us automatically. Awakening the Kundalini in just this way is the specialty of a Siddha Guru, a Yoga master with the unique ability to activate anyone's reservoir of psychic energy simply through contact with his own fully active Shakti. In this science, our Kundalini does not become active only after years of self-effort, but instead is ignited immediately, at the very outset of our practice; and this ignition is not a result of any personal effort at all on our part—it's strictly a gift from the Siddha Guru, who has the ability to awaken a seeker's dormant Shakti at will, and to do so in such a way that the intensity of its activation is perfectly suited to the capacity of each individual.

To illustrate how Kundalini-awakening on other paths compares to the way it occurs in Siddha Yoga, the following analogy is the one most often used: If we think of the sleeping Shakti as an unlit candle—since both represent dormant energy—we can then say that on other paths this candle is activated in some way similar to rubbing two sticks together, while in Siddha Yoga it's ignited simply by bringing it into contact with another candle which is already lighted.

In the preceding chapter the section on yogic kriyas explained how this awakened energy works as ''the fire of Yoga'' to burn up all our impurities, causing spontaneous activity during meditation in the form of physical, mental and emotional kriyas, and also automatic changes of behavior in our daily life as our character weaknesses are gradually removed. Since there is no need for arduous practices in Siddha Yoga, the outside world need never be considered a distraction on this path, for the activated inner Shakti will continue her work of transforming us even as we go about our normal daily activities of social, family and professional life.

Under the expert guidance of the Siddha Guru, our own inner Shakti—which is nothing but the dynamic aspect of our own inner Self—determines both the speed and potency with which she unfolds and operates inside us, always working at the precise pace and in the manner most appropriate to our unique needs and capacities. Thus, throughout the entire process of spiritual unfolding in Siddha Yoga, there is never any danger whatsoever to the practitioner, for our inner transformation is not directed by some external will, nor are we left completely to our own fallible intellectual devices; rather, the entire process is supervised by our own inner portion of the cosmic Self, and since this is the same intelligent force which created the entire universe, it can certainly be trusted to see that our relatively modest needs are met with absolute safety and precision.

3. Self-Effort, Ego-Surrender and Grace

Having first examined Siddha Yoga in the light of other *Kundalini-oriented* paths, let's now broaden our scope and consider how this Yoga relates to the entire field of spiritual science. For the purposes of this examination, we will divide all valid spiritual sciences into two main categories according to the primary means relied upon for the attainment of Self-realization. In the first type, which we will call "self-effort paths," the individual's will assumes most of the responsibility for instigating and sustaining the process of spiritual unfolding; while in the second type, which will be designated "ego-surrender paths," this responsibility is mostly deferred to a higher authority—the cosmic will.

As mentioned a few pages back, in Siddha Yoga both the awakening of Kundalini and its subsequent ascension to the sahasrara are accomplished through the latter means, for on this path, after ignition has been effected by the Siddha Guru's will, all we need do is defer responsibility for the ensuing process to the inner Shakti's supreme will, which is the will of our very own Self.

Though the Kundalini-Shakti is supremely intelligent, she is also supremely indifferent as to whether we choose a path which brings her power under our own direction, or one which permits her to guide herself to a reunion with Shiva in the sahasrara. Should we choose to rule over her, then naturally the responsibility for unfolding her properly is also ours; but if we choose instead to let her take command, then she will gladly accept full responsibility for leading us to the final goal with ease and safety.

Today's seeker will readily accept the practicality of approaching any goal through personal effort, for our modern society has been founded upon the belief that no material achievement is out of reach for anyone willing to strive hard enough for it. But when it comes to the concept of *surrender,* many of us turn our noses up, for we too-often equate the word with negative connotations such as self-abasement, submissiveness, groveling, disgrace and shame. In the realm of spirituality, however, surrender means something else entirely.

In an earlier chapter we saw that our limited self is a product of our ego, the part of us which considers itself to be separate from the rest of Creation. In spiritual science, the term ''surrender'' refers to ego-surrender; it denotes the voluntary giving-up of this self-limiting instrument which constantly says, ''I am this, but I am not that,'' and identifying instead with that part of us which says, ''I am everything, and everything is my Self.'' Most of us have been educated to think of our ego as the most valuable aspect of our inner being, thanks to the theories of analytical psychology; but spiritual science looks upon the human ego with quite different eyes. Modern psychoanalysis views the ego as an instrument to be strengthened during therapy, and considers the loss of ego to be a pathological condition; in fact, the language of this modern mind-science will permit the loss of ego to be discussed only in terms of illness, because psychoanalysts feel that ego-loss can never be a beneficial occurrence. Spiritual scientists, however, while agreeing that the *in*voluntary disintegration of ego may indeed be pathological, insist that there is an alternative situation in which the willful surrender of ego can have immensely positive results.

According to the yogic scriptures, the following formulas accurately portray the function of ego in our being:

$$God + ego = man$$

$$man - ego = God$$

To quote the poet-saint Eknath Maharaj: ''Eliminate your ego and whatever remains is God.''[18] Spiritual surrender, then, means the giving up of our own smallness by surrendering our limited I-awareness or ego to our divine Self, or God. In this type of surrender we do not give up freedom, we give up oppression. Through ego-surrender we become free of what is preventing us from possessing the entire universe. The ancient yogic texts also say this: "As long as you have ego, you will exist in just a tiny corner of the cosmos, but when you become free of ego the entire cosmos will be found to exist in just a tiny corner of your being."[18]

As explained earlier, this trading-in of our miniscule ego in return for one of cosmic proportions does not mean that we in any way lose our awareness of personal identity; it simply means that our I-awareness becomes bigger and bigger until it becomes all-inclusive. Once we have grown to encompass the whole of manifest Creation, who knows what evolutionary vistas may then become opened to us?

Now that we have hopefully eliminated any wrong understanding concerning the true nature of spiritual surrender, we almost immediately find ourself confronted with an even more formidable concept which figures prominently in virtually every spiritual science:

Divine Grace

Any dictionary will tell us that *Grace* is divine assistance given us for the purpose of regeneration or sanctification. Though this definition may at first sound too suspiciously religious to figure prominently in any science, it is not at all inconsistent with the model of Creation presented us by yogic philosophy. According to this ancient system of knowledge, the dynamic, Shakti aspect of Shiva continually performs five basic actions: (1) She creates, bringing objects into manifest existence; (2) she sustains, causing such objects to remain manifest for a time; (3) she destroys, returning objects to their potential state once more; then (4) through her power of concealment, she hides the essential divinity of all her creations by willfully assuming limitations and obscuring the fact that she herself becomes the very objects which she makes manifest; and (5) through her power of Grace-bestowal, she casts off her assumed limitations and reveals her true nature to those purushas which attain sufficient worthiness.

If this power of Grace-bestowal were not among the basic

functions of universal consciousness, we would never be able to realize our divine essential nature, no matter how hard we might try. If we recall the story of *The Secret Key* we will remember that it was only out of compassion that Ishwara chose to hide the key to the Self in a place where we could eventually find it. If such a key did not exist, what hope would we ever have of finding it?

The important question to consider here is, "Who or what is it that determines the exact moment we become worthy of Grace; and who or what decides precisely how much Grace we are worthy of receiving?" Many modern students of spiritual science are fond of casting this process in purely mechanical, impersonal terms, describing Grace as a natural force which manifests impartially in direct proportion to each individual's capacity to contain it. They feel that Grace, therefore, is always available to each of us in full measure; the more receptive we are to it the more we receive; and our receptivity can be increased through the willful performance of the practices prescribed by spiritual science.

Religious metaphor, on the other hand, portrays Grace-bestowal as an act of divine compassion dispensed by a cosmic overseer who judges the quality of our every deed and rewards us according to His desire to do so and not out of obligation. Viewed in this light, then, Grace is not the automatic fruit of certain efforts we put forth; it is not something the cosmic Self is bound to dole out to us in return for specific services rendered, for God is totally free to give or not give as He pleases; He is not obliged to deliver His favors automatically upon demand by us mere mortals. He bestows His grace upon us only when He is pleased with our efforts and thinks us worthy; then and only then will He permit us to experience His presence inside us and throughout the world.

Which view is the correct one? According to Yoga, both are correct in their own way: Divine grace *is* an all-pervasive force which can indeed be invoked by any of us through certain practices, but exactly *when* our efforts will earn us Grace, and to what degree it will then manifest in us, are determinations which are not within our power to make—at least, that is, they are not controlled by that part of us which we identify with the pronoun "I."

Yogic texts state that generally we become worthy of receiving

Grace when our good karmas (actions which are in harmony with our true nature) roughly balance out our bad karmas (past actions not in tune with our essential nature). Since our limited self is quite obviously not equipped to discern when this occurs, such determinations must be left to some aspect of higher consciousness, and whether we choose to call this judicial power God, supreme Shakti, the inner Self or some comparable appellative is just semantics.

Viewed in this context, Self-realization becomes impossible without divine grace, which therefore must be considered an essential aspect of every valid spiritual path, though some disciplines use terminology which is more scientific and less religious. With this understanding it can now be stated that no matter what means a spiritual path employs, its ultimate purpose is to invoke the cosmic power whose function it is to reveal essential Truth. This cosmic power, which Yoga calls *kripa*, or Grace, causes the Self to become revealed by activating the dormant Kundalini inside us.

Siddha Yoga is sometimes referred to as the Yoga of Guru's Grace because in it the divine grace which awakens our inner Shakti comes to us through a Siddha Guru. Although it may appear that the Guru dispenses this Grace indiscriminately, while on other paths each aspirant must earn it through self-effort, this must not really be the case, for it would be contrary to natural law; therefore, we may assume that even the Grace received "spontaneously" in Siddha Yoga must still be a reward for meritorious actions performed previously—perhaps in past lifetimes.

We can now see that all valid spiritual sciences share the exact same ultimate goals: (1) the activation and complete unfolding of Kundalini, (2) the invocation of divine grace, and (3) the attainment of perfect Self-realization. Since such paths differ only in the means which they employ to reach these common goals, the best way to shed more light upon the special character of Siddha Yoga is by next comparing it to other spiritual sciences in terms of their methodology.

Self-Effort Versus Ego-Surrender

Truly speaking, all spiritual sciences utilize both self-effort and ego-surrender to invoke the cosmic power of Grace-bestowal, but each path prescribes these ingredients in varying proportions, placing more emphasis upon one approach or the other. In the main, the following differences will be observable between those sciences which favor self-effort and those which attach more importance to ego-surrender:

1. As discussed in the preceding chapter, paths which rely mainly upon self-effort must prepare all aspirants with extreme care, which means that novices are generally required to practice an extensive system of exercises and moral observances before the process of inner transformation can be initiated in earnest. Paths favoring ego-surrender, however, seldom demand such preliminary austerities.

2. Spiritual sciences which emphasize self-effort usually prescribe elaborate systems of difficult techniques which must be mastered, while those which emphasize ego-surrender require far fewer, more simple practices.

3. On self-effort paths, every aspirant must proceed step by step through a precise series of stages, each of which must be mastered through specific techniques before the next higher level can be attempted. This set sequence must be gone through in the proper order by all aspirants, regardless of their initial aptitude. Therefore, even the most adept initiates must be prepared to devote a certain length of time (usually three years, minimum) to attaining the highest goal on such a path.

On paths of ego-surrender, however, there is no mandatory progression of levels, and so it is possible, in theory at least, to attain the final goal instantly; at any time, from the moment one's practice is initiated, it is possible to leap to the very top of the mountain without having to conquer every cliff along the way.

At first glance such a prospect may sound fantastic, but

we must remember that Self-realization does not really involve attaining something that we don't already have, for the Self is fully manifest inside us at this very moment. All we really need do to become Self-realized, then, is to rid ourself of all the false, obscuring notions which are keeping us from perceiving our true nature, and this does not require the acquisition of any new skill, but the simple letting go of all those concepts which are obstructing our perception of the Truth. Acquiring new skills may take time, but letting go of old ideas can be accomplished in an instant. Hence, the primary practice on such paths is learning to surrender our present identifications which are based upon self-limitation and replacing them with ones which remove this self-imposed handicap.

In following such a basically techniqueless path, progress depends primarily upon constant refinement of our attitudes and understanding, making them reflect true reality more and more, and "false reality" or illusion less and less.

4. The final general comparison which can be drawn is in the area of possible regression during practice. In self-effort-oriented sciences, prolonged striving is generally required, and this must be sustained without fail, especially after the basic levels of Self-realization have been attained, for until the very ultimate state is reached on such paths, there is always a possibility that its aspirants' determination or discrimination may suddenly fail, thus causing them to become stuck or even sending them tumbling backward down the mountainside.

On surrender paths, however, no personal effort need be directed specifically toward the attainment of Self-realization; rather, it occurs naturally as an automatic effect of our inner Shakti's merger with Shiva. Since it is the very nature of an awakened Kundalini to seek reunion with her cosmic mate, on paths which rely upon her will there is never any danger that once she is activated she will ever decide to stop short of her ultimate goal, veer erratically off course, or return to the muladhara chakra and go back to sleep.

The question may naturally arise at this point as to why any-one would choose to tread a path emphasizing self-effort when the same results can be achieved by favoring ego-surrender, without austerity or risk. The fact is that many people, simply by their very nature, cannot relate effectively to the concept of ego-surrender. Moreover, many seekers actually thrive upon self-effort and find the rigid demands of such disciplines to be both challenging and exciting.

However, it must also be noted that because of prevailing attitudes these days, many of us have been raised to look upon all avenues of intense self-effort as being somehow more noble than alternative routes, precisely because they are more taxing and risky; hence, people who are not really cut out for such approaches are often attracted to them, with disappointing results. To avoid such a possibility, it may be wise to remind ourself here that ego-surrender is not a passive approach, nor is it in any way less noble than that of self-effort. Though each demands a different type of courage, both demand the same amount.

On self-effort-oriented paths we must bravely keep our nose to the grindstone and expend a lot of blood, sweat and tears in order to reach the goal, while paths favoring surrender require us, at some point, to completely let go of our present identity—every-thing we think we are—in order to discover who we *really* are, and this too takes enormous bravery. Ego-surrender involves an extremely courageous gesture which has a parallel in modern psychoanalysis called *sacrificium intellectus;* it is a condition which obliges us to completely abandon ourself to the ongoing process, as to the current of a rushing river, without knowing where it will take us, without having a clear chart of the course ahead, without the solace of sure knowledge beforehand about exactly what we will eventually attain in return for giving up everything we now possess.

4. A Path of Integration

Originally there existed only one, all-inclusive spiritual science, a single pathway leading seekers to the pinnacle of Self-realization. Over the course of time, the masters of this primal science have deliberately isolated, one by one, its various aspects, expanding each into a valid spiritual path in its own right.

Of the many branch sciences which have evolved in this way to date, most have been expressly devised to suit the unusual needs of seekers living in a specific culture at a particular point in history. Such trails, having been blazed with a unique historical situation in mind, can usually be recognized because of their relatively short lifespan; they are well-traveled for a time, but then they become anachronistic and eventually slip into obscurity.

In addition to these, however, there are a few offshoot sciences whose purpose is to provide a more timeless utility, and these generally tend to retain their popularity throughout the ages. Such paths are those which seem to have been tailor-made for certain types of individuals—namely, those who exhibit unusually intense inclinations toward such pursuits as intellectual reasoning, emotional expression, or physical activity.

To typify this more enduring group of spiritual sciences, let's look at the Yogas of India, the country generally considered to be the homeland of the original mother science from which the others have sprung. Currently there are scores of Indian Yoga systems being taught throughout the world, and they all profess uniqueness in some way, but upon examination most of these diverse paths can be categorized among just seven basic approaches to Self-realization. These elemental schools of Indian Yoga are often distinguished by the following titles: Raja Yoga, Hatha Yoga, Laya Yoga, Mantra Yoga, Jnana Yoga, Bhakti Yoga, and Karma Yoga.

Where, we may now wonder, does Siddha Yoga fit into this picture? If these seven paths are seen as specialized branches stemming from a single, all-inclusive mother science, then the most accurate way to view Siddha Yoga would be to identify it with that original integrated science from which the others have been derived. The masters of the Siddha Path teach that their science does not stand apart from other Yogas, but rather encompasses them all. In effect, Siddha Yoga represents a return to the very foundation of spiritual science, an integration of all specialized approaches into a path of balance, harmony and universality.

This claim of all-inclusiveness is substantiated by the demonstrable fact that in Siddha Yoga, during the unfolding and ascension of our Kundalini-Shakti, any of the effects which are the specialties of other Yogas can manifest within us automatically. To illustrate this, let's briefly survey the seven special sciences and see how the particular benefits and techniques of each can occur spontaneously during the practice of Siddha Yoga.

Although for simplicity's sake we are limiting our survey to schools of Yoga which are indigenous to India, it may still be said with reasonable safety that all spiritual sciences throughout the world have been fashioned through some blending of these seven basic approaches to Self-realization. Of course, it's important for us to remember that the distinctions to be drawn here are by no means black and white. Just as a biologist cannot dissect and analyze a living organism without killing it in the process, we cannot hope to dissect Yoga into constituent parts without sacrificing much of its vital essence.

Spiritual science is an organic process; it is not inert and rigid dogma. All Yoga masters—even those of the same path—present their teachings in a unique way, varying their guidance in accordance with factors far beyond the scope of ordinary comprehension. Thus, it is impossible to precisely categorize the characteristics of any spiritual path. Still, there is some value in our attempting to dissect, analyze and categorize such subjects in some logical manner, for this device permits us to encapsulate voluminous material within a few brief chapters, even though the oversimplification required distorts a bit and robs our topic of some vitality. This text, then, must be perused with somewhat the same attitude we have when we look at a caged eagle: realizing that the creature has been confined for our convenience, we must not forget how much more magnificent it is when it exists unfettered in the wild.

Our survey now begins with a quick rundown of those basic approaches which emphasize self-effort over ego-surrender. Once again, the reader is urged to bear in mind that (1) every valid path requires *both* self-effort and ego-surrender in various proportions, and (2) a spiritual science which employs one of these seven basic approaches as its primary focus will usually utilize supplementary elements from some of the other approaches as well.

Basic Paths which Emphasize Self-Effort

1. Raja Yoga—The Science of Willful Mind-Control. Back in Part Two we saw how stabilization of the mind permits us to experience the Self. In Raja Yoga, the mind is forcibly restrained by act of will, a precise and delicate process implemented by difficult mental exercises which were equated earlier with "trying not to think of a monkey." The primary technique employed on this path is a type of meditation which, because of its highly sensitive nature, must be practiced completely without distractions; therefore, aspirants must first engage in an often extensive phase of preliminary practices aimed at purifying and stabilizing the body, senses and emotions.

Raja yoga meditation is primarily the practice and mastery of intense mental-focusing exercises which increase in subtlety by stages, the gradual result being a systematic elimination of all random mental activity. In time, the diligent practitioner learns to harness the power of the mind and focus it upon a single point, just as the normally dissipated power of the sun can be intensified by focusing its rays through a magnifying glass. After prolonged performance of forceful concentration and mental-purfication practices, the practitioner's Kundalini-Shakti is gradually drawn out of its dormant state and put to work as *manas-shakti* (mind power), which then can be willfully directed in any way the seeker chooses, thereby gaining access to a vast range of psychic powers (siddhis), plus all the transcendental states of samadhi, including the supreme state of perfect Enlightenment, called *Kaivalya* in this tradition.

This path relies mainly upon self-effort for its attainments, with ego-surrender employed in a subsidiary capacity until the final stages of Enlightenment, when it then becomes an essential implement in the practitioner's ascension to Kaivalya. Thus, the type of seeker most likely to find this path appealing would be one who is very strong-willed, rational, dispassionate, introverted, and oriented toward psychology.

Raja Yoga is said to be encompassed by Siddha Yoga in the sense that once the dormant Shakti has been awakened by the Siddha Guru, it can cause the spontaneous occurrence of the full range of Raja Yoga benefits, including the control of body, mind, senses and emotions, plus the attainment of siddhis, all the levels of samadhi and, of course, the ultimate state of Kaivalya.

2. Hatha Yoga—The Science of Physical Culture. In a previous chapter we made a detailed examination of the human structure, discovering that each of us is a complex system of four different bodies, of which two—the physical and the astral or subtle body—operate in extremely intimate relationship. Anything which affects the physical body produces a corresponding effect upon the subtle body, and vice-versa. Since our subtle body contains all our life-force, or prana, and since this prana is the power which normally operates the mind and all our other psychic functions as well, it is therefore possible, through repeated specific manipulations of the physical body, to influence the subtle-body prana in such a way that it in turn causes the mind to become stabilized and the dormant Kundalini to become active.

Toward these ends, the Hatha Yogin employs a wide range of rigorous physical techniques (called *asanas, mudras* and *bandhas*), coupled with strenuous breathing exercises (*pranayama*), and topped off in the later stages with Raja-Yoga-like meditation practices.

This path appeals most to physical culturists with strong, healthy bodies and a natural inclination toward intense self-discipline and physical exertion.

Aside from the ultimate rewards common to all other valid paths, Hatha Yoga techniques thoroughly strengthen and purify both the physical and subtle bodies, resulting in such additional boons as rejuvenation, longevity, perfect health, inordinate strength, extraordinary endurance, uncommon dexterity, and complete willful control over all bodily functions and processes.

During Siddha Yoga meditation, many Hatha Yoga practices often occur spontaneously as the awakened Kundalini manipulates the subtle-body prana, which in turn affects the physical body, causing physical kriyas in the form of the involuntary performance of even the most difficult and advanced Hatha Yoga techniques. In this way, without having to deliberately practice the austere Hatha Yoga exercises, Siddha Yoga practitioners may experience some of the same physical benefits automatically.

3. Laya Yoga—The Science of Inner Nada. The word *laya* means "absorption." On this path, the goal is for the mind to become absorbed into its source (the Self) through willful concentration upon subtle inner sounds, called *nada,* which arise from the heart chakra during meditation. In its initial stages, this science employs techniques similar to those of Hatha Yoga, though not as intense, to cleanse and stabilize the body, mind, senses and emotions so that the inner nada may be perceived and concentrated upon without distraction. As the mind becomes captivated by these sounds they become more and more subtle, luring the mind to ever deeper levels of awareness until the very source of one's being is reached. At this point, the limited self becomes absorbed in its true nature, and Self-realization is attained.

Kundalini is awakened through special advanced techniques in the final stages of this Yoga, and as she activates the chakras all their wondrous contents become available for exploration. Thus, during Laya Yoga meditation, practitioners experience divine melodies, visions, tastes, fragrances and feelings, and are given access to all the different planes of objective reality, which they may tour to their heart's content. In this Yoga, meditators perceive their supracausal body—the body of the inner Self—as a scintillating blue dot or pearl, which explodes upon final Enlightenment as the individual's consciousness surrenders its limited form and becomes all-pervasive. Because this path employs Hatha-like means to attain mystical experiences, aspirants who choose its approach are generally inclined toward physical exercise and have a strong interest in occultism.

One of the most important experiences in Siddha Yoga is considered to be the spontaneous appearance of the Blue Pearl during meditation. In addition, practitioners of this science may become gifted with any of the other Laya Yoga experiences, depending upon the extent of their interest in such things and also in accordance with their needs as determined by the unfolding inner Shakti.

4. Mantra Yoga—The Science of Sound Vibrations. Since we are all made entirely of vibrating Consciousness, we are profoundly influenced by every other pattern of vibration which touches us. On the path of Mantra Yoga, practitioners strive to synchronize the vibrations of their own consciousness with those of higher (cosmic) consciousness by repeating, mentally and vocally, special syllables which contain innate transforming energy. Such syllables are called "spiritual *mantras*"; they are unique patterns of sound capable of producing dramatic evolutionary effects upon the repeater, provided their inherent enegy has been activated, either through initiation by a Yoga master or through the aspirant's intense self-effort. The primary demands of this practical science are patience and perseverance, for although a mantra is guaranteed to bestow specific rewards upon anyone who repeats it in the prescribed manner, the number of requisite repetitions usually runs into the millions.

Because the use of mantra is so simple and surefire, mantras are employed in almsot every spiritual science; but Mantra Yoga can also be practiced as a complete science in itself, in which case it involves many other subsidiary techniques, including preliminary practices similar to those of other self-effort paths, and also the extensive use of devotional rituals. All the benefits of this Yoga are derived from different types of mantras, each of which has the power to yield a particular boon such as Kundalini awakening, a specific siddhi, nadi purification, etc.—all the way up to the supreme attainment of complete spiritual enlightenment.

During Siddha Yoga meditation, practitioners often utter unfamiliar mantras out loud involuntarily, or they find themselves spontaneously tuning in to strange and beautiful mantras being chanted by ethereal voices somewhere deep within their being. In addition to these automatic manifestations, mantra repetition (*japa*) is also an essential practice performed deliberately in Siddha Yoga; therefore, this mysterious subject will be dealt with in greater detail later, at which time we will look into exactly how such a deceptively simple technique can be so effective in producing such a vast range of benefits.

5. Jnana Yoga—The Science of Intellectual Reasoning. In essence, this is a path cut specifically for seekers who are primarily thinkers—that is, those who possess a great amount of subtle reasoning power and who wish to attain divine knowledge by means of intellective processes. Of course, as with other self-effort systems which all rely heavily upon various combinations of mind-, will-, character-, and body-strength, this path also requires aspirants to undergo an initial period of preparatory exercises before the specialized area of practice may begin.

The stated goal of Jnana Yoga is to achieve and then maintain a continuous awareness of ultimate reality, and toward this end its aspirants are provided with a practical discipline which consists mainly of (1) the acquisition of indirect knowledge by first hearing universal truth explained by an adept master, and (2) attaining direct knowledge and experience of this Truth through meditation practices which focus upon contemplation and analysis of, and eventually the direct perception of, the supreme cosmic principles under examination. Jnana Yogins experience Kundalini awakening as intellectual illumination, and her union with Shiva as the attainment of pure knowledge—meaning wisdom obtained through direct perception of Truth—as a result of their intense, willful refinement of their subtle intellect.

In Siddha Yoga, one of the spontaneous windfalls which the

awakened Shakti bestows is the automatic occurrence of intuitive flashes giving the meditator sudden and profound insights into the fundamental nature of reality.

Basic Paths which Emphasize Ego-Surrender

Because the whole of modern culture is founded upon the sanctity of logic and reason, most of us will find it easier to understand the effectiveness of the above approaches to Self-realization than we will those paths which are rooted more in mysticism. Even the word "mysticism" impresses most of us as meaning something ethereal and eerie, whereas it simply refers to the doctrine of belief which holds that direct knowledge and experience of ultimate reality is attainable instantaneously, through insight or intuition, in a way which differs markedly from the usual way we perceive or understand things.

As mentioned earlier, on such a path the aspirant endeavors to go directly to the goal without having to master elaborate techniques or progress step by step through a series of increasingly higher states of awareness. Mystical paths prescribe ego-surrender as the primary means of establishing direct communion with the cosmic Self, and to this approach they add just a few basic techniques, such as japa and meditation, as the only essential willful practices. Japa and meditation help purify the aspirant's mind and focus it in the direction of the Self, and surrender does the rest.

This approach may at first sound simplistic when compared to the intricate and precise sequence of steps laid out by every science of self-effort, but the fact is that among all the many aspirants who attain Self-realization primarily through personal effort, one common experience stands out in the light of our present discussion: Once practitioners of a self-effort approach finally reach the ultimate goal, they are often struck with the startling revelation that *none of the arduous practices they performed in order to get there were really necessary.*

What is mean by this, of course, is that these beings have personally experienced what we have been seeing proclaimed throughout this book: that there is really nothing to attain because the Self is already attained—it's right inside us, on the other side of all the false notions we've been storing in our mind in order to give ourself some feeling of personal identity until we can discover who we really are. Seeing all this with perfect clarity at last, every realized being understands that all we really need do to attain the Self is to simply discard all those false notions; then the Self will stand revealed at once. Meanwhile, those of us who still stand on the dark side of our false notions continue to swear that many of them are valid, and because of this wrong understanding we choose to cling to them throughout our quest for the Self, thereby setting ourself up for all sorts of unnecessary ordeals.

A few of us, however, possessing characters which are not so rigidly geared to logic, reason, and the preservation of our false self-image, soar straight to Liberation both naturally and easily by way of such surrender paths as Bhakti and Karma Yoga.

1. Bhakti Yoga—The Path of Divine Love. This approach to Self-realization focuses upon surrender through selfless devotion to the cosmic Self, or God, and as such it is usually categorized in the area of religion rather than practical science. Still, spiritual seekers in whom devotional attitudes come naturally or are easily cultivated may indeed approach this path scientifically. To do so, aspirants must first feel a particular affinity for the cosmic Self in some form which can be visualized, be it a divine incarnation such as Krishna, Buddha, Christ, etc., or one of the many gods and goddesses which religions throughout the world revere as embodied aspects of the cosmic Self. Next, this divine embodiment is made the focus of intense devotion through such willful practices as prayer, chanting, offerings and sacrifices. Throughout each day, Bhakti practitioners strive to perceive everything in the world around them as manifestations of their divine beloved; anything pleasant that is seen, felt, tasted, smelled or heard is immediately acknowledged as the result of intimate contact between the devotee and the chosen deity in various guises. Mantras are repeated with the understanding that they are nothing less than the deity itself in the form of sound. Thus, when spiritual devotion becomes intense enough to invoke the cosmic power of Grace-bestowal, the Bhakti

Yogin will automatically become gifted with spontaneous meditation, Kundalini awakening, and Self-realization. Because intense devotion has the power to make many of us forget ourselves completely, this path teaches devotionally inclined aspirants to become lost in divine love, thereby surrendering all their false ego-identifications. As soon as this occurs, Bhakti practitioners realize that the external deity they've been worshipping is none other than their own inner Self.

In Siddha Yoga, experiences of divine love well up from within spontaneously, and often Siddha meditators burst into joyful tears or laughter, or find themselves involuntarily performing beautiful dance movements which are love-mudras characteristic of ecstatic Bhakti Yogins.

2. Karma Yoga—The Path of Selfless Service. What the Bhakti Yogin accomplishes through devotional practices, the Karma Yogin gains through the performance of egoless actions. Acknowledging the fact that everything in Creation is a divine emanation of the cosmic Self, Karma Yogins realize that all actions also belong to that divine Self, and with this understanding they perform ceaseless work, usually for the benefit of others, and always with the attitude that they are not really the doer but are just an instrument of the divine will which is working through them. Working with meticulous efficiency and no concern whatsoever for the fruits of their labor, Karma Yogins become lost in selfless service until eventually they are graced with the realization that the Creation which they serve, as well as its Master, are both in reality their very own Self. On this path, too, aspirants with a natural inclination toward selfless service can deliberately set about to become Karma Yogins by willfully practicing self-sacrifice and meditation. When this Yoga becomes perfected in them, the ultimate spiritual attainments come automatically through Grace-bestowal, as on the Bhakti Path.

In Siddha Yoga, as our awakened inner Shakti gifts us with increased understanding and experience of our true nature, an attitude of selfless service automatically begins to pervade our daily life. All our worldly activities—our work, recreation, and pursuit of personal relationships—gradually begin to lose any taint of selfish desire and become instead pure acts of celebration performed with joyful recognition of the one divine Self that resides in everyone and everything.

These, then, are the bases upon which it is stated that Siddha Yoga includes all other Yogas. Such an assertion, however, does not mean to imply that the goal of this science is in any way superior to that of any other valid path. The distinction being made here is simply this: while the paths outlined above feature specialized approaches to Self-realization, the Siddha Path represents a harmonious balance among all these basic approaches. Beyond this, each of us must make our own determination about which of these alternatives is best suited to our needs and capabilities.

Meanwhile, having examined the general field of spiritual science and Siddha Yoga's relationship to it, we may now begin to focus more sharply upon the precise terrain of the Siddha Path.

5. Siddha Yoga

In Chapter Three we saw that Siddha Yoga is a path which emphasizes ego-surrender over self-effort, while in the previous chapter we found it described as a science which offers a balance of all the various specialized approaches to Self-realization. If Siddha Yoga is a path of balanced integration, we may now wonder why it favors ego-surrender over the equally essential ingredient of self-effort.

The resolution to this apparent paradox appears in Chapter Two of this section, in which we learned that on the Siddha Path our Kundalini is awakened for us by the Siddha Guru, right at the outset of our practice. On most other paths, the activation of the inner Shakti is effected only after much self-effort has been expended in the form of difficult exercises aimed at strengthening and purifying our instrument to make it capable of housing an awakened Kundalini. Once the inner Shakti has been safely aroused from dormancy, however, the emphasis of every valid spiritual science shifts from self-effort to ego-surrender, which we found earlier to be essential for the attainment of Self-realization.

Thus, since on the Siddha Path no effort is required on our part for the safe activation of our dormant Kundalini, our attention may be immediately focused upon ego-surrender, and it is toward this end that we should direct most of the effort we expend.

As we have already seen, spiritual surrender involves the giving up of our limited self, or ego, which means the letting go of all the false identifications standing between us and the experience of who we really are. It doesn't matter whether we choose to surrender to the cosmic Self or the inner Self, for in the end both of these aspects of divinity will prove to be identical.

While on some paths the ego is annihilated through self-denial, Siddha Yoga accomplishes equally effective results through self-affirmation. By constantly acknowledging and identifying with the internal aspect of divine consciousness—the inner Self—the ego is gradually elevated and eventually transformed from a faulty instrument which reflects all sorts of false identities to one which is so refined and pure it lets our true identity shine through. Instead of being asked to deny or ignore ourself, the Siddhas counsel thusly: "Honor your Self, love your Self, serve your Self, worship your Self, meditate on your Self—because your God, in the form of absolute consciousness, dwells within you as the real you."

This self-affirming approach appeals to many present-day seekers, particularly those who would otherwise not feel much attraction to paths which emphasize ego-surrender over self-effort. On the Siddha Path, the successful attainment of Self-realization need not include the loss of ego through intense devotion, nor its sacrifice through prolonged selfless service; instead we may opt to supersede it gradually through right understanding, replacing it with deeper and deeper levels of true Self-awareness. Through a special combination of ego-surrender, divine grace, and self-effort, each of us is carefully transformed into a fully liberated being, approaching the final goal methodically but always with the understanding in mind that at any moment it may become possible for us to suddenly let all the obstacles just fall away, permitting us to leap right to the top of the mountain with a single, giant stride.

"How Do I Surrender to My Self?"

It's easy to talk about that magical, mystical moment when we will suddenly soar to Self-realization instantaneously through total ego-surrender, but as most aspirants soon discover, it is not always so easy to make that moment happen. Spiritual surrender is a bit more tricky than simply saying to our inner Self, "I give up!" Expressing the desire and intent to banish ego from our being is, of course, an essential part of this surrender, but it's just the beginning; the true test of our capacity for surrender comes when we attempt to implement our intent by actually eliminating ego from all our thoughts and actions.

This is easier said than done. From a philosophical viewpoint, the discarding of our ego should take no time at all, for it is we who are clinging to the ego and not the other way around. From a practical viewpoint, however, it's not so simple. At first, many of us won't even know how to distinguish our ego from the rest of our being, let alone how to remove its influence from all our thoughts and actions. Thus, for most of us the accomplishment of ego-surrender will require some study and practice; we must study the true nature of the ego and the Self with someone who has personally attained complete surrender, and then we must put this understanding into practice in our everyday life, deliberately learning to perceive everything from the viewpoint of the Self, and to act accordingly. The moment at which our practice becomes spontaneous and natural is the moment of true spiritual surrender; instead of merely practicing at identifying with the Self, we simply become the Self. In other words, we become Self-realized.

The main requirement for true surrender, then, is right understanding and this can be attained only when our intellect is both sharp and receptive enough to recognize eternal truth when it stares us in the face. Keenness of intellect alone is not enough, for then we tend to become enamored of our own pet theories and unreceptive to new ways of looking at things; nor is openness alone sufficient either, for then we become too naive and gullible, accepting everything we're told as gospel. Before we can develop right understanding, we must possess complete intellectual receptivity to unusual ideas, coupled with keen discrimination which enables us to recognize not only universal truth when we encounter it, but also the illusion of truth as well.

If we have already developed such an intellect before we receive Grace from a Siddha Guru, then he need only remind us of our true identity and we will realize the truth of it immediately; we will attain Self-realization instantaneously. But if our intellect is at all clouded or unreceptive, then despite our learning about who we really are, we will resist the Truth and continue to cling to our old distorted concepts about it, in which event the process will take more time.

Charting the Path of the Perfected Masters

The ever-present possibility of instantaneous Enlightenment is only one of several features which make the exact route of the Siddha Path impossible to clearly chart. Another factor which greatly affects its course is the early and effortless awakening of Kundalini, after which she actually assists us throughout our ascent to the goal, selecting a unique route for each of us in accordance with our special needs and capabilities.

Since Shakti is the mother of the entire Creation, there is no limit to the range and combination of experiences she may provide to followers of the Siddha Path. One of us may soar directly to Shivahood, without any intermediate experiences or attainments, while another may explore every subjective level of Consciousness and every objective realm of manifest Creation, being gifted with the sequential activation of all the chakras and the resultant psychic powers, plus any or all of the special benefits which can be obtained on other spiritual paths.

But this is not the only way that Siddha Yoga may include the other yogic paths. Not only does it integrate the entire spectrum of spiritual sciences automatically, it may also do this in a more deliberate way as well. Although in this science only a few formal techniques are considered absolutely essential, the Siddha Guru may also prescribe a wide range of supplementary practices which each of us may employ to insure our balanced development and to accelerate the spontaneous process. Though these techniques may be employed as mandatory practices on other paths, in Siddha Yoga, unless the Guru personally instructs us to perform one or more of them fully, they are to be considered supplemental aids into which we may invest as much self-effort as we wish.

Because this path minimizes obligatory practices, each of us is able to find our own special combination of ingredients to assure the swift and successful completion of our spiritual journey. If we are nonreligious, Siddha Yoga gives us the space to pursue the inner Self in the form of ultimate truth, supreme reality or cosmic consciousness; if we are religiously inclined, we may seek our goal in the form of the Christ, Allah, Krishna, or any other deity we choose. Finally, we are also free to pursue our goal as leisurely or as adamantly as we like; we may devote our entire life to the practice of Siddha Yoga and thereby attain the goal as fast as possible, or we may mix our spiritual practice and our worldly pursuits in any proportion that pleases us.

By now the reader will have some appreciation of how difficult it is to pinpoint the Siddha Path with great precision, and there is still one final point to be made before our portrayal of this Yoga's enigmatic side can be said to be complete. In the introduction to this book we saw that the term "Siddha Yoga" means the Path of the Perfected Masters, and refers to spiritual guidance received through a Siddha Guru, who belongs to an elite lineage of Yoga masters possessing very special psychic powers, or siddhis.

Since each and every Siddha Guru prescribes a unique combination of philosophy, psychology, rituals, and techniques most appropriate to the time and place in which he is functioning, this Yoga has never appeared in exactly the same form twice, though it always bears the tell-tale earmarks of spontaneous Kundalini awakening and the automatic manifestation of all the Yogas from within during the course of spiritual practice. In addition, each Siddha Guru often assigns this particular version a special name; hence, this path has been identified by many different titles throughout the centuries, including such designations as Maha (great) Yoga, Kriya Yoga (the Yoga of spontaneous purification), Sahaja (natural) Yoga, Gurukripa Yoga (the Yoga of Guru's Grace), and Shaktipat-Kundalini Yoga (that path on which Kundalini is awakened by the transference of Shakti from a Siddha Guru to an aspirant).

Because of its inherently nebulous nature, not much has been written about this path throughout history, aside from frequent references to it in many ancient scriptures. Since each aspirant attains the highest goal by his own unique route in Siddha Yoga, it is even impossible to generalize about the stages one goes through on this path, especially considering the always present possibility of instantaneous Enlightenment through total ego-surrender.

Muktananda's Siddha Yoga

The particular brand of Siddha Yoga which we have been examining throughout this book is that of Swami Muktananda Paramahansa, and this specific combination of Kashmir Shaivism, Vedanta, spontaneous Kundalini activation, ego-surrender and willful self-effort is currently receiving the most far-reaching acceptance and the widest acclaim of any other Siddha Yoga in history.

Not long ago, great beings were crucified for publicly teaching spiritual truth. In bygone days it seems that just a small percentage of people were capable of understanding and appreciating such teaching, so most valid spiritual sciences were highly esoteric, "underground" paths. Until not long ago, for example, during a typical Siddha Guru's entire ministry he would initiate no more than a handful of aspirants, and because of this most people never knew that such a path even existed. The Guru would quietly select those whom he deemed ripe for spiritual awakening, and he would activate their dormant Shakti in secrecy, guiding each disciple to maturity in the inner sanctum of some hidden monastery or mountain cave.

Thus, this Path of the Perfected Masters has been generally unheard of throughout past ages, but today it seems that times have changed, for Siddha Yoga is now being made openly accessible to every interested seeker throughout the world. Perhaps the reason for this is that humanity today is more highly educated, more interested in spiritual growth, and more receptive to unfamiliar ideas; hence, more people than ever before are capable of understanding and appreciating spiritual truth.

Because of this increasingly favorable climate, many ancient spiritual sciences have recently come out of hiding; and yet, even though Siddha Yoga is among the last of these to become publicly available, its growth has been truly phenomenal, and one of the primary reasons for this is its extremely practical philosophy.

Many spiritual sciences are based upon philosophies which, though perfectly valid, take either a dualistic approach which views Creation as being separate from the Creator, or they portray the world as an illusion. Even though such views are perfectly accurate from certain viewpoints, most people living in the world today would find it quite difficult to maintain the type of awareness and attitudes which such philosophies recommend.

Spiritual paths based upon dualistic philosophies, for example, require us to view the world as being very real but distinctly separate from the Self; thus, on such paths we would have to completely sever any involvements between our soul and the objective world in order to attain Liberation. While such an approach may be fine for certain intellectuals and those for whom the world holds no particular appeal, most of us would find it extremely inconvenient if our worldly activities and relationships had to be viewed as impediments to our spiritual growth. In the same way, paths based upon philosophies which describe the world as an illusion would not seem very practical to the majority of us who live and work in a world which appears to be quite substantial indeed.

Viewed in this light, Baba Muktananda's choice of Kashmir Shaivism as the keystone philosophy of his Yoga has made the Siddha Path appealing to vast numbers of us instead of just a very few. Because Shaivism portrays the world as constantly changing but still very real and not at all separate from its Creator, this philosophy permits the practice of an awareness and attitudes which are very easy for most of us to adopt, namely that everything in Creation is divine consciousness, already pure and perfect, and all we need do is learn to perceive and experience things as they really are. Thus, instead of our worldly life becoming an obstacle to our spiritual unfoldment, in Muktananda's Yoga the world becomes our spiritual classroom in which we constantly practice looking upon every aspect of our daily life (including our work, relationships, recreational activities, etc.) as well as every object (animate or inanimate) as manifestations of the same all-pervasive Consciousness. In short, we learn to see the Self in everyone and everything.

According to Baba Muktananda, on the Siddha Path our daily

life becomes our religion, our home becomes a sacred place of pilgrimage, our friends and loved ones become gods and goddesses, and all our practical affairs become sacred acts of worship. In this way, not only does this path promise supreme enjoyment at the culmination of our spiritual odyssey, it also promises that the journey itself will be more of a joyful and exciting adventure, rather than a painful and depressing ordeal.

Once an Australian reporter asked Muktananda this question: "Baba, can you *see* God?" The Siddha smiled at her with such bemusement as to suggest that anyone would have to be joking to ask such a thing. "That's a baby's question," he told her in a gentle, grandfatherly tone, and then he added, "When I look at *you,* I see God."[18] The fostering of just such an attitude is perhaps the most essential practice in Siddha Yoga, as well as the one which yields the greatest rewards most quickly, for this path relies more upon the constant refinement of outlook and understanding than upon the practice of elaborate techniques.

The only techniques considered indispensable in the practice of Siddha Yoga are meditation on the Self, the repetition of a special mantra, and right understanding. The manner in which meditation is practiced in Siddha Yoga makes it a natural and spontaneous occurrence rather than a willful, contrived performance. After the Siddha Guru has activated our dormant Kundalini, all we need do to practice meditation is to sit in the prescribed manner and then just put ourself completely into the supremely capable hands of the unfolding inner Shakti. Basically, then, to practice Siddha Meditation means to simply refrain from all random external activity so that the inner Shakti can go about her work with greater efficiency. Since this Shakti is the dynamic aspect of our inner Self, all we need do is center our awareness on the work she is doing inside us at the moment, and we are thereby performing perfect meditation on the Self.

If she gifts us with Hatha Yoga experiences in the form of physical kriyas, we witness those with interest; if she causes Laya Yoga to occur, gracing us with divine visions or subtle sensory delights, we enoy them; if she decides to fill us with the heavenly love of Bhakti Yoga, or to astound us with the divine knowledge of

Jnana Yoga, or daze us with the thoughtless state of Raja Yoga, with great contentment we accept whatever comes, knowing that she is always giving us exactly what we need. When her work proves too subtle for us to perceive with our unrefined awareness, and there seems to be nothing going on inside us dramatic enough to rivet our attention, then we can just sit silently and repeat our Siddha mantra, which has the power to intensify the Shakti's activity inside us.

We can now summarize the various elements of Siddha Yoga by saying that on this path (1) the Siddha Guru begins the process of Self-realization by awakening our inner Shakti, then (2) meditation, mantra repetition and the practice of right understanding sustain this process, while (3) supplementary practices accelerate it by helping to strengthen and purify our body, mind and heart, thereby increasing our capacity and worthiness for Grace.

In Siddha Yoga as in any other spiritual science, the time required to reach the goal depends upon both the intensity of our desire to attain it, and the intensity of the means which we employ toward that end. After Kundalini awakening, then, Siddha Yoga initiates are expected to at least sustain the required daily practices as much as possible, and if these essential obligations are diligently honored, aspirants are generally expected to attain Self-realization by the end of their current lifetime, and this time-span can be even further reduced if they are willing to invest more self-effort in the performance of supplementary techniques. The exact nature of these optional practices will be discussed in detail later; meanwhile, in summing up the role of self-effort in Siddha Yoga, we can say that although it does not play a causative part in the attainment of either Kundalini awakening or Self-realization on this path, it is decidedly required in order for a practitioner to sustain, support and expedite the automatic process which has been initiated by the Siddha Guru.

Now that we have seen how Siddha Yoga compares with other types of spiritual science, it's time to focus our full attention upon the Siddha Guru, without whom this path quite literally does not exist for any seeker. Only a Siddha Guru can initiate a spontaneous process of spiritual unfolding inside us; only he can then show us how to accelerate this process to its maximum intensity; only he can assume full responsibility for our complete safety every step along the way; and only he can provide us with a guarantee that he will not let us get stuck somewhere short of the ultimate attainment. Thus, he serves as not only the master architect of the entire Siddha Yoga structure, but its very foundation stone as well. Trying to understand this path without studying the Siddha Guru would be like trying to understand day and night without studying the sun.

6. The Guru

In Washington, D.C., there once lived a minor government official whose hobby was detecting and analyzing counterfeit money. To keep himself supplied with specimens for study, he persuaded a Treasury Department friend to occasionally slip him a few bogus bills from the many which the government confiscated each year. Every time the amateur criminologist got his hands on some phony currency he would spend hours poring over it, carefully cataloging all the flaws he could find, taking great pride in his self-styled ability to spot even the minutest imperfections.

One day his friend sent him a pair of fifty-dollar bills, along with a note challenging him to determine which of these counterfeits was the product of a newly exposed ring of ingenious foreign criminals. Delighted with the opportunity to show off his prowess in this area, the armchair criminologist launched his investigation with great relish, but his enthusiasm waned somewhat as he quickly discovered that the problem his friend had posed was not the least bit challenging to him, for even the most superficial examination showed one counterfeit to be far superior to the other. The inferior bill was the typical work of American amateurs, he immediately decided, for its flaws were easily detectable by any savvy bank teller; but the other phony was a veritable work of art. So skillful was its printing, engraving, paper construction and ink mixture, it would have surely appeared genuine to anyone but an expert in the field of counterfeit detection. Of course, under *his* masterful scrutiny several subtle defects slowly came to light, and these he smugly detailed in a brilliant report which he was certain would flabbergast his Treasury Department friend.

As soon as his analysis was complete, he dropped by his friend's office and plopped his report upon the desk, along with the extraordinary bill, and announced triumphantly, "The people who made this note are the most brilliant counterfeiters in history!"

His friend looked at him strangely, glanced through the report, and then with great concern said, "That's a pretty serious accusation. You see, this bill came straight from the U.S. Mint. I sent it to you as a gag." At that he broke into uproarious laughter.

Needless to say, it was the pseudo-criminologist and not his friend who came out flabbergasted. Nonetheless, as the story goes, rather than admit that his assessment of the currency had been foolish, he refused to believe that the bill was indeed genuine, and to this very day he brags about the time when he detected a bogus note which even the Treasury Department had thought to be authentic!

The moral of this story is especially significant when applied to the subject of spiritual guides: That is, it's very wise to be able to recognize a counterfeit, but only if we don't forget how to identify the real thing when we see it as well. Some people nowadays are of the opinion that all gurus are fakes, thereby forgetting the obvious fact that imitations exist only because their genuine counterparts also exist. What would be the point in making fake money, for example, if there were no such thing as real money in the world?

Is a Guru Really Necessary?

With so many counterfeit spiritual guides popping up all around us nowadays, it's little wonder that many of us get leery every time we hear the word *guru*. Such an attitude of skepticism is, in fact, recommended by Yoga, as long as it does not get carried to the sort of extreme illustrated in the above story. Because there are so many imitation gurus around, however, we might well pause to wonder if it's truly worth our trouble to shop around until we locate one of the rare authentic masters.

In this regard, there is one point on which every valid spiritual science is in agreement: It is essential for every person seriously

seeking Self-realization to receive personal guidance from someone who has already attained it; otherwise all attempts at meaningful progress become practically futile and decidedly risky. Of
course, many naive seekers ignore this sound advice, and some
even go so far as to avoid *all* external guidance, meaning that they
become, in effect, their own gurus. Such an unfortunate situation
can be best characterized by paraphrasing a well-known admoni-
tion of the legal profession: Just as the lawyer who represents
himself has a fool for a client, so too the seeker who guides himself
has a fool for a guru.

Who among us would ever consider trying to master any art,
science, fine craft or athletic skill without assistance from those
who have already gained supremacy in it? Even those of us who
boast of being ''self-taught'' usually mean that we have become
adept at something by studying it on our own in books; thus, here
too we have been guided indirectly through books written by
predecessors who have already become accomplished in that field.

While we're on the subject of books, let's consider the relative
merits of using them as a means of spiritual guidance as opposed to
having a personal relationship with a living master. To begin with,
we must first ask ourself whether our interest in Self-realization is
mainly intellectual or mainly practical; in other words, do we just
want to learn *about* Self-realization, or do we want to actually *attain*
it? Most spiritual sciences agree that books are fine for elementary
research by dabblers who are not yet sold on Self-realization, but as
soon as we go beyond mere speculative interest and decide to
actively work toward attaining personal Liberation—which means
that we must now participate in some system of practical discipline
whose techniques must be adapted to suit our specific needs and
capabilities—it becomes imperative for us to put ourself under the
watchful eye of a living expert who is both learned and experienced
enough to show us exactly how we should proceed toward our goal.
Of course, once we obtain the direct guidance of an adept master,
books can often serve as helpful supplementary aids, but it's generally advisable to limit such study to the titles which our guru
recommends as being compatible with the path we are following.

One characteristic common to all perfected spiritual masters is that, though they all teach the same universal truth, each does so in a unique way, employing a particular reference-frame and idiom designed to suit the time in which they are living, the culture in which they are functioning, and the specific seekers they are guiding. Thus, however much inspiration we may derive from reading about past masters and their teachings, if we then attempt to observe the technical disciplines which these masters once recommended, we are likely to discover that although such practices were undoubtedly the most appropriate and effective ones at the time they were taught, they are not equally suitable for a seeker living in modern-day society.

For these and other reasons to be discussed shortly, spiritual scientists advise all serious seekers of Self-realization to find themselves a living, expert guide. The classic manner in which this guidance is obtained involves the following four steps: (1) We must first select a spiritual path whose approach is to our liking; (2) next, we must locate a perfected master who gives initiation and guidance in that particular science; (3) then we must spend time with this master, studying his character and teachings, until we are satisfied that he is a truly perfected guide with whom we feel compatible; (4) finally, we must establish a guru-disciple relationship with him.

The Guru-Disciple Relationship

Since most of us hear much more about the antics of false gurus than about the doings of authentic perfected masters, many of us carry in our minds a greatly distorted impression of the guru-disciple relationship. The bond between a true guru and his true disciples is decidedly *not* like that of a master and his slaves, with the disciples groveling at their guru's feet, waiting on him hand and foot, hoping that someday he will grant them Liberation because they have served him well. Nor is this special relationship like a spiritual fan-club in which a charismatic figure is fawned over by moon-eyed groupies whose only desire is to be looked upon with favor by their lord and master. It is also not comparable to the bond between a military leader and his followers, in which the disciples are held in line by force and are promoted on the basis of their ability to follow, blindly and without hesitation, every command of their superior.

If we had to pick the worldly relationship which is most comparable to the classic guru-disciple bond, it would probably be the one existing between an expert mountain-guide and a dedicated student climber. A serious spiritual seeker is like a climber who wishes to conquer the highest mountain in the world, but has neither a knowledge of the best route to take, nor a sufficient degree of skill required to make the ascent safely.

Faced with such a challenge, we as average climbers would have several possibilities from which to choose. We might, for example, elect to try the ascent completely alone, or we might opt to band together with other climbers whose skill and experience nearly match our own; but in either case, the odds in favor of a successful climb would be extremely slim. We may also choose to take along a book written by someone who has previously conquered the mountain, but a guidebook cannot take into consideration such vital factors as our particular strengths and weaknesses as climbers, nor can it anticipate such current ascent factors as weather changes, alterations in the mountain due to landslides, erosion, etc. Finally, we may of course choose to find ourself a living expert willing to personally accompany us all the way to the summit, and this is obviously the most sensible option of all.

In shopping around for such a guide, chances are we would not be too concerned with whether he is physically attractive or charismatic; nor would we demand that he be dressed a certain way or that ''he'' be a member of any particular race, sex or religion. Instead, our primary requirement would undoubtedly be that he must have personally reached the peak in question and must thoroughly know the way to get there. The other essential requirement would be that he must be a fully accomplished teacher of climbing, as well as a master climber himself, thus able to pinpoint our strengths and weaknesses and, with these in mind, select an ascent route most suitable to our unique capabilities, and also teach us whatever additional climbing skills he knows will prove to be essential along the way.

In our pursuit of spirituality, as in any other pursuit, a guide with consummate knowledge and experience can save us a great deal of wasted time and effort, as well as needless suffering and frustration. Such a guide can steer us clear of dead-end paths which have already been explored and rejected by our predecessors; he can advise us how to direct our energies most effectively, show us short-cuts, help us out of predicaments, force us to unlearn old habits which would eventually prove to be impediments on the climb, and teach us new habits, the practice of which may seem pointless and unrewarding as we scale the easygoing foothills, but which will prove to be great blessings when we reach the thin air and craggy cliffs near our awesome destination.

Just as a student mountain-climber must make a personal commitment to stick with his or her chosen guide throughout the entire ascent, so too must a disciple agree to accept one guru's guidance for the duration of the spiritual journey; otherwise there can be no true guru-disciple relationship. Since each guru approaches Self-realization via a different course, any seeker who attempts to reach this goal by following the guidance of more than one guru is like a climber trying follow guides who are scaling different sides of a mountain; or, to use the analogy preferred by the yogic sages, such a seeker is like a traveler trying to cross the ocean with each foot in a different boat—a voyage which will invariably end with a dunking not far from shore.

Until we are completely certain that we have found a guide whom we want to follow steadfastly until our inner unfolding is pronounced complete *by him,* we do not have a guru and the guide in question does not have us for a disciple. Every true guru has both "disciples" and "devotees." Among his devotees may be included people who are convinced of his authenticity but have little or no desire to work toward Self-realization, and also those seekers of Enlightenment who are still testing him (and perhaps testing other prospective gurus as well) by spending time with him, analyzing his character and teachings. Disciples, however, are spiritual aspirants who have decided to stop testing the guru and have authorized the guru to begin testing them instead.

Once a genuine guru-disciple relationship has been firmly

cemented, our climb toward Self-realization begins without delay, and during the ensuing climb both the guru and the disciple must accept certain serious responsibilities. Like a mountain guide, a guru is committed to looking after the needs of his disciple 100% of the time, but he cannot be expected to carry us up the mountainside on his back; this climb must be a shared effort in which both guru and disciple work in close cooperation throughout. The guru agrees to accompany us every step of the way, warning us the instant we set foot off the proper path, pointing out steep shortcuts along the way and teaching us techniques for scaling them, steering us around pitfalls, removing doubts and anxieties with the strength of his knowledge and experience, inspiring us by his own example, and even clearing away many obstacles which lay strewn along the path before us.

It is *not*, however, his responsibility to make the climb for us—it's up to us to keep scrambling upward, putting one foot in front of the other—and it is also not his job to coddle us along the way, for the object of our climb is not to become more and more dependent upon our guide, but to become more *in*dependent as the ascent progresses. A disciple's initial dependence upon the guru is, by mutual agreement, strictly temporary.

Even though a true guru is an unconditional servant of his disciple, it is still the guru who commands the disciple, and not the other way around. In the same way, a mountain guide is under the employment of the climber who hires him; but still, because the guide alone knows how to reach the goal, as soon as the journey commences it is he who takes complete charge of the ascent. Therefore, we must implicitly trust our guide to decide at every juncture exactly which course is best for us, and should we ever decide to wander off on our own for any reason during the ascent, we must be prepared to assume full responsibility for any delays or discomforts we may suffer as a consequence.

What a disciple derives from this relationship is obvious, but what, we may well wonder, does the guru get out of it? At this point our running analogy of a mountain guide completely falls apart, for in that worldly relationship the guide usually offers his services in return for some material consideration, whereas a true guru has no material needs or desires. Since he is by definition a fully Self-realized being, he is therefore the enjoyer of supreme happiness and fulfillment; thus, having attained a personal fortune of truly cosmic proportions—including limitless existence, power, wisdom and bliss—he would hardly be interested in leading us to the enjoyment of that same state in return for whatever payment, material or otherwise, which we might be able to give him.

According to yogic scriptures, there is only one reason why a being who has evolved into complete union with Shiva would undertake to guide us to this same attainment, and that reason is compassion. It is out of Shiva's compassion that the office of Guruhood even exists, otherwise we would have no Enlightened guides to show us to Liberation; and it is out of personal compassion that a particular Self-realized being consents to hold this office and function as a guide for others.

And what do such beings demand from us in return for their priceless guidance? Their primary demand is worthiness—an eagerness for spiritual growth and a receptivity to their teachings—and it is also traditional for them to expect some symbolic material sacrifice in the form of money, goods or services, which they never use personally but disburse in charity or direct toward the upkeep of their teaching institution.

Though most beginning seekers obtain guidance from many different types and grades of spiritual guides, any commitment of discipleship should be reserved until contact is made with a fully perfected master of the path we wish to follow. If we are serious seekers, we will have little difficulty identifying an outright counterfeit when we encounter one, but much more subtle discrimination is often required when it comes to determining whether a being who is obviously more highly evolved than we are has indeed attained the ultimate pinnacle of Enlightenment. To arm ourself with sufficient understanding to make this difficult judgment, let's now focus our investigation upon the nature of a fully perfected spiritual guide, the holder of an official cosmic office which in Yoga is identified by the title of *Sadguru*, meaning "true guru."

The True Guru

The Sanskrit word *guru* consists of two syllables which stand for "darkness" and "light" respectively. Thus, the Sadguru is one who leads us from darkness into light; in other words, he takes seekers who are in the dark about their true nature and leads them to an awareness of the Self's pure light of divine consciousness.

The most fundamental point which must be understood about the Sadguru is one which most seekers tend to forget: *The true guru is not a person, but a cosmic power*.

Remember a few chapters back when we examined the five cosmic functions which Shiva performs through his dynamic aspect, Shakti? There we saw that this supreme Self creates, sustains, destroys, conceals its true nature, and reveals itself again through the bestowal of Grace. To perform these five actions, Shiva is said to manifest five special cosmic powers, and that power whose function it is to bestow Grace is called "The Guru."

According to Kashmir Shaivism, the Sadguru is a cosmic principle which can be identified as that part of the divine will concerned with the bestowal of Grace upon anyone who demonstrates sufficient desire to perceive the highest truth. As such, the Sadguru is not a person but a cosmic power; however, when the divine will singles out someone who has attained Self-realization and enlists that being to serve as a channel for the dispensation of Grace, then that perfected master is also referred to as a Sadguru, by virtue of the cosmic power vested in him.

The question may arise at this point as to why the cosmic will needs a physical instrument, in the person of an Enlightened being, in order to make Grace available to us. The moment we become worthy, why can't Grace simply manifest inside us spontaneously, descending upon us straight from the cosmic Self, perhaps by way of our inner Self, instead of having to be delivered by a human embodiment of the Guru Principle? The answer, Yoga tells us, is that Grace does not in fact need such a physical instrument as a transmission medium; indeed, many of us receive small amounts of Grace directly from the Self occasionally, every time our karma, worthiness and receptivity permit us to glimpse the bliss that is our essential nature. The problem with receiving Grace in this direct way is that most of the time we don't recognize it as Grace at all, and instead attribute the effects we feel to some external thing.

In certain rare instances throughout history, when really large infusions of Grace have suddenly descended upon people "from out of the blue," such events have proven to be quite disconcerting and often terrifying, for the recipients had no understanding of what was actually happening to them. We can only imagine how we ourself would react if we had absolutely no knowledge of the sort of information we've been covering in this book, and suddenly one day we felt a tremendous eruption of energy inside us, accompanied by violent physical, mental or emotional kriyas. Though these would simply be signs of our organism's reception of Grace and subsequent movement toward Self-realization, we would probably not appreciate them as such at all, but would instead assume them to be signs of physical illness or mental imbalance.

It is not God who needs the physical Guru to dispense Grace—it is *we* who need him. By providing the physical Guru as the primary medium through which we receive Grace—especially moderate and intense infusions of it—the divine will has anticipated our possible confusion and has seen to it that its blessings are delivered to us by a specially trained emissary who can not only give us the Grace, but can also give us right understanding to go with it, so that we will appreciate the gift for what it really is, instead of interpreting it negatively out of ignorance. A living Sadguru is therefore looked upon as a seeker's greatest gift of Grace, and it is said that such a Guru's guidance cannot be obtained unless an aspirant has already attained a high degree of spiritual worthiness through the expenditure of personal effort.

Signs of a Sadguru

Truly speaking, all Self-realized beings radiate Grace—meaning that a receptive seeker in any such being's presence can have an experience of that being's state and become drawn automatically closer to the Self; but an Enlightened being who is also a Sadguru controls important additional powers in that not only can he bestow Grace, along with the understanding required for us to truly benefit from receiving it, he also has the authority to show us exactly what to do to earn more and more of it, and he alone can lead us all the way to permanent establishment in the ultimate state of Grace: Self-realization.

The person of a Sadguru is paradoxical in that he is at the same time both human and divine. He is human in that he still retains many personality traits which characterized him as an individual before Self-realization, and he is divine in that he has become an embodiment of the fifth cosmic function of Grace-bestowal.

In addition to being fully realized, a Sadguru must also have the specific authority to initiate seekers in a traditional spiritual science, and must be able to lead them all the way to the topmost peak of Self-realization via that path. As a fully perfected master of a particular spiritual tradition, each Sadguru must have a ''pedigree'' which proves him to be a bona fide descendant of an authentic lineage of perfected masters of that tradition. Regardless of the spiritual path in question, each Sadguru must have been the disciple of another Sadguru of the same tradition; hence, no perfected master may be self-proclaimed, but must be pronounced to be such by an already recognized Sadguru.

Furthermore, a true guru must have the ability to activate mantras, making their dormant shakti available to his disciples so that they may supplement their self-effort with mantra power. A Sadguru must also have complete knowledge of the ultimate truth and be able to teach this knowledge in such a way that his disciples can not only understand it intellectually, but also practice this understanding in daily life and eventually experience this Truth personally through direct perception.

Other characteristics a true guru must display are flawless discrimination, a razor-sharp intellect, and mastery of the scriptures which support his path. Such a Guru must be a living embodiment of his teachings; he must be completely without trace of ego, exhibiting no attachments whatsoever to worldly things; and he must be in total command of his body, mind and senses. He must be completely satisfied within himself, never trying to attain satisfaction in any way from his followers, and he must never solicit either personal service or worship. A true guru's main purpose is to put us in touch with our own inner Guru, not to make us become dependent upon him. A true guru must be able to uplift everyone who follows him; he must be able to help those who are grounded to become airborne, and those who are airborne to go ever higher.

A true disciple, on the other hand, never forgets that the Sadguru is an external symbol—in fact a living embodiment—of the same Self which exists inside each one of us. Thus, to show such a being reverence, devotion and respect is a simple acknowledgment of this fact; to serve and honor him is, in effect, serving and honoring our own Self, and it is also an outlet for expressing our gratitude for the uplifting guidance he gives us.

In addition to the above list of qualities to look for in a Sadguru, the yogic sages have also provided us with some suggestions on how to recognize a false guru as well. They advise us, for example, to steer completely clear of any professed guru who teaches hate, prejudice, violence or wanton behavior, condones the use of drugs or intoxicants, encourages cultism or engages in politics, shows disrespect for ancient scriptures or the teachings of great beings, employs brainwashing or coercion on his followers, cuts them off from the outside world, breaks up families, or denies the public access to his spiritual community.

Now that we have sketched in the general characteristics of all true gurus, let's focus exclusively upon the unique qualities possessed by Sadgurus of the Siddha Path.

The Siddha Guru

In addition to those qualities which are universally possessed by all true gurus, a Siddha Master displays two more distinctions which give him a special place among Sadgurus. First, because the Siddha Path is one of integration, a Siddha Guru is a master of not just one but many yogic sciences. Secondly, he alone possesses a supreme psychic power called *Shaktipat*, which enables him to instantly awaken and control anyone's Kundalini, simply through an act of his will. The word *Shaktipat* means "the descent of cosmic power," and the particular power which the Siddha Guru causes to descend upon us is the power of Grace.

Though all true gurus on every path have some power to willfully bestow Grace, only a Siddha Guru has the full potency of cosmic Grace at his command. By simply willing it, a Siddha Guru can effect any degree of Kundalini activation he wishes, in anyone he chooses. What's more, he can willfully control anyone's inner Shakti once it has been awakened; he can willfully remove any internal or external blocks impeding a practitioner's progress toward Self-realization; he can willfully increase or decrease the intensity of an awakened Kundalini; he can willfully cause automatic meditation to occur in anyone at any time; and he can willfully bestow, upon anyone he chooses, virtually any meditational experience he wants them to have, including physical kriyas, divine visions, and even the temporary immersion in samadhi states.

In fact, so total is his command of spiritual energy, a Siddha Guru can even effect complete and permanent Self-realization in anyone instantaneously, though examples of this are extremely rare because recipients of such a boon must necessarily possess extraordinary karma. Siddha Gurus, then, belong to an elite "Shaktipat Lineage" of true gurus, and each must be specially endowed in order to so completely command the full power of cosmic grace.

The manner in which a Siddha Guru bestows Shaktipat upon a disciple may vary. Often he may do it by touching us physically, usually on the head, chest, or base of the spine; but there are many other ways he may employ to bestow Grace, for the real working force behind Shaktipat is the Guru's willful intent: He simply has to wish it and the bestowal occurs.

Thus, when a Siddha Guru consciously intends to transmit his Shakti into someone, he may use any vehicle he cares to, such as a physical touch, a word, a look, or just a thought. If he wants to, he can even transmit his Grace telepathically, halfway around the world; he can send it to one disciple through the person of another disciple; or he can send it through a photograph or any other object of his choosing. The means he selects are the ones which he determines are most appropriate to each specific situation.

To illustrate the fact that it is the Siddha Guru's intent and not his actions which determine his bestowal of Shaktipat, we need only point to Baba Muktananda, who uses a wand of peacock feathers both to bless people who come to greet him, and also to transmit his Shakti when he gives Shaktipat; thus this same action has a completely different significance in the two situations, the reason being that his intent is different in each.

The Siddha Guru Lineage

Tradition states that this lineage began when Lord Shiva himself took human birth eons ago, and since that time the lineage has grown like Shiva's family tree, with each Siddha Guru passing the Shaktipat office to one, and occasionally more than one perfected disciple. Figure 16 on the following page simulates what this tree might look like, with its roots planted in the formless reality—the primal Guru Principle—while its trunk springs into the world as divinity incarnate, from whom all descendant Siddha Gurus then branch upward, with a host of non-guru Siddhas (fully perfected beings who do not function as Gurus) issuing forth as the fruit of the Shaktipat Lineage family tree.

As this schematic indicates, at some point in the early history of the Siddha Guru lineage, some Guru transformed more than just one of his perfected disciples into Siddha Gurus; thus, at this point, the tree trunk begins to branch out into sub-lineages. This branching out has occurred periodically throughout history until, by the time we arrive at the present day, we see that there are many sub-lineages of Siddha Gurus represented on the family tree. As the top of the tree indicates, not all of these sub-lineages need be active at the same point in time. Though tradition states that there will always be at least one Siddha Guru alive on earth to keep the "master lineage" unbroken as well as to give Shaktipat and personal guidance to worthy seekers, there need not always be a living guru in each and every sub-lineage. Thus, when a Siddha Guru leaves his body, he need not immediately leave behind a fully perfected Guru as his successor. Often, in fact, he will continue to guide his disciples personally from more subtle realms after his passing; then, when he deems that the time is right, he may descend into the world again temporarily, in any form he chooses, and ordain the next Siddha Guru in his particular sub-lineage.

At some points in history, many sub-lineages will be active concurrently and a number of Siddha gurus will be found to be functioning in the world simultaneously, while at other times (such as the present) Siddha Gurus will be found to be in extremely short supply. Perhaps one reason why there are so few around today is

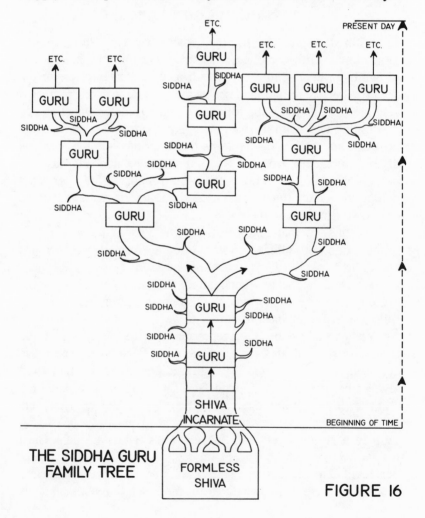

THE SIDDHA GURU
FAMILY TREE

FIGURE 16

because modern technology permits one such master to become accessible to vast numbers of seekers. In the few decades during which Baba Muktananda has been functioning as a Siddha Guru, for example, he has circled the world several times and initiated hundreds of thousands into Siddha Yoga, a feat which would have required the services of a great many Siddha Masters before the age of jet planes and electronic communications.

Since Baba Muktananda is recognized the world over as a living yogic saint and Siddha Guru, let's take a brief look at his particular guru-ancestry in the light of what we've just been discussing about lineage.

Baba Muktananda was commanded to Guruhood by his Guru, Bhagawan Nityananda, one of the most renowned and revered Siddhas in the history of India. Even now, two decades after Nityananda's death, though the samadhi shrine in which he is buried lies a tough two-hour drive from the city of Bombay, its tiny village of Ganeshpuri is visited by hundreds of pilgrims daily— enough to support commercial round-trip bus service from Bombay every hour from morning to night.

Before Nityananda left his body on August 1, 1961, he conferred upon Muktananda the title of *Paramahansa*, signifying the attainment of perfect Enlightenment, and then empowered him to function as a Siddha Guru. Thus, Baba Muktananda now stands as the current patriarch of a Shaktipat-Guru lineage which includes such venerable sages as Vasishtha, Vyasa, Suka Muni, Gaudapada, Shankaracharya, Hastamalaka, and Nityananda's Guru, Ishwara Iyer.

Traditionally, most Gurus make deathbed proclamations regarding their immediate successors, if any. Surprisingly, however, in May of 1982 a hale and hearty Muktananda ceremoniously instated a pair of future standard-bearers for his lineage. They are the youthful Swami Nityananda (namesake of Baba's Guru) and his older sister, Swami Chidvilasananda. Though both are only in their twenties, they have studied and practiced Yoga intensely under Baba's guidance since childhood.

Is the Guru a Miracle Worker?

When we first come into the presence of a purported Sadguru, our initial concern as prospective disciples is the proving to our own satisfaction that he is indeed an authentic perfected master. Such an endeavor often turns out to be frustrating, however, for one of the most maddening qualities of a true guru is that he will seldom openly display the awesome cosmic powers he commands.

Instead of being willfully invoked by him, these powers will often seem to serve him spontaneously, creating minor miracles around him constantly, and because most of these miracles are rather subtle and seem to occur through sheer coincidence, they easily escape the notice of all but the keenest observers. If we have very sharp perception, however, we will soon begin to notice that the life of everyone who comes in contact with such a being—and this includes our own life as well—begins to change in some profound and positive way. Though sometimes such changes are cataclysmic, most often they are deceptively subtle, so we may fail to observe these minor miracles if we're too busy expecting something much more spectacular to happen.

Guru-watching is a very subtle, tricky business. As we watch such a being diligently, straining to catch some tiny clue to help us fathom his true spiritual state, our baffled and frustrated mind may often cry out, *If you're really a Siddha, why do you bother walking to the door when you have the power to walk right through the wall instead? Why do you travel in an automobile when you could just as easily teleport yourself with psychic power? If you really have all the powers in Creation at your beck and call, why can't you even cure your own illnesses, grow new teeth when the old ones fall out, or perform some stupendous miracle on international television so the whole world will immediately become convinced of who you really are?*

Such thinking reveals a very basic misunderstanding about the nature and role of a Sadguru. Guruhood is indeed a divine office which can be filled only by a being who has earned the command of special powers through extensive self-sacrifice and personal effort; and yet, a true guru's primary function is leading his disciples to

Liberation, so he will seldom use his powers for any other purpose. Rarely, if ever, will he invoke them even to alleviate his own personal ailments brought about by residual karmas which must work themselves out before he can leave the earth plane. Though undeniably there have been some Sadgurus throughout history who have deemed it necessary to perform such healings and other public miracles, this behavior is exceptional and not in itself a sign of true guruhood.

Another important reason such a being will usually avoid all public displays of psychic power is that it is not the function of a Sadguru to sell himself to prospective disciples: in fact, one of the primarily ways the worthiness of seekers is tested is by requiring them to judge the quality of a guru by means which demand great sharpness and subtlety of intellect.

Every serious seeker of Self-realization knows that it does not take a Sadguru or even a Realized being to perform miracles, and therefore we should not attach much importance to the possession of siddhis. Psychic powers manifest automatically during the pursuance of any valid spiritual science and are not always indicative of high spiritual attainment. In fact, it can generally be stated that serious seekers become less and less inclined to exercise psychic power the closer they come to the final goal.

Though at first this may strike us as mysterious, its logic rests upon the simple fact that a fully Enlightened being experiences total identification with Shiva. Those of us who have not yet attained this state have a severely limited perspective on reality; thus we may well be sitting around right now, fantasizing about the day when we finally reach Siddhahood and will immediately begin to perform stupendous feats such as moving mountains; but when that long-awaited day at last arrives, when we have achieved complete identification with the universal Creator, when we have finally realized that every mountain was placed in its original position by none other than our very own Self, chances are we will also then realize that we have already put everything in our Creation exactly where we wanted it in the first place, so we will no longer have the desire to change anything.

When any human being attains Siddhahood, it's as if Shiva

himself has come into the world and assumed a human form, simply for his own amusement. According to Kashmir Shaivism, in fact, Shiva resides in every object in Creation at this very moment, so this means that Enlightened beings are not the only ones among us who are essentially Shiva in a human form: *we all are*. The only difference is that those who are Self-realized experience this essential truth all the time, and the rest of us do not.

Since most of us do not consciously experience our "Shivaness," let's just imagine for a moment that we really are Shiva walking around in a human body, perceiving everything around us to be various forms of our own Self. This being the case, why would we now decide to walk through walls and miss the bliss of walking through doors? Everything being equally blissful, why would we want to teleport ourself to our destination instead of walking or riding in a car? Why cure our illnesses or grow new teeth when both good and ill health, real and false teeth, are equally our own blissful Self? If God Himself were to choose to take a human form simply to enjoy His own Creation, would He then have to behave in superhuman ways in order to have fun? Or would he get an even bigger kick out of just doing all the things that ordinary humans do?

If God wants to fly in the sky, why should He choose to do it in a human body when He can simply become a bird? In the same way, if He wants to be invisible, He can become the air; if He wants to appear beautiful, He can become a flower; if He wants to exhibit great strength, He can become a hurricane. Perhaps, then, when He chooses to become a human being He is perfectly content to walk on His own two feet, wear false teeth, catch cold and talk about the weather just as do the rest of His human creations. This is why Enlightened beings usually behave in a very human way rather than a superhuman one, despite whatever powers they have come to command during the course of their spiritual practice.

In the case of a Sadguru, however, there is one sure way in which a seeker can test such a being's power. Since a true guru employs his siddhis only for the benefit of his disciples, the one act of his which will consistently stand out as an observable demonstration of his power is the act of spiritual initiation. This is particularly true of a Siddha Guru, who initiates with his unique power of Shaktipat. Since Shaktipat awakens a seeker's dormant Kundalini, and since this book has outlined in detail the specific evidences of such an awakening, we should now be able to observe such evidences in those disciples who have been initiated by a Siddha Guru. If we do not see unmistakable signs, in the company of a guru, that he has the power to completely awaken and control the Kundalini with absolute authority and safety, we can legitimately assume that he is not a Siddha Guru.

There is an ancient yogic aphorism which makes the amazing claim that the true guru is greater than even God Himself. The explanation which then follows states that although God is able to turn Himself into every living creature in the cosmos, only the Sadguru is able to turn a living creature back into God. Here, of course, the terms "God" and "Guru" signify two of the five cosmic functions of Shiva, "God" being his creative power and the "Guru" being his power of Grace-bestowal as explained earlier.

When this cosmic Guru Principle begins to function through an individual who has attained Self-realization, that person becomes empowered to lead others to Enlightenment. We have already seen that, theoretically at least, just a single moment in the presence of such a being is sufficient for any of us to become completely Liberated; in practice, however, because of our lack of receptivity, this process is usually extended into a period of years.

Thus, once we find that we do not miraculously attain instantaneous Enlightenment upon receiving initiation from a Sadguru, an extended guru-disciple relationship then becomes essential, during which the Guru prescribes certain practices designed to increase our receptivity to Grace. The length of time it then takes us to become Self-realized depends upon the type of techniques employed and the intensity of our desire to reach the final goal. This period, lasting from spiritual initiation, through our performance of prescribed practices, and ending at the moment of perfect Enlightenment, is known in Yoga as *sadhana*.

Part Five

Sadhana:
The Practice of
Siddha Yoga

1. Right Effort:
The Essence of Spiritual Sadhana

The Sanskrit word *sadhana* literally means "the way to achieve." *Yoga sadhana,* then, is "the way to achieve Self-realization"; it is our willful performance of practices prescribed by a Sadguru for the explicit purpose of evolving to the ultimate level of spiritual enlightenment.

According to the law of karma, everything that comes to us in life does so only because we have earned it with our own personal effort, either in this present incarnation or in some previous existence. The most important detail to bear in mind about this aspect of karmic law is that every single effort of ours—no matter how big or small—is unconditionally guaranteed to yield a result which is entirely appropriate to that effort. Therefore, whenever we strive for some specific goal we must be sure to invest only *right effort*; that is, we must be certain that the effort we put forth can be depended upon to produce only the desired result.

For example, no matter how hard we might desire to bake a cake, our goal can never be reached if we insist upon investing all our effort into following only recipes for pie. This is where the essential element of the Guru enters into a successful sadhana; it is his responsibility to see that we follow the right "recipe," combining only those ingredients which will result in the attainment of Self-realization and not some lesser goal. Once these proper ingredients are assembled, all we need do is bake them in the oven of sadhana until we obtain the desired result. On paths which rely mainly upon self-effort, most of our oven's heat must come from the burning of our own personal energy, while on the Siddha Path our awakened Kundalini furnishes much fire of its own.

An essential point to bear in mind about spiritual sadhana is that the disciple and not the Guru determines the length of time it takes to become Self-realized. On any path—Siddha Yoga included —the duration of our sadhana depends upon our initial worthiness (meaning the extent of our receptivity to Grace), our strength of determination, and the potency of the means which we employ. But because Siddha Yoga is a path which relies more upon ego-surrender than self-effort in the attainment of supreme spiritual evolution, the primary personal striving required of Siddha students is that of becoming adept at spiritual surrender, which is nothing more than learning to identify with the Self instead of the ego. To facilitate this adjustment of personal identification, we are advised to practice just a few simple techniques.

The moment we accomplish perfect surrender, our awakened Shakti will lead us automatically to Self-realization; thus, depending upon just how much talent we have for surrender, our journey to the top of the mountain can take anywhere from a few seconds to several lifetimes. This much is certain, however: no matter how long our sadhana may take, it cannot begin until our dormant Kundalini has been activated by a Siddha Guru.

Shaktipat: The Beginning of Siddha Yoga Sadhana

Regardless of which spiritual science we may elect to practice, our sadhana cannot officially begin until we are initiated by a master who has himself become perfected on that same path. In Siddha Yoga, our initiation into sadhana occurs the moment we receive Shaktipat, the awakening of our sleeping Shakti through an infusion of spiritual energy from a Siddha Guru.

Shaktipat is the keystone of Siddha Yoga. It marks our entrance onto the Siddha Path and insures us that all our future efforts in sadhana will be augmented by the Kundalini's work within us. Once activated by a Siddha Guru, the inner Shakti becomes a wise and powerful ally in our conquest over bondage; immediately she proceeds to aid us in our systematic removal of all the obstacles which block us from the perception of essential divinity, a process which gradually brings us deeper and more frequent experiences of ultimate reality until at last we reach a complete and permanent realization of the Self.

In a previous section we saw that the true activating force behind Shaktipat is Guru-sankalpa, meaning that the transmission of a Siddha Guru's Shakti occurs any time he expressly wishes it. Thus, the most efficient vehicle of transmission is pure thought, but often the Guru will employ some sort of perceivable gesture as well, such as a look, a word, or a touch, and occasionally he may even elect to transmit his Shakti through some external vehicle. When he does this it is not because he wishes to flaunt his power in public but because most initiates become more receptive to Grace when they can actually perceive the Guru transmitting his Shakti in some noticeable way.

The main external vehicle which Baba Muktananda favors for the transmission of his Shakti is an event called a Siddha Meditation Intensive. This is generally presented as a two-day program of information, instruction and practice during which Shaktipat is made available to everyone who attends and actively participates. In accordance with Muktananda's explicit wish, the Intensive format itself has become a vehicle for the transmission of cosmic grace; thus, Shaktipat initiation occurs spontaneously at such a program, regardless of whether or not the Guru himself is physically present.

If this Intensive format were to be "borrowed" by unauthorized personnel and presented to unknowing seekers without Muktananda's knowledge and consent, the absense of Guru-sankalpa would prevent the occurrence of Shaktipat at such a program. How, then, can we be sure that such a publicized Muktananda Intensive, at which Baba is not to be physically present, is indeed a bona fide vehicle for his Shakti? To protect the public from such a possibility, every authorized Siddha Yoga teacher carries official credentials; furthermore, all such teachers, who must be specially trained and specifically authorized to conduct Siddha Meditation Intensives and courses, are registered with the Teacher Training Office of the SYDA Foundation, whose regional headquarters are listed in the back of this book. Anyone wishing to affirm the authenticity of a particular Siddha Yoga Intensive or Meditation Course may do so by calling or writing the nearest ashram or foundation headquarters.

After Shaktipat

The moment we receive Shaktipat, we become destined to some-day reach full blossom on the Siddha Family Tree. Shaktipat, then, is like a priceless inheritance bequeathed to us by our Siddha ancestors. If we choose to accept this inheritance purely as a windfall, feeling no personal responsibility to nurture and revere it, its worth will be considerably diminished. If, on the other hand, we look upon it as a golden opportunity, an advance against future efforts in our sadhana, then it will become a family heirloom of inestimable value. As Goethe very wisely pointed out: What our ancestors have earned through their own personal effort and then passed on to us, must be re-earned with our own effort before we can truly possess it.

Through Shaktipat, the cosmic Guru Principle bestows upon us the initial spark of Grace, without which the Self could never become revealed; after this, it then becomes our duty to continue to bestow Grace upon ourself through sadhana, personally building that divine spark into a conflagration which finally consumes the entire mountain of our ignorance as well as all our past and future karmas, setting us completely free.

Depending upon our state of physical and mental purity at the moment of Shaktipat, ignition of Kundalini may occur within us to any degree from extremely mild to extremely intense. The analogy most often used to explain how this works likens Shaktipat recipients to pieces of firewood, and the Guru's infusion of Shakti to a flame that's placed beneath them. Some sticks are still green (filled with impurities), so the flame only causes them to smolder faintly, while others are well-seasoned (free of impurities) and immediately ignite with great force. The same fire is applied to each piece of wood, yet some burst into flame at once while others take varying amounts of time to ignite.

Sadhana is the process of removing our impurities and seasoning our instrument so that it will more quickly become consumed and transformed by the fire of Yoga. On paths which emphasize self-effort over ego-surrender, this seasoning must be accomplished by our own striving alone, and Kundalini ignition usually occurs only when we are completely purified. On the Siddha Path, however, ignition is effected through Shaktipat at the very outset of Sadhana, and then the smoldering Shakti begins to help us burn away our impurities with her own heat, which gradually intensifies as the process of purification progresses.

If we expect the awakened inner Shakti to do all this work herself, however, our progress will be very slow indeed. To hasten our ascent to Shivahood, we must willingly cooperate with her through-out the transformation process by supplementing her activity with some effort of our own, and this self-effort should be directed not only toward helping her to eliminate impurities from our instrument, but also toward minimizing the amount of new impurities we continue to collect.

Since the duration of our spiritual journey depends largely upon the amount of personal striving we are willing to invest in it, let's now examine the types of right effort which Muktananda prescribes in order to shorten our sadhana as much as possible.

2. Essential Daily Practices in Siddha Yoga

As we have just seen, Siddha Yoga sadhana begins with Shaktipat, and this is the first unique characteristic of discipleship under a Siddha Guru. After Shaktipat initiation, the Siddha Guru pre-scribes whatever basic practices he considers vital to our spiritual unfolding. Because Baba Muktananda's Yoga is primarily a path for people living active worldly lives rather than monastic ones, there are only three essential techniques which he advises us to practice on a daily basis, two of which may be exercised right in the midst of our worldly activities. In addition, Baba also recommends several supplementary practices which are equally beneficial to our sadhana, but which may be performed whenever we can spare some time from our weekly duties.

In this section, we will first examine the three techniques which Siddha students are encouraged to practice daily. These are (1) mantra japa, (2) formal meditation, and (3) right understand-ing. Mantra japa is the repetition of a spiritual mantra which has been given us by the Siddha Guru; formal meditation is the practice of periodically turning our awareness inward, as described at the outset of this book; and the practice of right understanding is really just another form of meditation on the Self, performed with our awareness turned outward instead of inward.

The primary purpose of these three exercises is to purify the mind, turn it away from self-limiting things, and focus it toward the Self. Beyond this, everything else is accomplished through the work-ings of our awakened Kundalini. Since aspirants on this path are advised to invest the bulk of their self-effort into the practice of man-tra japa, formal meditation, and right understanding, it's important for both prospective and established practitioners to fully appreciate the true meaning and significance of these primary tools.

I. Mantra Japa

It is a primary contention of both modern science and yogic philosophy that everything we experience in life takes substantial form inside our mind. Back in Part Four, Chapter Three, we saw that our mind-stuff is like magical modeling clay, constantly molding itself into countless forms in reaction to many types of stimuli.

The manifestation which we identify as "a tree," for example, may be experienced by us in a variety of ways: The tree may actually be standing before us, it may be a recollection of some tree we have stood before in the past, or it may even be a complete mental creation which has never existed except in our imagination. In any case, unless our mind-stuff assumes the form of a tree, we can never experience it. Thus, our experience of reality is determined solely by the forms our mind assumes, and these forms will accurately reflect the true nature of things only to the extent that our mind is able to properly interpret the stimulation it receives.

This notion is a central one in Siddha Yoga's philosophy, for if indeed we can experience only the forms which our mind assumes, then *we can never experience the Self until our mind-stuff actually assumes the form of the Self.* According to Yoga, the easiest way to accomplish this is through the repeated contemplation of a "pure object"—that is, one which embodies the Self as closely as possible, as opposed to an "impure object" which tends to entrap us more deeply in the illusion of individuality and limitation. For as long as we can keep our attention focused upon one of these pure objects, the mind becomes temporarily pure; and when we can manage to completely fill our mind with such an object, without intrusion by other mental images or thoughts, we will then experience a sense of merging with that object, at which point we will realize the Self. Of the different types of objects available to us for spiritual contemplation, the yogic sages tell us that the purest one is a mysterious sound-form called a *mantra*.

Earlier we defined the spiritual mantra as a series of special sound-pulsations which have the capacity to modulate the vibrational pattern of our entire being, gradually causing us to resonate with ever purer frequencies of universal consciousness. This description is certainly not inaccurate, but it barely scratches the surface of a mantra's true significance, for a mantra represents an awesome and profound energy phenomenon whose roots go back to the very core of Creation. Mantra japa is generally considered the most useful and powerful tool in all of spiritual science, with effects so beneficial and far-reaching that on most paths the attainment of Self-realization is, practically speaking, considered impossible without it. To understand exactly what a mantra is, how it works and why, we must begin our investigation at the very essence of reality.

As we saw in Part Three, the ultimate reality is characterized by yogic science as an eternal union between two apparent opposites, Shiva and Shakti. Shiva symbolizes that aspect of reality which can be described as quiescent Consciousness, forever changeless and unmoving, while Shakti represents dynamic Consciousness, ever changing and in motion. To the normal human intellect, which functions in three dimensions only, this idea that the same cosmic consciousness can be absolutely still and in motion simultaneously is impossible to comprehend. Only through sadhana, which removes mental limitations and enables us to function in higher dimensions of reality, can we gain an improved perspective from which all apparent opposites will be found to be merely different aspects of a larger whole.

Meanwhile, if we search our gross physical world for something roughly equivalent to this Shiva/Shakti concept, the closest we can come is the phenomenon known as rapid vibration or oscillation, in which the two opposite states of movement and stillness alternate repeatedly in quick succession. Modern physicists have found that vibration is the primary characteristic of the physical universe, and spiritual scientists further assure us that this phenomenon is essentially nothing less than pure consciousness in motion. *This postulate, stating that the entire Creation is at heart nothing but Consciousness in the form of vibration, is the very first foundation stone upon which the science of mantra rests.*

The second foundation stone of mantra philosophy is the principle which establishes an unbreakable link between vibration and sound. This yogic principle states that *all movement produces sound, and all sound is accompanied by movement.* Again, our modern scientists know this to be true throughout the physical universe, and the yogic scientists assure us it is also valid in all the more subtle realms of Consciousness. The range of sound which falls within normal human hearing is but a minute fragment of the stupendous spectrum of cosmic sound emanating unceasingly from every tiny portion of every stratum of manifest Creation. For example, the vibration of atoms, which accounts for the predominant type of sound on the earth plane, occurs at frequencies which are thirty-four octaves beyond our range of hearing.

According to Yoga, then, sound is the second essential characteristic of vibration, the first being the repetitive alternation between movement and rest. Sound and movement are thus inextricably united; one cannot exist without the other, so anything which vibrates produces sound—and this holds true regardless of what is vibrating, be it a galaxy, an atomic particle, an entity in a world more subtle than our own, or even pure, unmodified consciousness. Earlier we saw that even in our Western Bible, in referring to the initial vibration which marked the very onset of Creation, calls it ''The Word''—a word, in essence, being nothing but a specifically meaningful sound.

Kashmir Shaivism states that before this current universal cycle got underway there was no movement or sound anywhere; there was just quiescent Consciousness, or Shiva. Then came The Word, or Spanda-Shakti—the initial creative force which arose from the static depths of Shiva and threw the entire mass of all-pervasive consciousness into a state of stress, causing it to stir en masse.

Back in Part Three we illustrated this by employing the analogue of a large vessel filled with clear water. Like Shiva, this water remains invisible as long as it is still; only when it becomes agitated, like Shakti, does it take on a form which is perceivable by us—otherwise our vision passes through it unobstructed. When this vessel of still water is suddenly jarred by a force comparable to the initial creative impulse, at first all the water particles move in unison; but then, as the initial stress-wave bounces off the vessel's sides, a great number of reflected waves travel through the water, and these begin to interact with one another, forming interference patterns which become increasingly complex. Soon the entire mass of water is filled with an infinite array of unique and ever-changing vibrational patterns, each caused by the interaction of countless water particles moving in every conceivable direction. In a similar way, when the universal mass of consciousness begins to vibrate in an infinite variety of ever-changing patterns, an endless succession of objects springs into temporary existence.

When viewed in terms of vibration, then, the entire cosmos becomes nothing but a unified field of vibrating Consciousness which, after being set into motion by a single "push" or "creative urge," has self-interacted into an infinite system of correlated forces. These forces are continually interacting to form an endless, ever-changing array of vibrational patterns, each of which exists only until it transmutes into a different pattern, becomes absorbed into a larger pattern, or breaks up into smaller patterns.

As long as any one of these patterns maintains its individuality it is said to be an object of manifest Creation, and if it falls within the range of our sensory perception, we identify it as an object of some sort—a "rock," perhaps, or a "tree," a "person," a "star," etc. Thus, each object in existence is simply a partial experience of the entire field of vibrant Consciousness, a portion in temporary stress due to the interaction of forces which have come together at some particular place to form a unique vibrational pattern.

Anyone with a knowledge of music knows that each musical tone is the product of a specific frequency of vibration, and this exemplifies the yogic contention that each unique vibrational pattern in Creation generates its own special sound pattern as well. This sound pattern is similar to a musical chord in that it is a blend of sounds produced by the vibrational forces which have interacted to manifest that particular object. Thus, Yoga states that *every object in Creation has both a body of substance and a body of sound.* Yogic scientists refer to this sound-body as the object's "natural name."

This leads us to the third foundation stone upon which the science of mantra has been built. This principle states that since the substance-body and the sound-body of any entity are inseparable, it follows that, whenever we construct any object, its corresponding sound-body automatically springs into existence; conversely, *if we could somehow produce a sound pattern identical to the natural name of any object, the thing itself would automatically be projected into susbstantial existence.* It does not take much imagination to see that the implications of this latter contention are truly staggering.

At first glance such a suggestion sounds like something right out of *The Arabian Nights,* but Yoga assures us that it's true. In fact, this principle forms the underlying basis for many of the superhuman psychic powers which come to those who attain higher states of consciousnness along the spiritual path.

Though sound-bodies cannot be perceived by normal human ears, a person whose psychic senses have been activated through sadhana soon becomes capable of functioning in the primal realm of causal vibration; indeed, this is how natural names were discovered in the first place—they were directly perceived by yogins who had achieved superhuman states of consciousness. Once any of us learns to operate on the level of natural names, we then become able to produce pure sound-bodies with our own consciousness completely at will, meaning that we have the power to create any object or manipulate existing ones in any way we choose.

Eastern tradition states that many of the ancient wonders of human construction, such as the Egyptian and South American pyramids and the Great Wall of China, were built with the assistance of natural name. The Indian scriptures even describe a terrible ancient war which featured weapons powered through the invocation of natural name; such military use is said to have reached supremacy with the development of something called a "Brahmastra" or "weapon of the Absolute," which makes our current-day nuclear missiles sound like pea-shooters by comparison, for the Brahmastra supposedly had the power to destroy *the entire universe*. Fortunately for us all, this truly ultimate weapon was itself destroyed before it could be put to use.

Ancient texts of nearly every culture are replete with similar tales of awesome power, suggesting that at one time the technological use of natural name was a fairly frequent occurrence. Today, however, such wondrous feats of metaphysics have been all but forgotten, surviving mainly in the form of eerie myths about ancient sorcerers who could perform all kinds of incredible magic simply through the incantation of certain mysterious sounds. Mantra technology, it seems, has now become a lost art, as modern science is currently preoccupied with energy sources which are mundane by comparison.

There is still, however, one scientific field which has not lost access to the power of natural name, and that is the field of spiritual science. In Yoga it is known that natural name, in addition to being useful to practitioners who have already attained exalted states of consciousness, can also be adapted in such a way as to provide great help to those of us who are still in lower stages of the climb toward Self-realization.

Since advanced practitioners who can perceive pure natural names do not do so with their physical sense of hearing but with a psychic apparatus which is much more subtle, it follows that such subtle sounds cannot be duplicated by so gross an instrument as the human voice; still, when advanced yogins return to worldly consciousness, they can try to *approximate* as closely as possible the pure natural names they have perceived in their elevated state, thereby transmitting at least some measure of their transcendental experience to those of us who have not yet gained the ability to rise above worldly awareness. Such approximations of pure natural names are known in Yoga as *mantras*.

By way of illustration, say we suddenly attain a samadhi state in which we can actually perceive the pure sound-body of Spanda-Shakti, the initial creative impulse which has set this entire cosmic cycle into motion. This natural name of Spanda-Shakti, this "Word" which the Bible marks as the beginning of Creation, occurs on the most subtle level of reality, where the concept of sound is almost nothing like we conceive it to be here on the gross physical plane. Yet, when we return to worldly consciousness and try to describe this experience to those who have not yet enjoyed it personally, we will want to approximate that subtle sound in some way with our physical voice. According to Yoga, the utterable sound which we will find most closely approximates an accurate verbal reproduction of Spanda-Shakti's natural name will be the syllable *Om*. This particular mantra, then, is the *approximate* natural name for the primal vibration upon which the whole of Creation rests, its pure, natural name being inexpressible in gross human speech.

Every mantra is said to have an approximate form on each plane of existence and therefore may be thought of as an unbroken, interconnected series of increasingly gross sound-patterns, starting in the realm of pure natural names and ending on the earth plane. The mantra which we utter with the human voice, then, is a sound-body that is directly connected to a pure natural name by a chain of progressively more subtle links stretching through all intervening levels of reality. Yoga states that through the continued repetition of a mantra it is possible for any spiritual aspirant to progress gradually to more subtle forms of that particular sound-body, following the mantra chain, link by link, until eventually the natural name at its source is reached, at which point the essence of that mantra will assume substantial form for the repeater.

In the lexicon of yogic science there are said to be 70 million spiritual mantras, each one an approximate natural name of some aspect of the cosmic Self. Most of these mantras are in Sanskrit, said to be "the language of the gods" because it is built around approximate natural names. Sanskrit is a Vedic language comprised of three types of verbal structure: (1) approximate natural names which are also called *bija* or "seed" mantras; (2) certain combinations of sounds which are not bijas individually but naturalize one another as an effect of their combination, thereby becoming approximate natural names; and (3) a large number of sounds and names which are employed to explain the meanings and applications of the first two categories, and which themselves only remotely represent natural names.

Most spiritual mantras fall into the second category, their

effectiveness reliant upon the overall sound-pattern produced by a particular combination of syllables uttered in a specific order. *Om Namah Shivaya*, for example, is one such mantra which approximates the natural name of the first universal principle; thus, any of us who persists in following this mantra all the way back to its absolute sound-body will not only attain Self-realization, but may also cause the cosmic Self to appear before our very eyes in a substantial form made out of our own mind-stuff. Such a divine revelation occurs through the same process of perception described in Part Three, Chapter Four, and it is one reason why it is said that the goal of sadhana is to make the mind take the form of the Self.

As long as a practitioner is able to hold an absolute name in his consciousness *with creative force*, the substantial form which corresponds to it will continue to remain in manifest existence. This, by the way, is said to be exactly how the supreme Shakti keeps her entire Creation intact for the duration of the universal cycle; in an aspect known as *Matrika-Shakti*, she creates and holds all natural names in her active consciousness, and as long as she does this all the objects of Creation continue to exist. As soon as she lets these sound-bodies slip from her awareness, however, in effect absorbing all sounds back into their potential state, the cosmos disappears. Thus, the yogic scriptures state that the entire universe is mantra.

Mantra japa is guaranteed to yield concrete results, provided our mantra is properly repeated the required number of times. The main stipulation to this seemingly easy task it that the requisite number of repetitions traditionally runs into the millions.

Fortunately, however, Yoga advises us that there are ways to accelerate the effects of our japa. The most important of these is to have our mantra japa initiated and guided by a perfected Yoga master, a being who is in personal contact with the realm of pure natural names. Japa performed with a mantra from some other source reaches fruition slowly through the repeater's investment of "sadhana-shakti," which is the power of the individual to realize through self-effort; but a mantra obtained from a Sadguru actually supplements our effort with inherent power of its own. This additional energy is known as ''Mantra-Shakti,'' and it is activated by the Guru himself at the moment of mantra initiation.

A mantra which has been enlivened by a Sadguru's transforming Shakti is called a *chaitanya mantra,* meaning one which has become imbued with life, while mantras which have not been so enlivened are known as *jada,* or inert, mantras.

The presence of Mantra-Shakti gives a tremendous boost to our performance of japa. With each repetition of a chaitanya mantra, its all-powerful shakti combines with our sadhana-shakti, which is imperfect and meets with obstacles; thus, any effort we invest in japa is intensified dramatically. According to yogic texts, the pure consciousness which is the essence of mantra can be realized most easily when our sadhana-shakti unites with Mantra-Shakti through japa with a chaitanya mantra.

To illustrate how different a mantra is when it's "alive" compared to when it's inert, let's imagine that we wish to take a long trip and for our vehicle we may choose between two available automobiles. From all outward appearances, both cars seem to be identical—same year, same make, same model, same colors and accessories; in fact, there is only one small difference between these two vehicles: one has fuel in it and the other doesn't. The car without fuel is like a jada mantra; we could climb into it and apply all the right effort in the world—turning the right knobs, clicking the right switches, pushing the right pedals—and still that inert vehicle is never going to contribute any power of its own to our journey; in fact, the only way we'll ever get it to go anywhere is by investing our own self-effort in pushing it. No vehicle can propel us up a mountainside unless it contains accessible power which can be activated through our own right effort. A chaitanya mantra contains accessible power because the Guru has enlivened its inherent consciousness, "filling its tank" with Mantra-Shakti.

Yoga also suggests another way for us to accelerate the progress of our japa: In repeating a mantra we should try, as much as possible, to involve the mind as well as the voice. Earlier we saw that a mantra is an approximate natural name which is connected to a pure natural name by a chain of increasingly subtle links. At one end of this chain lies our goal—pure natural name—the most subtle form of our mantra, while at the other end lies the approximate natural name which we utter with our physical voice, and this is the grossest form of the mantra. Since the time it takes us to follow a mantra back to its source depends largely upon the number of links between us and our goal, and since the mantra which we repeat mentally is more subtle than its spoken form, japa performed mentally will bear fruit more quickly than mere oral pronunciation with no attendant mental involvement.

According to Yoga, there are four primary stages of progress in japa, each one corresponding to one of the four bodies which make up our human being. This means that, as we follow the mantra chain to progressively more subtle links, we will experience our japa occurring in progressively more subtle bodies. From the physical body, where repetition takes place at the lips and tongue, japa eventually passes to the astral body, at which point japa becomes seated in the throat area. When the mantra moves to the causal level of our being, japa is experienced in the area of the heart and, at the supracausal level, the navel area. These four areas do not correspond in any way to the various chakras, since each mantra-seat is in a completely different body, while all the chakras reside in the astral body alone.

When the mantra begins to move to more subtle bodies, progress accelerates considerably. Yogic texts estimate that one repetition of the mantra at the throat (astral body) level is equal to about 1,000 repetitions at the physical level, and one repetition at the heart (causal body) level is equal to about 1,000 repetitions at the throat level (or about 10,000 physical repetitions). The supracausal level, of course, is the level of pure natural name, so when the mantra reaches this level its essence, the Self, is realized.

The Sanskrit word *mantra* literally means "the thought which saves." What mantra saves us from, Yoga explains, is all the pain and frustration which automatically befall anyone caught in the illusion of individuality; then, as if that were not enough, it goes on to save us from Illusion itself, transforming our distorted perception of reality into the unerring vision which comes with absolute knowledge. Just as certain sound vibrations can shatter glass containers, the vibration of a mantra can shatter all the veils of ignorance which contain and limit us, thus revealing the divine Self which is the real essence of our being.

Some texts describe mantra as Shakti or divine power in the form of an idea clothed with sound; others describe it more simply as the Self in the form of sound. The important point to remember here is that a mantra is not merely a symbol which represents the ultimate reality, it is the sound-body of supreme reality itself. Thus, whenever we repeat a mantra we must realize that we are not just talking or thinking *about* the Self, we are actually making the Self assume a substantial form right inside and all around us. Of course, it will take patience and perseverance in our performance of japa before the time comes when we will actually be able to perceive the presence of the Self in concrete form. Just as a sculptor patiently chips away at an amorphous lump of stone until the desired form is gradually liberated from its granite confines, with each repetition of our mantra we "chip away" at those parts of our being which encompass our sense of limitation and separateness, until eventually the hidden Self within us begins to manifest in a form which is discernable to us.

To define a mantra as "the Self in the form of sound" may give rise to some confusion for those of us who recall the yogic contention that not just mantras but everything in Creation is the Self or supreme consciousness in one form or another. The distinction to be made here is that, while all the objects of Creation are indeed the Self in the form of those objects, a mantra is the Self in a pure form. To realize the Self in some limited form, such as an apple, we may do so at once simply by using our mind, senses and attention; but the objective of japa is to realize the supreme Self in its universal aspect, clothed only in its essential nature. Just as the goal of the word "apple" is the limited Self in the form of an apple, the goal of a mantra is the all-pervasive Self in its pristine form.

En route to the ultimate goal of Self-realization, there are many intermediate benefits which can be derived from mantra japa. Modern scientific research has produced a mass of findings which support the ancient yogic contention that sound vibrations can have a profound effect upon our emotions, our mind, and even our physical body. According to Yoga, the sounding of different letters sets up unique patterns of cerebral agitation and also causes different parts of the body to resonate as well. In the East, mantra japa has long been considered to be an effective combination of psychotherapy and physiotherapy, since its performance cures mental anguish and even physical disorders which are the result of certain imbalances in the vibratory structure of our being.

While modern medicine has basically a negative orientation (its primary focus is on what's *wrong* with us), mantra japa involves the completely positive approach of filling the mind and body with a repetitive positive thought (the mantra); thus, instead of putting energy into negativities and thereby possibly strengthening them, with mantra japa we put all our energy into something positive, thus allowing negativities to simply atrophy through lack of sustenance. The continual repetition of a mantra washes the body and mind with waves of harmonious vibrations which gradually smooth away any eccentricities in our vibratory pattern.

Mental purification is a primary concern of sadhana, and mantra japa is the easiest way to accomplish this. Instead of bringing all our mental functions under control through force, japa takes advantage of the mind's natural tendency to think, the result being that the mind actually purifies itself. Every thought we think is impressed upon our mind in the form of a memory, which is like a small groove cut in our mind-stuff; and the more we repeat that same thought, the deeper this ''groove'' becomes. Then, when we try to still our mind—in meditation practice, for example—all these grooves which we have carved in the past begin acting like troughs which draw our attention to them, cluttering our awareness with all sorts of unwanted thoughts and mental images. Through mantra japa we solve this problem by deliberately carving a brand-new groove in the mind, constantly enlarging it until it is so huge that most of our mental energy automatically flows toward it every time the mind is passive. Eventually, this ''mantra groove'' will completely dominate all the smaller grooves, leaving only one thought in our mind when it is at rest—the thought of the Self.

In Siddha Yoga, as in most spiritual sciences, mantra japa is considered an indispensable ingredient of spiritual sadhana. Since the Siddha Guru is a fully perfected Yoga master, the mantra we receive from him is chaitanya—enlivened with his transforming Shakti—and this makes it an especially powerful aid in our climb to Self-realization. The mantra which Baba Muktananda dispenses is *Om Namah Shivaya,* a very popular mantra in the East, but in this case it is given added value by the Shakti which he awakens in it. This mantra, in fact, is the one which Muktananda's Guru—Swami Nityananda—gave to him; it's the mantra which led Muktananda himself to Liberation.

A chaitanya mantra such as this is such a valuable asset to sadhana that traditionally Sadgurus have issued them quite sparingly, only after seekers have convincingly proven their seriousness through extensive self-effort and personal sacrifice. Baba Muktananda, however, is a notable exception in that he offers a chaitanya mantra to virtually anyone who wishes it, free and clear. To obtain mantra initiation from him, all we need do is pick up his personally authorized mantra card at any accredited Siddha Yoga ashram or meditation center.

On other paths, initiates are often assigned different mantras in accordance with their individual needs, but on the Siddha Path such an approach is unnecessary. In this Yoga, since our supremely intelligent Kundalini-Shakti is at work inside us from the very outset of our japa performance, the Guru need simply prescribe for everyone a single mantra aimed at nurturing and increasing the intensity of our awakened Kundalini. She, in turn, exercising perfect discrimination, will then go to work inside us, determining her priorities in strict accordance with our unique requirements. Thus, even though we may all be using the same mantra, its effect upon us will vary so that we will each get exactly what we need.

Beginning Siddha Yoga students who have received mantra initiation are advised to practice their japa during formal meditation twice a day, silently pronouncing the words over and over at whatever rate seems most comfortable. Above all, we should remember that japa with a Siddha Guru's mantra is a form of

Shaktipat; the more japa we perform, the more Shakti will be put to work inside us, bringing us closer and closer to the Self, so we should not become surprised or dismayed if occasionally we experience spontaneous yogic kriyas which are manifestations of awakened Kundalini.

Our japa practice need not be restricted to formal meditation periods, either. The mantra may be repeated silently or aloud, listened to via tape recording, written repeatedly on paper, or chanted in a group. It should accompany us throughout our entire day, whether we are brushing our teeth or washing dishes, walking on the street or riding in a car, waiting for a bus or lying in bed before we fall asleep; persistently we should continue to carve that mantra-groove deeper and deeper into the mind.

In addition to a mantra being the sound-body of the Self, it also possesses a conceptual meaning which can serve the mind as well. *Om Namah Shivaya,* for example, means "I bow to the Self." Therefore, when we repeat this mantra during our introspective formal meditations, we can remind ourself that we are bowing to the Self within our own being; and when we repeat it during times when our attention is focused upon the outer world, it can serve as a reminder that the same Self is inherent in everything we see, hear, taste, touch and smell.

Mantra japa is a universal panacea; it cures whatever ails us. It's a natural tranquilizer, a gentle antidote for anxiety, boredom or depression, a perfect centering device for helping us to operate at peak efficiency—and ultimately, it's the key which can open the door to eternal bliss. Now that we have examined its true significance in our ascent to Self-realization, let's turn our attention to the second essential practice of Siddha Yoga sadhana.

II. Formal Meditation on the Self

Also called "sitting meditation," this practice is an essential ingredient of sadhana on every spiritual path and has been dealt with extensively in other sections of this book. As we will recall from those discussions, formal meditation is a technique which involves the deliberate minimizing of all physical and mental activity while our awareness is directed inward for a specific period of time each day. The benefits of such practice, both to sadhana and in our worldly life, have also been detailed earlier, and the very fact that we have continued to peruse this book indicates that we have already begun to appreciate the value of introspective meditation practice.

Our main objective here, then, is to distinguish between Siddha Yoga's approach to formal meditation and the same technique as it is practiced in other spiritual sciences. This distinction is the result of two primary factors: First, the Siddha Path is one which emphasizes ego-surrender, while most other spiritual sciences rely mainly upon self-effort; and secondly, because Shaktipat occurs right at the outset of Siddha Yoga sadhana, students of this path always have the awakened Kundalini as an active partner in their meditation practice.

On paths such as Raja Yoga, where self-effort is emphasized over ego-surrender, formal meditation practice involves the willful inducement of progressively higher states of awareness through the systematic mastery of a specific sequence of arduous techniques. Each time practitioners of such paths sit for meditation, they must proceed, step by step through all the levels they have already mastered, until they arrive at the one on which they are currently working. Each time a new level of awareness is reached, continual practice is required to first become established at that level, then to break through it and climb to the next higher one. With repeated practice, aspirants gradually become more and more adept at running the sequence of previously mastered stages, shortening the time it takes them to reach the most elevated state they have so far managed to attain. If such practitioners do not maintain the utmost diligence and determination throughout their meditation sadhana, they face the ever-present danger of becoming stuck at some level short of the ultimate one, or even regressing. Thus, in the practice of formal meditation on a path emphasizing self-effort, willful striving cannot cease until the aspirant attains the highest pinnacle of Enlightenment.

In Siddha Yoga, on the other hand, the experience of expanded consciousness need not be willfully induced through systematic striving, but instead occurs spontaneously as a result of the awakened Shakti's work within us. Though we are encouraged to invest self-effort in our formal meditation practice on this path as on any other, here we need not rely so much upon personal striving in the attainment of a transcendental state. In fact, it would be more accurate to say that in the practice of Siddha Meditation the willful performance of any technique is merely a way of investing our time profitably until our awakened inner Shakti graces us with automatic meditation.

On the Siddha Path, techniques are nothing more than supplemental aids; all willful practice is to be abruptly suspended the moment we perceive that the Kundalini-Shakti has taken the reins of our sadhana for a while. At this point, our main responsibility is to just sit back and enjoy the ride.

Once we have received Shaktipat, we may rest assured that our active Kundalini is always performing her transformation work inside us. Still, at some times when we sit for meditation her activity may be so mild or subtle that it will be imperceptible to us, while at other times it may be quite dramatic and intense. For this reason, there appear to be two distinct varieties of formal meditation in Siddha Yoga.

The first variety occurs during sittings when we experience no noticeable indications of the Kundalini's work within us. At such times our meditation practice becomes similar to the conventional type in that we willfully apply some prescribed technique designed to still the mind and activate more Shakti. The second variety—and this is the one generally referred to by the term Siddha Meditation—occurs when our Kundalini's activity is intense enough to be perceived by our physical senses, in which case all willful practices are abandoned and we simply witness the automatic process unfolding from within. Spontaneous yogic kriyas and elevated states of awareness occur during this type of meditation, and it is at such times that surrender supercedes self-effort in Siddha Yoga sadhana.

Thus, in the practice of formal meditation on the Siddha Path, willful techniques are employed only when the inner Shakti's work is too subtle to enthrall our physical senses. For such occasions, Baba Muktananda prescribes a variety of meditation practices, and to illustrate their scope we will now examine five of these.

1. Mantra Japa. Since this subject has already been discussed at length, its methodology and value as a meditative aid need not be further elaborated upon here.

2. Witness-Consciousness. This practice involves a continued effort to observe, from the viewpoint of the Self, rather than the limited ego, everything that naturally occurs to us throughout our meditation period. There is no attempt to willfully control the mind; we neither suppress nor invite mentation, but instead we simply witness whatever thoughts, images or sensations that well up from the depths of the mind, and we remind ourself that each of these experiences is nothing but the all-pervasive consciousness in a different form. Nothing that falls within the range of our perception, whether emanating from inside of us or from the environment around us, is either resisted or rejected; everything is acknowledged as an emanation of the Self. This type of practice is simple but extremely rewarding, and it, too, has been previously examined (see Part Two, Chapter Three).

3. Saguna Dharana. This Sanskrit term refers to the practice of concentration (*dharana*) on the pure Self with form (*saguna*) as opposed to the formless Self (*nirguna*). Because the formless Self is impossible to conceptualize, this practice calls for the fixing of our attention upon some physical object which represents the pure Self, thus presenting our mind with a pure object upon which to dwell. Since our mind-stuff actually takes the shape of everything upon which we focus our attention, this practice effectively causes our mind to assume a form symbolic of the Self; thus, it is a very beneficial meditation technique.

Yoga advises that the best object for this purpose is the physical person of an Enlightened being, because anyone who has attained perfect union with the supreme Self quite literally becomes a physical embodiment of that pefection. Whereas a mantra is the sound-body of the Self in *audible* form, a Self-realized being is like a *yantra*—the Self in a *visible* form. Saguna meditation may be practiced with our eyes closed, the object of concentration being visualized in the mind, or with our eyes open, in which case we simply gaze at the actual form itself. For this latter practice, the object may be physically present or even depicted in some form such as a photograph, statue, etc. In Siddha Yoga this practice is always performed with a firm understanding that the object of our concentration is essentially an embodiment of our own inner Self.

4. Ajapa-Japa: The Hamsa Mantra. Baba Muktananda stresses this meditation technique as being of particular importance to practitioners of Siddha Yoga. In order to ensure the quick fruition of *ajapa-japa* practice, Siddha students are advised to obtain special initiation into this technique by attending a Meditation Intensive.

Ajapa-japa literally means "the japa that is not japa"; in other words, it refers to a type of mantra repetition in which the mantra is not actually repeated by the meditator. *Hamsa,* the mantra utilized in this practice, is interchangeable with its reverse form, *So'ham. Hamsa,* or *So'ham,* is the seed mantra (approximate natural name) for the process we know as "breathing."

This means that each time we inhale and exhale, our own breath-cycle produces the sound-body of the *hamsa* mantra, a process outlined in the mantra section of this chapter. Because *hamsa* is the breathing process in the form of sound, all we need do to practice japa with this mantra is simply to become aware that it is always being produced inside us with every breath we take. Rather than mentally pronouncing this mantra, we merely observe our breath with the awareness that the *hamsa* sound-body is contained in every cycle. According to Kashmir Shaivism, if we project an awareness of the syllable *ham* (pronounced *hum*) into each inhalation, and *sa* into each exhalation, the intensity of the awakened inner Shakti will become increased.

When first applying this technique, many meditators find that there seems to be too subtle a distinction between the act of "hearing" the mantra in the breath and that of deliberately repeating it in the mind. For this reason, Muktananda teaches that in the beginning it is permissible for us to actually repeat the mantra to ourself during meditation, matching the syllable *ham* with every in-breath and *sa* (or *so*) with every out-breath. Because Muktananda has expressly approved this mantra for willful repetition by his students, its use brings all the benefits ascribed to a chaitanya mantra earlier in this chapter, for the Siddha Guru has enlivened it with his potent Shakti. When repeating this Sanskrit mantra willfully, it is beneficial to remember its English translation, ''I am that,'' meaning ''I am the Self.'' Of course, this is only its conceptual significance; of much more importance is an understanding of its essence.

To appreciate the essential significance of *hamsa,* we must now return to our examination of pure ajapa-japa, the technique in which this mantra is simply experienced as identical to the breath, rather than willfully repeated in the mind. To begin with, the breathing process must be recognized as a vibratory cycle; that is, it meets both criteria which Yoga sets forth to define the phenomenon called vibration: Our breath cycle consists of (1) sound (the sound-body *hamsa*), and (2) repeated alternation between movement (inhalation and exhalation) and rest (the point at which the breath reverses its direction). The concept of movement, we will recall, corresponds to the cosmic principle known as Shakti—the Self in the form of ever-changing, objective Creation; while rest, or stillness, corresponds to Shiva—the Self in its formless, changeless aspect.

Thus, if we were to observe the breathing process, not only with an awareness of its movement aspects (*ham* and *sa*), but also paying particular attention to the tiny point of rest that occurs each time the air-flow is reversed, we would then be concentrating on both aspects of the one supreme Self. During ajapa-japa practice, this minute point of stillness is to be concentrated upon as it exists within us after each inhalation and outside of us after every exhalation, like a speck of dust that is drawn in with the air we breathe and then expelled with our next out-breath. Gradually, as we become able to focus more of our consciousness upon it through repeated practice, this tiny point can become a portal through which we may enter and immerse ourself in Shiva's pure being.

For as long as we are able to focus our awareness unwaveringly upon this miniscule gateway, our breathing will become suspended naturally, and time will stand still while we enjoy an ecstatic dip in a luminous sea of immortality, the pristine essence of our own true Self. Such are the fruits of ajapa-japa, one of the most subtle and sophisticated meditation techinques taught by Baba Muktananda.

5. Matrika Meditation. This is a special practice which involves observing the workings of our mind with an awareness of the true source from which our thoughts arise. According to Kashmir Shaivism, this source is not the mind, but the Matrika-Shakti, a creative power of the Self. The word *matrika* literally means "little mother," but here she is "little" in the sense that she is so inconspicuous as to be imperceptible to us; therefore, the Matrika-Shakti is that aspect of the Self which, unbeknownst to us, gives birth to all the sounds which we identify as alphabetical letters— sounds that are combined in the mind to form our every thought and every syllable we utter.

As we already know, Yoga states that each human being is a miniature version of Shiva, the universal Self. Therefore, this Matrika which resides within our being has a cosmic counterpart as well, and we have already touched upon this subject in the section dealing with mantra japa. Briefly then, the universal Matrika is that aspect of the supreme Shakti which produces the initial creative impulse known as Spanda. At the supracausal level of Creation, no sound exists except in potential form; Matrika still carries her sound-child inside her. At the causal level, she gives birth to the primal sound *Om*. This great mantra contains the most subtle essences of all the fifty basic sounds which form the very foundation of Creation. At this point the universe is merely one undifferentiated mass of moving Consciousness, but then, at the astral level, each basic sound takes on its own separate existence, and all of these begin to combine and interact in an endless variety of sound patterns known as natural names. On this level, the universe consists mainly of sound-bodies, like objects of imagination. Finally, at the physical level of Creation, the gross forms of these objects appear. This is why the cosmic Matrika is called the unknown mother who gives birth to the manifest universe.

In the same way, within each of us there is said by Shaivism to exist a microcosmic Matrika which is the true source of the mental universe to which each one of us is confined until we realize the Self. At the supracausal level of our being, she is in her potential state; at the level of our causal body she issues forth the subtle essences of all the basic sounds; and at the astral level these sounds become the letters of the alphabet, interacting and combining to form words, phrases and sentences, as well as their corresponding mental images. Finally, at the physical level of our being, these sounds spring forth as spoken speech.

Matrika-Shakti is like a ceaseless fountain of sounds, constantly filling our mind with letters which combine to form words and mental objects. Of course, through our power of intellect we can willfully order up whatever words or images we care to, but even when we have no such intention it seems that such things persist in popping into our mind completely uninvited.

This phenomenon can be witnessed most effectively during formal meditation practice, when our explicit intent is to minimize mental activity as much as possible. What we quickly discover at these times is that, even though we command the mind to become still, it rebelliously disturbs our quietude with an endless parade of images and thoughts which we seem helpless to control. The reason for this, Yoga tells us, is that our mind is filled with a multitude of desires and past impressions which we have planted there throughout many lifetimes. Thus, even during times when our mind seems empty for a while, this is only because these desires and impressions have all temporarily retired to seedlike dormancy. Sooner or later, one or more of these seeds is bound to sprout, completely on its own, and we will find our attention being drawn to some corresponding mental object.

These seeds are in our mind because in the past we have taken a lot of time and trouble to plant them there and nurture them with our own precious energy. Today, the natural karmic process which we began with our past thoughts and actions simply continues to unfold and fructify spontaneously; as soon as each seed is ripe, it sprouts—and if this happens to occur during our formal meditation practice, our sitting will become disturbed by mental agitation. If our attention is not disciplined, it will immediately become captivated by this agitation, in which case we will soon find ourself being swept away in a flood of interrelated thoughts and images. A perfect example of how we become completely possessed by this process is the dream state, in which we lose all contact with physical reality and get trapped in a mental world which is fashioned solely by the desires and impressions that are sprouting in our mind.

The key to Matrika meditation practice is understanding that the mind is not the creator of our inner world of thoughts and images; it is merely a vessel which contains and influences them. Once we know that the true source of our entire mental contents is the Matrika aspect of our inner Self, then we can begin to utilize this natural process to distinct advantage in our sadhana.

In one type of Matrika meditation, for example, our intellectual ability to willfully manipulate the Matrika is employed in a way which makes her assist us in our quest for Liberation. The mind, after all, is like an enormous room filled with many different objects—some worrisome, some frightening, some pleasurable, etc. If there is no light cast upon these objects, however, none of them will be perceptible to us, so none can cause us agitation. The light which illuminates the objects of our mind is the light of attention—our ability to focus our awareness. When our attention is undisciplined, it gets pulled here and there by every tiny stimulus which arises in the mind; but by exercising control over our attention, by learning to pinpoint it and keep it concentrated steadily upon one thing, we can choose to perceive only those mental objects which lead us closer to Self-realization, leaving all the other ones in darkness. Just as we use the Matrika to fill our mind with concepts of limitation and duality, we can also use her to fill our mind with pure objects such as our mantra.

The objective of Matrika meditation practice, then, is to transform "the unknown mother," who is a root cause of our bondage, into a mother who is known and understood, at which point she becomes a means of Liberation.

Though all of the techniques just described are easy to perform, it would be quite difficult for us to master any of them if our practice were supported solely by our own self-effort. Fortunately, in Siddha Yoga we need not be at all concerned about mastering such techniques, for our attainment of Enlightenment is not contingent upon the mastery of anything but surrender to the Self. On this path, techniques may be performed with neither concern for our progress nor expectation of any reward, for because we have an awakened Kundalini as our sadhana-mate from the very outset of our practice, we can rest assured that she is always at work inside us, amplifying the effects of all our willful efforts and insuring that our spiritual unfoldment proceeds with optimum speed and safety.

To practice Siddha Meditation, we need simply sit for whatever duration we wish each day, without making any advance conditions about what we want our meditation to be like. If we find that the inner Shakti's work is imperceptible to us at this time, we then reach for some prescribed technique with the firm understanding that such self-effort practice constitutes a period of intense sadhana which moves us a considerable distance along the path to Liberation.

If, on the other hand, when we sit for meditation we discover that the inner Shakti graces us with spontaneous experiences of some sort, then we merely defer to her and witness her activity in whatever form it takes. Thus, we accept with gratitude the gifts our active Kundalini bestows on us, be they the physical kriyas of Hatha Yoga; the inner visions, sounds, aromas, tastes, etc., of Laya Yoga; the profound insights of Jnana Yoga; the ecstatic emotions of Bhakti Yoga; or the complete stillness of Raja Yoga. To display resistance, annoyance or anxiety whenever such automatic events occur indicates a lack of understanding about the process unfolding within us, and a lack of faith in our own inner Self's ability to determine the best course for this unfolding to take.

Perhaps the most difficult thing to grasp about Siddha Meditation is its simplicity. In practicing formal meditation on this path, the main lesson most of us must learn is how to stop *trying* to meditate. Trying to enter meditation is like trying to fall asleep; the harder we strive for it, the farther away it gets. By far the most effective way to get Siddha Meditation to visit us is essentially the same way to get sleep to visit us: we make ourself as mentally calm and physically relaxed as possible. To quote Baba Muktananda: "Siddha Meditation should happen on its own. You should just sit quietly and watch the Self meditate on itself. Don't try to meditate. Just turn within and let the inner Shakti teach you meditation. If this type of meditation does not come naturally, then take the support of the mantra or some other technique."[18]

This completes our examination of the second essential ingredient of Siddha Yoga sadhana. On the Siddha Path, mantra japa and formal meditation work in concert to accelerate our spiritual unfoldment, each technique serving to enhance the other's potency in many important ways. For example, through japa our meditation practice receives a welcome energy boost in the form of constant infusions of Mantra-Shakti; and, conversely, through formal meditation practice we sharpen our ability to focus our attention, which in turn makes it possible to project more consciousness into our mantra repetition, thus causing our japa to bear fruit more quickly.

We will recall, however, that there are not just two essential practices in Muktananda's Siddha Yoga. Let's now see how the inclusion of a third technique enriches sadhana on this path.

III. Right Understanding

On other paths, this technique is sometimes referred to as "meditation-in-action." It is primarily intended for use when we are actively engaged in our normal day-to-day activities. Basically, the practice of right understanding involves a continuing endeavor to look at life from the yogic point of view; that is, in addition to the way our ego perceives things, we also try to maintain an intellectual understanding of their underlying reality as outlined in the philosophy of our path. This practice is enormously productive in a variety of ways.

If Siddha Yoga were a path primarily for recluses, then mantra japa and formal meditation practice would be sufficient sadhana after Shaktipat; but this is a spiritual science geared especially for people who are disinclined to turn their backs upon the world; it is a path for those of us who feel determined to realize the Self right in the midst of family life, while pursuing a career and otherwise relating to our fellow humans in an intimate and meaningful way.

However, because the world is not as it appears to be, our involvement in it must be accompanied by a correct understanding of its true nature, or else our worldly life can be quite detrimental to our sadhana. To live in the world without true knowledge of it can only cause us pain and further bind us, but through the practice of right understanding a seeker of the Self can transform what would normally be a jungle filled with pitfalls into a spiritual classroom as well as a garden of endless delight.

In the same way that we combine mantra japa and formal meditation to greatly increase the impetus of our Siddha Yoga sadhana, by adding the regular practice of right understanding to both of these our progress is accelerated even further. Moreover, since this third essential technique is exercised primarily in the course of our regular worldly activities, the time demand it places upon our already too-short day is nearly negligible. Thus, two of the three essential daily practices prescribed for Siddha students may be performed right in the midst of our worldly activities; mantra japa may be employed during activities which leave our mind relatively idle, while right understanding may be practiced at any time, its employment designed to serve us particularly well when our mind is involved in making qualitative judgments and decisions which profoundly affect our life.

The practice of right understanding or meditation-in-action is really just another form of meditation on the Self, only here the object of our contemplation is the *outer* rather than the inner Self. In formal meditation we turn our awareness *away* from the external world in order to realize the Self within us, thereby overcoming the wrong understanding that we are limited creatures who are separate from our Creator. The practice of right understanding, on the other hand, is a type of meditation which we perform when our awareness is focused upon external things, in order to realize that everyone and everything around us is just as much an extension of the one, divine Self as we are, thereby overcoming the misconception that the universe is filled with diversity and is separate from us.

On the Siddha Path, the practice of right understanding requires us to constantly remind ourself of the underlying unity which exists throughout Creation; that the Self is the essential nature of every person, creature, and insentient object; and that this perfect, all-pervasive Self is the real doer of every action in which we take part, the real enjoyer of every experience that comes to us. Thus, by setting as its goal the realization that our entire world is a manifestation of the Self, the technique of right understanding actually gives us an opportunity to expand our daily meditation practice, beyond the one or two periods of formal sitting we squeeze into our busy schedule, to include every waking hour of our day.

Yet another benefit of right understanding practice is that it helps us to attain success and fulfillment in both our worldly and our spiritual lives. Spiritually, it presents us with the opportunity to turn our entire life into sadhana without ever having to withdraw from the world; and, when used as a complement to formal meditation practice, it enables us to greatly increase the effectiveness with which we function in the world. Siddha Yoga sadhana thereby enables us not just to explore our inner world, becoming peaceful and content within ourself, but also to make some meaningful contribution to the outer world as well. This aspect of right understanding practice entails learning to take whatever inner capabilities which unfold during formal meditation and put these to worthwhile use in our everyday life.

If we want to enjoy the very best of both worlds, ardently striving to realize the Self even while leading a full and rich worldly life, then we must practice both formal meditation and meditation-in-action; we must constantly increase our inner power and strengthen our ability to focus it through daily periods of intense introspection, and at the same time we must learn to maintain a meditative center throughout all our worldly activities, for which right understanding practice is a must.

An important point to remember here is that there is a crucial difference between the *practice* of right understanding and the actual *attainment* of it. To attain right understanding is to be Self-realized. If we are not Self-realized, the reason is that we possess *wrong* understanding, an ailment which can be remedied only through sadhana.

We have to practice right understanding because attaining it is not just a matter of pouring Truth into our mind. The problem is one of physics: we can't pour anything into a vessel which is already filled with something else. The mind is like a cup which is presently filled with the water of wrong understanding—concepts of self-limitation, duality, and diversity that destroy our perception of the all-pervasive, ever-present Self and make us think it's something else. In school we all learn a precept of physical science which states that "nature abhors a vacuum." That's a pretty strong word, *abhor*; it means that nature *detests* any truly empty space, and she will always rush in to fill one whenever possible. In the physical world, she fills every empty space with air, and in the spiritual world she fills such space with Truth—her own essence. So, just as all we need do to fill a cup of water with air is to pour out all the water, all we really have to do to fill the mind with right understanding is to simply pour out all its wrong understanding; then the Grace-bestowing power of the Self, which abhors a vacuum, will rush in to fill the empty space.

Indeed, the basic purpose of everything we do in sadhana is to rid the mind of all its wrong understandings, for these are the only obstacles which stand between us and Self-realization. The instant we accomplish this seemingly simple task, we attain Shivahood. No time restrictions whatever are placed upon us by the Siddha Guru; as far as he is concerned there is absolutely nothing preventing us from becoming fully Enlightened the instant we receive Shaktipat. All we need do is summarily banish all wrong understandings from our mind and our sadhana will be finished.

Unfortunately, though this is perfectly true in theory, in practice it does not often turn out to be so simple. What most of us experience after Shaktipat is that, no matter how fervently we try, it does not seem possible for us to merely dump our wrong understandings out of the mind. The "water," it seems, has turned to "ice"; the vessel of our mind clings tenaciously to its wrong understandings and simply won't let go. From the Guru's point of view, our position appears ludicrous; he sees us desperately struggling to free ourself of all our pain and suffering while at the same time obstinately clutching to our bosom the very burden which torments us, ferociously resisting his every attempt to pry it from our grasp. This burden is our limited ego—that part of us which identifies with our parcel of wrong understandings and makes us think the parcel is the *real us*.

From our own viewpoint, however, this situation seems quite reasonable. Our ego, after all, is the only *us* we know. Asking us to throw away all our present concepts about who we are appears to us a very terrifying and extremely dangerous act—comparable to asking us to throw away our soul. Right now, our ego is the only part of us that gives us any sense of personal worth. Sure, it may also cause us a lot of anguish and frustration, but at least it's better than nothing at all. "A bird in the hand is worth two in the bush," so why should we give up something already in hand—something which at least gives us some *occasional* pleasure—in return for some impossible-sounding dream of eternal bliss called the Self? After all, it's taken us a long time to collect our little parcel of understandings, right or wrong; we've grown attached to them and are not about to chuck them away just like that.

It's this kind of attachment to our present understandings that creates a need for sadhana after Shaktipat; otherwise, all the Siddha Guru would have to do is say to us, "You are the Self," and we would experience it immediately. Every willful practice we perform in Siddha Yoga is to loosen our attachment to our wrong understanding. All the energy we burn performing self-effort practices, all this heat of sadhana-shakti, goes into melting the ice of our wrong understanding, and evaporating it away to make room for Grace to flow into our life.

After we receive Shaktipat there is nothing more we need obtain in order to realize the Self, but there may well be things which must be gotten rid of. We alone are responsible for the time it takes us to realize the Self in Siddha Yoga. On this basically "tech-niqueless" path, the moment we eliminate our wrong understand-ing we are buoyed up by an influx of Grace and swept straightaway to the top of the sadhana mountain. At every moment of our Siddha Yoga practice, the pure and perfect Self is standing right before us, waiting to give us our birthright, the entire universe, and all we need do to lay claim to it is to surrender our present claim to the tiny world we now inhabit.

The sole reason for imperfect surrender is the presence of mental impurities in the form of wrong understanding, and to eliminate these we practice whatever techniques the Guru recom-mends for this purpose. We have already seen how japa is used to divert mental energy away from wrong understanding by "carving a mantra groove" in the mind through recurrent repetition. Then, during periods of formal meditation, we observe and learn to understand the workings of the mind, gradually gaining control over mental agitations which arise from wrong understanding and which disturb our equilibrium. Finally, in the practice of right understanding, we observe our reactions to external stimuli, recog-nizing that any inner turmoil which these elicit must be the result of wrong understanding; then we try to superimpose upon our mind the proper understanding in accordance with the teachings of our path.

The first prerequisite of right understanding practice, there-fore, is a firm intellectual grasp of Siddha Yoga philosophy, *as it is expounded by the Guru himself.* It is not enough for us simply to learn Vedanta and Kashmir Shaivism from some scholar who has in turn learned it from other scholars; we must receive our instruc-tion straight from someone who has personally attained Self-real-ization by following these same teachings. Only such a one is capable of instilling in us an absolute conviction of the philosophy's validity; only he will be able to keep us inspired, by his own example, to continue striving through thick and thin until we also obtain the same reward as he has. Unless the yogic philosophy which we are trying to imbibe has the Shakti of a perfected master behind it, sooner or later our initial enthusiasm will almost cer-tainly become overwhelmed by doubts arising from deep-seated wrong understanding, and we will then be wooed away toward what our mind assures us will be greener pastures.

Through study, inquiry and intellectual analysis of the master's teachings, we gradually develop an unshakable conviction that his understandings are more valid than our own. Japa and formal meditation help a lot here, for both practices increase our intellectual acuity—our ability to grasp subtle understandings—and our intuitive power to recognize Truth. But Yoga tells us that this type of philosophy must not just be tested intellectually; it must also produce practical benefits when applied to our daily life. If a philosophy does not noticeably improve our lot when put to practical use, then it is not a valid path for us, no matter how much truth it supposedly contains.

On the other hand, to have an intellectual conviction that a philosophy is valid and yet neglect to apply it in our daily life can be extremely detrimental to our sadhana. According to the teachings of this path, if we believe that everything in Creation is a form of the same universal Self, then we must try to put this philosophy into practice; otherwise, we are like the jeweler who, even though he knows that all his ornaments are made of the same pure gold, neglects to put this understanding into practice when he makes a sale; thus, he charges more money for a tiny image of a god than for a very large one of an animal, even though the animal contains more gold. Just as that jeweler must never let such concepts about a god being more valuable than an animal obscure his deeper understanding that both ornaments are made of the same gold, so too we must never let our personal value-judgments obscure our deeper understanding that everything in Creation is made of the same divine consciousness.

Once this lesson is learned, we must then learn to avoid the opposite extreme as well. For example, a person who lacks discrimination may now argue that since everything in Creation is the Self, which means that all objects and activities are equally divine, then no special effort need be made to obtain Self-realization; for sadhana, all we need do is recognize that everything is the Self, and as long as we keep this fact in mind, we may do anything we like. Such reasoning amounts to a license for unrestrained indulgence in either sense pleasures or behavior which is illegal, immoral or unethical; and though it may be embraced by pseudo-seekers looking to avoid self-discipline, it is based on wrong understanding.

The practice of right understanding is often compared to walking a razor's edge because it's so easy to lean toward one extreme or another in applying yogic philosophy to life. Though of course Shaivism teaches us to see the Self in everything, at the same time we must not forget that until we actually experience this cosmic unity directly, we will have to accept the fact that we are bound individuals who are still caught up in perceiving limitation in ourselves and diversity in the world around us. As long as this ignorance persists; that is, until we become Self-realized, our association with certain objects and activities will tend to lead us closer to Liberation while others will tend to lead us further away from it. Such differences are not inherent in the objects themselves, but are products of our own wrong understanding.

Sadhana is the process of favoring those objects and activities which serve to eliminate wrong understanding, and this process must be sustained until we are able to perceive, directly and permanently, the all-pervasive structure of supreme consciousness which underlies all phenomena in Creation. Moreover, from our present position of ignorance we are incapable of determining for ourself which objects and activities are aids to sadhana, and which are not. In this regard we must trust the Guru to decide what's best for us, for only one who looks upon our bondage from a position of total freedom can competently advise us about our course to Liberation.

The technique of right understanding can be practiced anywhere at any time. No matter what our situation may be at any moment of our daily life, we can always find some aspect of Siddha Yoga philosophy which will prove to be extremely helpful if applied with intelligence and discrimination. If, for example, we should happen to be experiencing mental hyperactivity, we can practice right understanding of the Matrika-Shakti which is the true source of all our thoughts, thereby establishing, between our ego and mind, a more realistic association in which mental agitations do not disturb our equanimity.

Similarly, should some aspect of our sadhana begin to trouble us, the practice of right understanding can provide the answer to any question or remove any doubt, provided we have a firm intellectual grasp of the mechanics and philosophy of the Siddha Path, knowing exactly how and why this yogic science works.

When possessions cause us discontent—either the desire to own them or the fear of losing them—we can practice the right understanding of renunciation, which does not mean that we must give up possessing things, but rather we must renounce being possessed by them. True renunciation is the giving up of our *attachment* to possessions, thus breaking their hold on us—their ability to affect us by their presence or absence. In this respect, the practice of right understanding means remembering that nothing can ever really belong to us anyway, for there is only one thing in all of Creation—the Self. To become a true renunciate we must practice discriminate enjoyment, neither craving nor despising anything, taking delight in the things which are with us, but never missing the things which are not.

When we are hurt or baffled by things which happen to us or others in the outside world; when we are agonized in our relationship with a loved one; when we are anxious about what decision to make or what action to take in a difficult situation, the practice of right understanding with respect to the yogic doctrines of reincarnation and karma can provide us with the enormous advantage of being able to view things from a higher perspective. When something pleasurable or painful suddenly descends upon us without any effort on our part, we can practice the right understanding that it is simply the fruit of some action we've performed at some time in the past. On the other hand, if we have to put forth effort to attain something, we can understand that in this case we are creating new karmas rather than paying off old ones; therefore, we will make certain that our present actions are always the sort that will yield us future fruit that is sweet instead of bitter.

In order to practice right understanding effectively, then, we must first implant in our mind a working model of true reality as it is described by the philosophy of our path; then, as we go through our daily life, we must constantly try to monitor our spontaneous reactions to things, using our intellect to determine whether or not these reactions are in keeping with our new philosophy. When we find discrepancies, we resolve to react differently to similar situations in the future. And, of course, we must always attempt to think and act with the awareness that everything in Creation is nothing less than supreme consciousness itself. In the words of Baba Muktananda, "The best meditation, the highest understanding, and the greatest worship is to see God in one another."[18]

The practice of right understanding is very much like learning a new language. In the first place, both pursuits involve a conscious effort to think about and express things in a different way from the one to which we've become accustomed. Secondly, just as the older we are the more ingrained our present language becomes (thus making it more difficult for us to learn a new one), the fact that we have been viewing ourself and Creation with wrong understanding for many lifetimes makes it very difficult for us to learn to see things differently. Thirdly, when acquiring a new language, we must begin by practicing a willful process of conversion which involves first mentally expressing in our *old* language what we want to say, and then translating it into the new one. With continued practice, this conversion process becomes quicker until eventually one day we spontaneously drop it and begin thinking directly in the new language. In the same way, learning to perceive reality correctly involves the initial practice of a conversion process in which we first perceive things in the old way and then make a conscious effort to look at them differently. Eventually, this repeated practice leads to a spontaneous dropping of the conversion process and we experience the direct perception of true reality; in short, we become Self-realized.

This completes our examination of the three essential daily practices of Siddha Yoga sadhana: (1) mantra japa, (2) formal meditation, and (3) right understanding. As our investigation has revealed, each of these practices is powerful enough to be a separate sadhana on its own, but when performed in concert they provide exceptional balance and great acceleration to both the spiritual and worldly growth of the Siddha student. So compatible and complementary are these techniques, in fact, that not only can they all be practiced every day, but also any two or even all three may be practiced simultaneously. For example, during the practice of formal meditation, we may elect to employ either the technique of mantra japa or that of right understanding (in the form of observing witness-consciousness). Similarly, in the midst of our daily activities, when we silently acknowledge the Self in everything we see by repeating *Om Namah Shivaya* with an awareness of its conceptual meaning, ''I bow to Shiva,'' we are effectively using our japa as a practice of right understanding.

Conversely, we can practice right understanding during japa performance by constantly remembering the inestimable value of our mantra and the profound effect its repetition is having at every level of our being. And finally, we can even use formal meditation as a practice of right understanding; when we are out in the world and find that we must make some important decision quickly, we can simply pause and close our eyes for a moment, turning our awareness toward the inner Self and permitting the decision to arise spontaneously from within rather than arriving at it through a lot of mental agitation. We'll find that the more we exercise our power of intuition in such ways, the faster and more reliable its responses will become. Thus, in many ways all three techniques may be interwoven throughout our daily life, thereby greatly increasing the beneficial effects of each moment we devote to sadhana.

And yet, the spectrum of techniques which may be employed beneficially by Siddha students does not end with just these three. For those of us who desire even greater balance and acceleration in our sadhana after Shaktipat, Baba Muktananda recommends several other important techniques which may be used to supplement our daily practices, and these may be fitted into our weekly schedule as often as we can find the time for them. Let's now extend our study of Siddha Yoga with a brief examination of these supplementary techniques.

3. Supplemental Practices in Siddha Yoga

The three practices detailed in the previous chapter constitute the *minimum* daily observances required in Siddha Yoga sadhana, which means that to insure steady progress on this path, each student is expected to invest at least as much personal effort as it takes to perform these three techniques regularly. Therefore, though the practices to be outlined in this present chapter have been categorized as supplementary, they should in no way be considered inferior to the first three with regard to their beneficial effects. In fact, Siddha students who desire to accelerate sadhana to the *maximum* extent are advised to regard *all* of these supplementary techniques as essential daily practices, along with the three already prescribed.

Quite naturally, of course, the vast majority of us will choose to fall somewhere between these extremes of minimum and maximum sadhana, trying our best to practice our mantra japa, formal meditation and right understanding every day, then augmenting these regular observances with those which are supplemental as often as we feel motivated or can spare the time.

Each of the supplementary "sadhana intensifiers" which Baba Muktananda recommends is important enough to merit as extensive an examination as we've already given to the basic three, but here we will just touch upon the more salient aspects of each in order to appreciate the comprehensiveness of Siddha Yoga sadhana and the perfect balance it instills in each practitioner throughout our spiritual development.

Satsang

The word *satsang* means "good company," and the practice of keeping good company is an important key to quick progress in Yoga sadhana. An old adage states that a person is known by the company he keeps, and this assumption has merit in two respects: firstly, we do generally tend to hang out with others whose goals are in line with our own, and secondly, the people with whom we keep company certainly do have a strong influence upon us.

According to Yoga, in fact, *everything* with which we keep company—every person, every object, every activity and even every thought—has a distinct vibrational pattern which affects our own vibratory field in some specific way, in effect modulating us upward (toward higher consciousness) or downward (toward lower consciousness). Loosely speaking, then, *all* sadhana practices are considered to be satsang, for when we spend our time with them we are in good company which modulates us upward. In the same way, if we want to make fast progress in our sadhana, we should try as much as possible to keep good company with regard to the personal relationships and activities we pursue, the surroundings in which we live, the books we read, the food we eat, and so on.

Of all these various things which modulate us, we are probably affected most by the people with whom we keep company, and since this is the case, it then follows that the best possible person for us to be with is an Enlightened being such as the Siddha Guru. The vibratory field of such a being is so pure and potent that it remains completely unaffected by the things around it, while at the same time having a profound effect upon everything with which it comes in contact. The people, animals and plants which live in his surroundings, and even inanimate objects—the very furniture and walls—become modulated upward by the powerful vibration which emanates from him. Thus, we too become uplifted in his presence, a presence which is not just limited to his physical being, but also pervades every atom of the atmosphere around him. So pristine is the Shakti which he radiates, those of us with sensitive perception can actually feel it, and sometimes even see it, as soon as we enter his environment. This uplifting effect is automatic and occurs in the presence of any Realized being; the only effort we need make to obtain this benefit is whatever effort it takes to transport ourself to the place where such a being resides.

If this Enlightened being also happens to be a Sadguru, however, the possible rewards of being in his physical presence do not stop here; but to reap these additional benefits we will have to put forth some extra effort, mainly in the form of right understanding practice. The best way to learn right understanding is to keep company with someone who already possesses it. Having completely realized the Self, a Siddha Guru projects his flawless understanding of reality into everything he says and does; therefore, if in his presence we deliberately watch and listen to him with rapt attention, this practice can have a profound remedial effect upon the way we perceive things.

It's possible to relate to the Guru in a variety of ways, any one of which is fine, provided it reflects our true feelings and is not merely a role we are playing in accordance with some concept about how we think we should act towad him. Most disciples find that they relate to the Guru most naturally by thinking of themselves as his child, his servant, or his pupil; but others spontaneously behave toward him as if they were his parent, a close friend, or even his beloved. This external aspect of the Guru-disciple relationship is determined solely by whatever karma, if any, exists between us and the Guru. If we have known him in previous lifetimes, there will probably be karmic debts between us and him which must be worked out before he leaves this world for the last time, so our external relationship will include some degree of personal interaction; but if we have no karma to work out with him, if our connection with him now is based purely upon the fact that we have become worthy of discipleship under a Sadguru and he is the nearest one available, then our external relationship will probably be more impersonal—the teacher-student type.

A Sadguru is essentially two entities in one body; he is both a person who has attained perfect Self-realization, and also a cosmic power—the Grace-bestowing power of Shiva. Thus, it is possible for us to relate to either one or both of these, depending upon our karma. For example, we could relate to just the person and not to the power of Guruhood working through him, in which case we would simply be working out karma with him and not doing sadhana at all. Secondly, we could relate to both the person and the Guru Principle simultaneously, which would indicate that we are not only working out past karmas with him, but doing sadhana as well. And finally, we could relate primarily to the Grace-bestowing Shakti working through him, interacting with the physical person more or less impersonally, in which case our relationship with him would be based entirely upon sadhana.

In the same way, the Guru may outwardly relate to us in a personal or impersonal way, but regardless of whether he treats us like a close friend or a total stranger, as long as we have received Shaktipat from him and are fulfilling our discipleship responsibilities by doing sadhana, we may rest assured that he too is fulfilling his responsibility of seeing that we get everything we require to complete our spiritual journey with speed and safety.

To sum up the benefit of satsang with the physical Guru, then, we can say that although simple proximity to such a being can automatically elevate our state, this effect will usually be just temporary unless we invest our own right effort into the situation as well. Disciples who are seldom able to be in the Guru's physical presence and yet still perform their daily practices diligently will progress infinitely faster than those who neglect their practices but are constantly at the Guru's side. Best of all, of course, are those disciples who ardently pursue sadhana in the presence of their Guru, for then the master's influence can work with maximum effectiveness.

The main purpose of satsang in Siddha Yoga sadhana is to maintain a solid connection with the Guru after Shaktipat. The influence which the outer Guru exerts upon our ego, intellect and heart lends enormous reinforcement to the inner Guru's work, giving our sadhana a one-two punch which blasts through obstacles with great dispatch.

Since most of us have worldly pursuits and responsibilities which render us unable or unwilling to live with the physical Guru full time, the general custom is to visit him as frequently as possible, exactly how often and for how long being dependent primarily upon how far away he happens to be. Baba Muktananda has made this as easy for us as possible by touring the world frequently, thereby making himself accessible to more people than any other Siddha Guru in history. Still, this means that the vast majority of Siddha Yoga students spend the bulk of their time away from the physical Guru; so how, then, can we effectively keep "plugged into" the mainstream of his Shakti throughout those periods when we cannot be with him in person?

If satsang with the physical Guru is not possible, the next closest thing is to attend one of his residential ashrams or group-meditation centers which are scattered throughout the world. According to Yoga, a Sadguru's ashrams and centers are to be considered extensions of his own body, which means that the same Guru Principle that functions through his body also functions through the teaching institutions which he has established. Each Siddha Yoga ashram and center—often called a "Siddha Yoga Dham"—is staffed by specially trained teachers and center leaders who maintain constant contact with the Guru, and he in turn employs his sankalpa to ensure that in each of these places his personal presence can always be experienced in the form of his spiritual power, or Shakti.

The principle vehicles which Muktananda employs to infuse his ashrams and centers with Shakti are the rituals which are regularly performed there. Since Baba himself and the science of Yoga both grew up in the East, these rituals are performed in Sanskrit and clothed in Eastern trappings; nevertheless, their sole purpose is to focus our awareness in the direction of the Self. Yogic ritual does have strong religious overtones, but if this type of spirituality is to be labeled as a religion, it must be understood to be the worship of the Self, which exists in *everything*—including all religions. Meditation on the Self is not the exclusive property of any sect; it belongs to everyone, just as sleep belongs to everyone. Just because we choose to decorate a bedroom in an Eastern motif, this does not mean that only Hindus can find sleep there; and, in the same way, the Eastern trappings of a Siddha Yoga Dham should not discourage anyone from honoring the Self there.

A group-meditation center is generally just a room or two in someone's private home or apartment in which a small number of local Siddha students gather one or more times each week to practice sadhana together and to share their spiritual experiences. An ashram, on the other hand, is a full-time residential community of Siddha students, managed by Muktananda's principle teachers and dedicated completely to the pursuance of Siddha Yoga sadhana. The only reason an ashram exists is for sadhana; since every activity which takes place there is designed to promote our spiritual growth, its environment is extremely pure, containing only things which modulate us upward. If we enter an ashram with the firm understanding that we are entering our own inner Self in the form of a building, everthing we experience there will have tremendously valuable significance to us.

For a few disciples, the ashram is their permanent home; for others it is a spiritual university at which they live and study for several months or years, and then graduate into the world to raise a family and pursue a career like everyone else, but with the priceless advantage of being able to stay in tune with the Self throughout all their mundane activities. Most of us, however, will use the residential ashram as a place of spiritual retreat to which we can withdraw for a few hours, days or weeks now and then, leaving all our worldly cares behind us temporarily and immersing ourself in the cleansing sauna of uninterrupted sadhana. Any time we need a spiritual boost—to help us over some obstacle or simply to ensure that our sadhana is progressing as smoothly as possible—the ashram is our spiritual clinic.

Whether our stay is for a long or short time, while we are in an ashram our number-one priority should be the pursuit of sadhana. In order to assure us of the maximum opportunity for spiritual growth throughout our time there, all ashramites are expected to consider as essential daily practices not only the three which were discussed in the previous chapter, but all of those being outlined in the present chapter as well. Thus, ashram life is often quite intense, but always guaranteed to be extremely beneficial.

Every meditation center conducts regular free programs of group sadhana, while each ashram offers such programs daily, as well as free lectures, personal experience talks, video tapes, movies, meals and special events. Both centers and ashrams hold frequent introductory programs and orientations for newcomers, and the general public is always welcome to attend any scheduled activity. Of course, the main tuitional program offered is the Meditation Intensive, Baba Muktananda's primary vehicle for Shaktipat; and in addition there are courses and workshops presented on a wide range of topics designed to eliminate our wrong understanding and further enrich our sadhana in a variety of ways. The money which is collected from these programs is used to maintain existing facilities, for charitable work, and to make Siddha Yoga available to more people throughout the world.

Regarding the value of attending ashrams and centers, Baba himself has said, "Often, in the course of our spiritual practice, we encounter a certain restlessness, anxiety and doubt due to impurities existing in the mind. It is precisely at this time that we need to direct our entire energy toward intense inner concentration. The effort which must be made is that of remaining open to the Guru, which is synonymous with remaining open to the inner Self. The prime function of a meditation center is to help seekers through these difficult times. At a Siddha Yoga Dham, the Siddha Guru's Shakti can be strongly felt, putting us easily into the meditative frame of mind. Here, other seekers and devotees—members of our spiritual family—gather. Although we can only go alone to the final goal, it is very helpful and meaningful, during certain stages of our sadhana, to share our inner world with spiritual friends."[18]

On many paths, practitioners are enjoined to keep silent about their spiritual experiences, but since Siddha Yoga is a "public Yoga," its sadhana progresses faster when we keep company with other Siddha students and share our inner world with them. To spend time with others who are engaged in the same process as we are, sharing our experiences with friends who have the right understanding and who strongly support what we are doing, is indispensable satsang, especially for those of us doing sadhana while living in the world.

Wherever a group of Siddha students congregates, there is a kind of "group shakti" which comes into play, a vital force which seems to act with a wisdom far greater than the sum of its parts, guiding the group's activities, and even its conversation, in directions which reveal important insights to each participant. Thus, in addition to the great love and joy which permeate group satsangs, this mysterious shakti, which seems to act in lieu of the physical Guru's presence, always makes certain that each of us gets precisely what we need, seeing that our questions are all answered, our doubts all removed; it even makes us feel uncomfortably out of place when we have drifted unknowingly from the smoothest, most rewarding course of sadhana, and it informs us in unmistakable terms exactly what we can do to make the necessary adjustments.

Without the satsang of fellow Siddha students to reinforce our sadhana, our constant associations with other worldly people whose goals may differ wildly from our own can quickly dull our discrimination and retard our progress considerably; for this reason, most practitioners of this Yoga make a point to attend group satsang at an ashram or local center at least once a week, to get a Shakti "boost" and to make sure their sadhana has not become bogged down unnecessarily.

Aside from the techniques we have discussed so far, the two main supplementary practices which group satsangs offer are called *kirtan* and *Guruseva*, both of which are generally more rewarding when performed with other Siddha students.

Kirtan

Fortunately, we have already examined in detail the true significance of mantra, for without such understanding it would be impossible to grasp the full importance of *kirtan* as an aid to sadhana. *Kirtan* is spiritual chanting—the repetitive singing aloud of certain approximate natural names such as *Rama, Shiva, Krishna, Narayana, Vasudeva, Govinda,* etc., which constitute various aspects of the cosmic Self, or God. In other words, when we chant we are not just singing *about* God; the sounds we are producing are God Himself—or at least as close as we can come to forming His actual sound-body with the physical voice.

Just as each spiritual mantra has a "seer"—a sage who personally perceives the pure natural name and then brings it back with him to the physical world in a form which is utterable by the human voice, so too each yogic chant has a seer as well—a Realized being who, in a transcendental state, has experienced the pure form of the complete chant and has passed it along to us in a form which we can sing. Thus, the structure of a yogic chant is not arbitrary in any way; all its elements are essential constituents of its overall vibratory pattern.

A spiritual chant is a specific type of mantra which need not be made chaitanya by a Guru in order to produce its desired effect; it need only be performed aloud with right understanding. Kirtan is usually practiced in a group because its vibratory strength increases by logarithmic rather than arithmetic proportions, meaning that when ten people participate, for example, the result is not just ten times as powerful as when only one person chants, but ten times ten, or one-hundred times more powerful.

In order for each participant to make the maximum contribution to the overall effect of kirtan, we are advised to keep our spine erect so that the chest can fully expand for optimal resonance; also, the chant should be sung loudly, but not raucously. Since the word sequence, melody and meter all contribute to a chant's effectiveness, variations and improvisations should be avoided; better results are obtained when the entire group sings with one voice, in perfect unison. Moreover, to assure ourself of maximum personal benefit from our participation in kirtan, the Siddhas advise us to sing straight from the heart as much as possible. If we remain constricted and closed-in while doing kirtan, our vibratory field will resist the beneficial modulatory effect of the chant; but if we become expansive and loosen up, the effects will be much more far-reaching.

The best way to open up physically during kirtan is to involve our body in the chant by swaying in time with the music, clapping our hands, etc. To become more open mentally, we need only maintain an understanding that the words we are singing are the Self in the form of sound. During the times when we practice our mantra japa, our objective is communion with the inner Self, while in kirtan the focus is the cosmic Self; of course, both the inner Self and the cosmic Self are essentially the same, but from the point of view of sadhana the two may be thought of as perfectly matched mates who have been separated through ignorance and who naturally long to reunite. Thus, if we sing with great sweetness and devotion, the outer Self which our song invokes will gradually, in effect, woo his mate from her hiding place in our heart.

One point upon which all yogic texts agree: in order to benefit from kirtan, we must participate enthusiastically. To attend a chanting session and yet not chant greatly diminishes the personal rewards to be derived, and whatever we do derive is obtained by what amounts to "stealing from the chant"—receiving the benefit of other people's effort without contributing any of our own.

A primary benefit of devotional chanting is that it opens the heart, making us able to give and experience love more freely, and mellowing the activity of the awakened inner Shakti. Although the chant is directed toward the cosmic Self, in effect it is a serenade to our own inner Self, who, like a bashful beloved, in time will begin responding to our sweet romancing.

Another important benefit of kirtan is its effect upon the external environment. First of all, it has a balancing and stabilizing effect upon the vibrational fields of every living body present; secondly, it purifies the atmosphere of the place in which it's performed, by neutralizing downward-modulating, "bad" vibrations and replacing them with "good" ones; and finally, it has a soothing effect upon the very forces of nature. Yoga contends that natural disasters are the result of imbalances among the forces of nature, imbalances caused by human thoughts and actions which are not in harmony with the natural flow of Creation. Kirtan introduces a pure vibration into the universal vibratory field; thus, it has the same effect upon nature as it does upon our immediate environment—it cancels out "bad vibes." In this way, the Siddhas tell us that impending natural disasters can actually be eased or completely averted through extensive group kirtans.

In addition to this type of kirtan, Siddha Yoga sadhana includes two others. The second type involves the regular chanting of the Guru's mantra, *Om Namah Shivaya*, thereby adding the benefits of kirtan to those of mantra japa. The third type is the performance of certain scriptural chants such as the *Guru Gita, Arati,*

Shiva Mahimnah Stotram, and *Shree Rudram.* These are long, epic-mantras whose profound significance and extensive additional benefits are detailed in the texts themselves, a translation of which accompanies the Sanskrit rendition in every Siddha Yoga chanting book. Though ashramites chant these texts together daily, many individuals and families who practice Siddha Yoga while living in the world also perform one or more of these regularly as part of their daily sadhana.

In the beginning of our kirtan practice, since chanting may seem rather alien to some of us, we may have to make an extra effort to fervently participate in this activity; but in time, the Siddhas guarantee us, we will begin to experience a tremendous upsurge of pure, unconditional joy, which becomes unleashed from our heart automatically whenever we throw ourself into a chant with complete abandon. Chanting, a primary technique in both the paths of Mantra and Bhakti Yoga, adds more purity and sweetness to our spiritual journey, and more love to our worldly life as well; thus, it is an invaluable asset to Siddha Yoga sadhana.

Guruseva

In Siddha Yoga, this is the term used to designate the practice of selfless service, a technique which is the specialty of Karma Yoga. Literally, *Guruseva* means "service to the Guru," but since the physical Guru is an embodiment of the cosmic Guru Principle which is an aspect of Shiva, and since Shiva is synonymous with God, the ultimate meaning of Guruseva is "service to God."

How do we go about serving God? According to Yoga, to do this we must (1) perform any work we do to the absolute best of our ability, with single-pointed concentration and with a feeling of devotion; (2) we must work with the attitude that we are not really doing the work, that in reality the part of us which we identify as "I" is but an instrument of God (or Shiva, the inner Self, etc.); and (3) whatever work we perform must be completed without concern for personal reward of any kind.

At first glance, all this will probably sound very unrealistic to most of us. For example, how does one go about balancing a financial ledger *with devotion,* and why would anyone even want to try? Why should we work with the attitude that we are not really doing the work, when in fact we know darned well we *are?* And why should we do work without regard for a reward of some kind, when this is the only reason anyone does work to begin with?

As substantial as these objections may seem to be, Yoga contends that they are all founded upon wrong understanding, and by now we should all be quite familiar with its logic: Since everything in Creation is God or Shiva, then any object with which we do work—be it a prayer book or a financial ledger—must be Shiva himself in this form; therefore, if we perform work with this understanding, every object with which we work becomes deserving of our devotion. Furthermore, if only Shiva exists and nothing else, then all actions must belong to him and him alone; thus, that part of us which thinks it isn't Shiva may also think that it's the doer of action, but in reality it is sadly mistaken on both counts. And finally, if all actions are Shiva's, then Shiva is the one who is really doing all our work; therefore, it is he who deserves to get whatever fruits such work may bring.

Ultimately then, selfless service is simply a practice of right understanding, for it involves the performance of all our actions with a correct understanding of the way things really are, despite how they appear to be. Admittedly, this particular type of right understanding practice is extremely difficult to sustain while engaged in our worldly pursuits, for it has been ingrained in us throughout our entire life—indeed, throughout many lifetimes—that the primary reason for working is for the rewards we may enjoy thereafter.

According to Yoga, the only reason a bound soul performs any action whatsoever is in order to fulfill desire. Any action performed with desire creates karma, and as long as we continue to create karma we must keep returning to this Earth Realm, which is the level of Creation at which karma is worked out. If we want to practice right understanding in this regard, we must realize that this world is not the appropriate realm for the fulfillment of desire; thus, if we try to appease our desires here, this place becomes a realm of pain and frustration for us.

The celestial plane called "heaven" in the West is the appropriate realm for desire fulfillment; any desire we do not act upon in the Earth Realm will be fulfilled in the heavenly one between our physical incarnations, Yoga tells us. If we try to fulfill them here and now, we will only create more karma, making ourself return again and again to endure more pain and frustration. Thus, if we must pursue a desire, the Siddhas advise us that we should pursue the desire for Liberation from this "veil of tears"; it's the only type of action which does not further bind us to the realm of karma.

As long as we continue to act in this world with a sense of personal doership and a desire for reward, we will never experience the absolute bliss of Liberation. However, as important as it is for those of us who seek Self-realization to adopt the proper attitude while engaging in the worldly work we do, if we try to accomplish this simply by performing our usual daily activities with an attitude of selfless service, we will probably discover this to be a hopeless endeavor. Our own wrong understandings in this regard are probably so deeply entrenched as to be almost invincible if besieged in their own territory; also, as we work in the world, we will usually find ourself surrounded by people who do nothing but reinforce our wrong understandings.

The only sensible way to gain a positive foothold in this type of right understanding is to begin by practicing it in a controlled environment, meaning one which is pure (upward-modulating), one in which the nature of the work is such that it is easy for us to maintain the proper attitudes while engaged in it, and finally, one in which everyone around us is also working with the same awareness of non-doership and non-attachment to its fruits. A Siddha Yoga Dham provides just such an environment.

The continued existence of each ashram and center depends upon the voluntary assistance of those who attend it. Just as we perform work around our worldly home, not for monetary or other reward but just because it's our home and the work needs to be done, so too we perform work around an ashram or center with the understanding that it is our spiritual home. Baba himself has said, "An ashram does not just belong to Swami Muktananda or the SYDA Foundation, it belongs to everyone who comes here."[18]

By practicing Guruseva at such a place, we learn to perform work simply for its own sake, and whatever fruits there may be as a result, we dedicate symbolically to the Guru—the physical Guru, the Grace-bestowing Shakti, God or the inner Self—whichever form we relate to best.

Even though we may perform such work without expectations of any kind, remarkable benefits seem to accrue anyway. By some mysterious process, whatever work we perform as seva seems to effect some corresponding beneficial change inside us. Thus, if we clean something in an ashram, something inside of us also gets purified; if we repair something in our local meditation center, some faulty inner mechanism becomes repaired as well. Perhaps this universally experienced phenomenon has to do with the fact that Guruseva eliminates wrong understanding, thereby permitting any internal obstacles—physical, mental or emotional—which are the by-products of that wrong understanding, to melt away.

So effective, in fact, is Guruseva as a sadhana tool, it can be employed exclusively to take us all the way to Self-realization. Some Siddha students with special inclinations derive so much enjoyment from this practice that they even try to shun all other sadhana practices and center all their efforts upon this one alone. Still, it's good to balance our Siddha Yoga sadhana with other practices, so Baba has usually insisted that such dedicated ''sevites'' forgo some of their work time in order to participate in the other ashram programs.

Our practice of Guruseva is, of course, not to be limited to Siddha Yoga Dhams alone. The object is to take the attitudes we develop while doing ashram or center seva and begin to apply these to all our worldly activities as well. True Guruseva is to act with the realization that Guru, God and Self are one-and-the-same and all-pervasive; then, as a result of this understanding, to perform our allotted duties with devotion, diligence, a sense of non-doership and without expectation of reward, simply accepting whatever comes to us—be it pleasurable or painful—as the just settlement of ancient karmic debts, having nothing to do with our present actions. Thus, all old karmas are resolved, no new ones are created, wrong understanding is erased, and the bliss of the Self is eventually regained.

Up to now we have been dealing mostly with supplementary practices which ideally involve group participation; but what if we are unable to attend group satsang regularly, either because there is no ashram or center nearby or because of some other circumstance? In such an event, we can still keep good company by reading Siddha Yoga books; we can receive the Guru's personal guidance by writing to him for advice; we can keep "plugged into" the mainstream of his Shakti by subscribing to the various magazines and newsletters which chronicle his activities as well as print his major talks and keep us up to date on what's happening in Siddha Yoga around the world; and finally, there is even a Siddha Yoga correspondence course, through which we can receive regular lessons designed to deepen our understanding and further our sadhana. These are all excellent ways for us to supplement our essential practices on our own, but the best one of all still remains to be discussed.

Moderation

Aside from the group techniques discussed above, the main individual practice with which each of us is encouraged to supplement our Siddha Yoga sadhana is the practice of moderation, which means the avoidance of excessive indulgence in sense-pleasures.

The moment many of us hear the word "moderation" used in connection with spirituality, the next words which often pop into our minds are "celibacy" and "vegetarianism," two notions which really seem to push people's anxiety-buttons nowadays. Perhaps if we first examine the yogic position on both these subjects we will be able to appreciate better the practice of moderation as it applies to spiritual sadhana.

To begin with, let us state that Siddha Yoga sadhana does not require us to be either celibate or vegetarian; it simply recommends that we understand the special needs of our system after Kundalini has been awakened, for the more we choose to respect these needs, the faster we will progress along the spiritual path.

In order to understand the effect that sexual intercourse has upon the process of Yoga, all we need know is that our sexual energy is the same energy which the awakened Shakti uses to perform her work inside us; therefore, the more of this energy that we disburse through sexual activity, the less will be available for the spiritual journey. Yoga does not moralize about sex; it merely concerns itself with the practicalities involved, and the practical facts seem to indicate that the more we can conserve our sexual energy, the faster our sadhana will progress. Few Yoga students are both willing and able to completely eliminate sexual activity from their lives; in fact, even the yogic definition of the state of celibacy permits the indulgence in sexual activity once a month between a husband and wife. Once we understand that our inner Shakti thrives upon the same energy which we expend during sexual contact, then quite naturally those of us who are dedicated to the quest for Self-realization will exercise great discrimination in the way we use this energy.

Our diet also has a profound effect upon the intensity with which the process of Yoga unfolds within us, for again the energy used to digest our food can also be used by our Kundalini for our spiritual strengthening and purification. Therefore, the best diet for a practitioner of Yoga is one which can be digested with the least amount of energy, yet supplies the maximum amount of nourishment to our system. Of all the foods available for the human diet, animal protein requires the most digestive energy for the process of assimilation; thus, for mainly practical reasons once again, Yoga recommends a diet which minimizes such foods, in order to make more of our precious prana available for sadhana.

In the same way, such indulgences as alcohol, tobacco and drugs not only damage the physical body, but also injure more subtle mechanisms within our psychic instrument—mechanisms which must function properly if we are ever to establish contact with the deeper levels of our being.

Many practitioners of spiritual science have the erroneous impression that sadhana "toughens" our body and makes it more resistant to abuse, but in fact, until we reach the final stages of our spiritual journey, our instrument actually becomes more *intolerant* of any kind of indiscretion. The practices of sadhana are designed to refine our body into an extremely sensitive and delicate instrument of perception which is capable of tuning into the most subtle levels of reality; such a precise instrument must be cared for more specially than a normal, low-performance human body, just as a finely-tuned, expensive sports car must be driven and maintained more carefully than a cheap subcompact model. Eventually, of course, when we become firmly established in the higher stages of our Yoga, we will command enormous power and possess invincibility, but in the interim we are as vulnerable as the tender, young sapling which needs a protective fence around it even though it is destined to become a mighty oak someday.

Exercise

Just as we can impede our sadhana through excessive indulgences which deplete our vital force, or prana, we can also retard spiritual progress by permitting ourself to become too sedentary. The energy level of the human body decreases through prolonged inactivity, in the same way that an automobile's battery loses power if it is not driven regularly.

The best way to generate more prana for our sadhana is to engage in some form of invigorating physical labor outdoors, at least every other day, for muscle tone begins to deteriorate after forty-eight hours without exercise. Such labor should not be overtaxing, but merely sufficient to warm up and tone our muscles, increase our circulation, and bathe our lungs in fresh air, without causing undue pain or stiffness.

If this type of work is not practicable, then some system of formal exercise may be practiced regularly. From the standpoint of Yoga, our goal should not be to develop huge muscles, for these tend to impair the body's flexibility, which may make it very difficult for us to sit for meditation; rather, as practitioners of Yoga we will be best served by a body which is strong yet flexible, with good circulation, good posture, and clear lungs.

The ideal exercise system for Siddha Yoga students should firm and tone our muscles, stretch our ligaments, loosen our joints, stimulate our organs and glands, increase our circulation, strengthen our lungs, improve our posture and eliminate nervous tension. Since the exercises of Hatha Yoga are designed to accomplish all these benefits, and yet are simple enough to be practiced by anyone, this system is the one most highly recommended by Baba Muktananda.

Although followers of the Hatha Path must master at least eighty-four such exercises through extreme ardency and perseverance, in Siddha Yoga we merely mean to supplement the inner Shakti's work with some personal effort of our own; therefore, the Siddha student whose body is in fairly good condition need only perform a few basic poses and breathing exercises, working on his own for twenty or thirty minutes each day or every other day, and perhaps supplementing this with attending a Hatha class once a week for more instruction and personal guidance. Hatha Yoga classes and courses are offered at every Siddha Yoga ashram and most meditation centers throughout the world.

These, then, are the means through which a Siddha student may further enrich and intensify his basic sadhana after Shaktipat. However, despite the many techniques which Baba Muktananda has recommended for us to practice, we must never forget that Siddha Yoga is at heart a "techniqueless" path, meaning that the willful performance of yogic exercises, though extremely beneficial throughout our sadhana, is not the means upon which we rely to finally gain reunion with the Self. On the Siddha Path, the vehicle which transports us to Self-realization is, from beginning to end, our awakened Kundalini-Shakti, and we are advised to make surrender to her our number-one priority. Thus, we should always be prepared to defer our limited will to her supreme will the moment we feel her assert herself within us—and this can happen at virtually any time throughout our sadhana.

As soon as automatic Siddha Meditation commences, all techniques are dropped. In the early stages of our sadhana this may occur infrequently or not at all, in which case we are instructed to simply pursue our technical practices as prescribed by the Guru; but as more and more Shakti becomes active inside us, our sadhana will become progressively more automatic and less reliant upon our personal effort. In the end, the final goal is reached completely automatically, our only contribution being total surrender to the ongoing process, without any reliance upon sadhana techniques at all. This is why Shaivism states that the goal of sadhana is not obtained by means of sadhana.

This point of complete surrender is eventually reached by practitioners on every valid spiritual path; but, whereas on self-effort paths it is reached only after we have mastered many techniques, in Siddha Yoga it can come at any time after we receive Shaktipat: to bring it on, all we need do is let go of all our wrong understandings. Baba Muktananda affirms this ever-present possibility of instantaneous Enlightenment by stating, "If you want to open yourself, open yourself. You don't have to do anything; you don't have to look for anything; you don't have to expect or even hope for anything; and you don't have to worry about when you will receive. You give with one hand and receive with the other simultaneously, for you are in reality both giver and receiver. Therefore, open yourself *at once;* God is standing right before you, waiting to give you back your very own Self."[18]

4. The Ups and Downs of Sadhana

From an emotional, mental and physical standpoint, doing sadhana is often very similar to riding on a roller coaster. Some of the time we're flying high, thrilled with joyful exhilaration, and at other times we're plunging downward, feeling physically ill, disoriented and afraid. The "ups" of sadhana are of course the result of our getting closer to the Self through right understanding, and the "downs" are caused by direct confrontation with obstacles which are solely the products of wrong understanding.

The first thing we are advised to bear in mind concerning this process is that obstacles are an essential ingredient of sadhana; if there were no hurdles to overcome, there would be no need for sadhana after Shaktipat. On the other hand, just because obstructions are an inherent part of sadhana, it does not necessarily follow that suffering is, too. According to the Siddhas, pain is not produced automatically when we meet with a difficulty; it is experienced only when we put up strong *resistance* toward adversity. Discomfort is a direct result of our perceiving an obstacle as something separate from the Self—something alien and malicious. The things which appear to us as hindrances are in reality only certain manifestations of Shiva which, through wrong understanding, we fail to recognize as such. The Siddhas tell us that when we learn to regard obstacles with right understanding, we will realize that they are actually our benefactors; they are the steps upon which we climb to reach our goal of Liberation. Knowing all impediments on the Path to be golden opportunities rather than worthless vexations, we will then strive to encounter them with devotion and enthusiasm, and as our resistance falls away, much of our suffering will go with it.

Insist as we might that the things which appear on the pathway before us—both in our sadhana and in our worldly life—have been deposited there by other humans, or gods, or demons, the fact is that according to the law of karma it is nobody else but we ourself who are completely responsible for whatever destiny awaits us. Whatever comes to us in life is a direct effect of our past actions, either in this or previous incarnations. We are the absolute masters of our fate, and there is no external will in all Creation to which we must respond as helpless pawns. Therefore, instead of wasting time complaining about our lot, we should cheerfully embrace whatever comes to us in life and figure out how to use it for our best advantage. This, say the Siddhas, is the secret of a creative sadhana which is lively, exciting and trouble-free.

The first major obstacle with which most of us must come to grips is our resistance to sadhana itself. After all, we have been plodding along aimlessly for countless lifetimes, looking outside for happiness and fulfillment, so when it finally dawns on us that what we seek is not out there at all but right inside our very own being, we should not be surprised if it takes some doing to turn our attention in the opposite direction from its usual mode of functioning. For this reason, sadhana practices do not generally become second-nature overnight; often we will have to make a willful effort to fit our spiritual exercises into our daily schedule, and in the beginning we may frequently fail; but through perseverance, with the help of our inner Shakti and reinforcement from the physical Guru and our fellow travelers on the Siddha Path, it is certain that eventually we will succeed in making our quest for Self-realization an indispensable part of our daily life.

Another important point to remember about our sadhana is that it, like everything else in Creation, is cyclical, which means that we will quite naturally experience periods of progress alternating with periods of apparent stagnation or even regression. The old adage about "one step backward for every two forward" pretty accurately characterizes the beginning stages of sadhana. To every one of us, the spiritual journey represents a venture into unfamiliar territory, and though there is really nothing at all to fear, most of us will experience some measure of anxiety when confronting the prospect of coming face-to-face with what we identify as "The Unknown"—even though this mysterious "unknown" which we view with so much foreboding will in the end turn out to be our very own Self. Until this unwarranted anxiety is eroded away through the practice of right understanding, periods of regression should be expected (but certainly not encouraged). As long as our organism wrongly interprets the unfamiliar inner world to be a threat of some sort, we will be compelled to keep retreating to what our ego considers to be safe ground, to which it will then obstinately cling until our more discriminating intellect drives us courageously forward into new territory once again.

On the other hand, in some of us the ego may become prematurely *obsessed* with sadhana, its zeal prompted not by the proper reasons at all, but by wrong understanding. At such times, the Guru (inner or outer) may find it necessary to temper our enthusiasm briefly, for our own good. For example, should we become overly enraptured by the promise of supernatural power, our inner Shakti may rescue us from this trap by temporarily souring our taste for sadhana. Another example might be a case in which we are enjoying a great many impressive meditation experiences, and our pride becomes dangerously overinflated as a result of this phenomenal progress; here, the physical Guru may opt to employ his power to halt our sadhana experiences until we gain enough right understanding to overtake and restrain our runaway pride.

In this way there are a lot of legitimate causes for our sadhana to slow down now and then, and often the explanation we decide upon for this does not reflect the true cause at all. But regardless of the reason for our apparent regression, it's not productive to feel sorry for ourself, and it's even worse to flagellate ourself with guilt. To help us keep our spirits up at such times, the Siddhas remind us that once we have received Shaktipat the awakened Kundalini never ceases working inside us, even during times when we stop doing sadhana willfully; instead, at such times she will continue somehow to utilize our everyday relationships and activities as a means to awaken and root out our wrong understandings. The Siddhas further advise us that the very quickest cure for all our spiritual doldrums is, first of all, to remember that even though such periods may seem as if they will continue forever, each is merely a temporary phase; secondly, we should try to stay firm at least in our *desire* for Liberation, even if for the moment we are not being very firm in our *action* toward it; and finally, we should endeavor to keep good company.

At times, even this sort of positive action may seem impossible for us to take; in fact, we may suddenly find ourself not just turned off by the idea of sadhana, but actually *opposed* to it. In the early stages after Shaktipat, it is not at all uncommon for us to find the most appalling negativities welling up from somewhere deep inside us, even to the extent of feeling violent hate for our daily practices, the Guru, God—anything connected with spirituality.

The reason behind such experiences lies with the fact that as soon as our inner Shakti becomes awakened by the Siddha Guru, she immediately goes about stirring up latent negativities so that she can eliminate them from our system. Since the hate of spirituality represents the most extreme type of wrong understanding, if there are any traces of such feelings still inside us when the Shakti is awakened, they are among the first impurities she sets about consuming with her cleansing fire, and as she roots them out in order to destroy them, we may briefly experience them in the form of negative thoughts, emotions or behavior. The best course of action to take, should we experience something like this at any point during our Siddha Yoga sadhana, is to first understand it to be the product of the yogic process unfolding within us; then, as negativities begin to manifest, we should simply witness them without attachment, knowing that they are not really part of us, but just some worthless, excess baggage which must be dragged out of the dark recesses of our mind in order to be disposed of.

The last main obstacle that we must overcome is impatience. Perhaps the Siddha Guru makes it a bit too easy for us to obtain Shaktipat, for instead of continually celebrating this priceless gift of Grace, we often grumble because we can't contain it all immediately. If we must dwell upon something, it should not be upon how far it seems we have yet to climb, but rather upon how far we have already risen, for the Siddhas state that in order to be worthy of an evolutionary boon as monumental as Shaktipat, we must have performed an extraordinary number of good karmas throughout this and previous incarnations. And even when we *do* think about the goal toward which we are striving, we should constantly remind ourself that it is much closer than it seems—as close, in fact, as our very own breath. Everything a Siddha master is, is right inside of us at this very moment, waiting for us to let it manifest itself.

Above all, we must remember that we are in good hands. A Siddha Guru is a master fisherman, and the catch for which he angles is our limited ego. Once his "hook" of Shaktipat is set in us, he will then give us all the play we need, waiting for us to tire ourself out swimming in this ocean of worldliness. But he will never permit us to become "the one that got away"; he is totally committed to landing us in his boat of Liberation as quickly as possible, but the harder we choose to fight him, the longer we will have to endure the anguish of this world. If we cooperate by swimming upward, we will always feel the gentle tug of his line, helping us to ascend and preventing us from sinking when we have to stop now and then to rest. Eventually, the pull will become so strong that all we need do is just relax and let him lift us from our sea of bondage, but until then we must keep swimming as often and as rapidly as possible.

Because most of the effects of sadhana are registered on levels of our being too subtle for our physical senses to detect, it may often appear as if our efforts aren't getting us anywhere at all, but if we persevere they are bound to pay off sooner or later. To illustrate this, there is the fable of two frogs who once fell into a pail half-filled with milk. The milk was too deep for them to stand up in, and too shallow for them to reach the top of the pail while afloat, so their only option was to start swimming, round and round. Soon they both became exhausted, and one of them, consumed by hopelessness and despair, just gave up and drowned. But the second frog refused to quit without a fight. "If I'm gonna go down," he decided, "I'm gonna go down trying!" So, for lack of any better effort to put forth, he just forced himself to resume his swimming, even though it didn't seem to be getting him anywhere at all. Before long, however, and to his extreme amazement, he noticed that the milk seemed to be getting thicker all around him; now it became considerably easier for him to stay afloat, but still he made himself continue swimming. The next thing he noticed was that a small lump of butter had begun to form in the middle of the milk, and as he continued to swim the lump got bigger and bigger, until—miracle of miracles—it actually became large enough for him to climb upon and leap to liberation!

The world is a lot like that pail of milk; it contains much sweetness, but if we imbibe too much, we drown in it; and the only way we can escape this misery is by a combination of determined right effort and the miracle of divine grace. But unlike that frog, we don't have to leave the world to become free of pain and suffering; we can enjoy the bliss of Liberation right here and now, in the midst of all our worldly pursuits. All we need is a spark of Grace and right understanding; then we will experience heaven on earth.

Such are the teachings of the Siddha masters. According to them, each of us who lives in the world, without Grace and bound by wrong understanding, is like a stray dog who, in search of sustenance, wanders into a hall of mirrors. Immediately this dog sees what he perceives to be another dog walking toward him. He barks, and the other dog barks, too; he shows his teeth and the other also snarls; he turns to flee, and yet another ferocious canine confronts him. Looking around frantically, he suddenly finds himself surrounded by wild-eyed adversaries which lunge toward him no matter in which direction he seeks escape, and finally, consumed by fear and exhaustion, he simply collapses and dies.

But with the Grace of the Siddhas bestowed through Shaktipat, and with the right understanding bestowed through their teachings, we can each become a wise and knowing sage; then, we can enter that same hall of mirrors, and this time we will find it to be a source of endless delight, for everywhere we look we will behold only the reflection of our very own Self.

Conclusion

Yogic legend maintains that once the ancient sage Vasishtha was confronted by a ravenous demon who threatened to devour him unless he could give a satisfactory answer to the following riddle: *What is the most bewildering mystery in all Creation?* Vasishtha's response was so impressive that the demon spared his life, so perhaps what he said will be of interest to us now as well, especially since he was one of the most venerable Siddhas in history, the composer of many scriptures and the Guru of Lord Rama himself.

The most bewildering mystery in Creation, according to Vasishtha, is the fact that human beings do not attempt to conquer their most terrible enemy of all time—Death. Even though we fear Death more than anything else in Creation; even though we see things being eaten up by it all around us every day; even though we know beyond the slightest doubt that it will come and claim us, too, at any time it wishes—perhaps tomorrow, perhaps even before we draw our very next breath; and even though the ominous specter of Death torments us, either consciously or unconsciously, through-out every single moment of our life, it's amazing that we choose to do so little to combat it. Like ostriches which bury their heads in sand when confronted with danger, most of us react to the prospect of our impending demise by simply trying not to think about it, while others are labeled as more noble because they act instead like sheep awaiting slaughter, docilely accepting their mortality and trying to face the inevitable end with as little fear as possible.

Even the demon of Death feels compelled to admit bewilder-ment at how we humans, as resourceful and industrious as we are, choose to submit so passively when we learn of its intention to devour us someday. Finding ourselves doomed to a cruel fate of surprise annihilation—meaning that at any time, in any place, completely without our consent or foreknowledge, Death is free to snuff us out in any of a million ways—the best we can come up with is an attitude of cold acceptance. Despite all the prodigious effort we expend to accumulate a few possessions which offer us some pleasure and comfort, why are so few of us willing to put forth any effort in an attempt to prevail against that wanton, dark marauder who gallops up at any time he pleases and mercilessly robs us of all the worldly wealth for which we've worked so hard?

More amazing still is the fact that for thousands of years all the world's greatest beings have taught that pathways to immortality do indeed exist and are available for anyone willing to make the journey; yet, rather than expend the effort, most of us are content to simply rattle around in Death's trouser pocket, like a candy morsel he can unwrap and consume whenever the craving hits him.

The Siddhas promise us that there is a door which leads to eternal life, that it is situated at the heart of every human being, and that it can only be unlocked with the key of spiritual sadhana. It doesn't matter which valid path we elect to follow, but this much is absolutely certain: just as nothing can ever come to an end unless it first has a beginning, so too, none of us can ever hope to complete a sadhana until we get around to starting one. Procrastination is the demon Death's best friend.

Of course, liberation from death is but one of the many boons of spiritual enlightenment, and the Siddhas advise us that this bountiful state of Self-realization can be attained only by those of us who (1) select a valid path which suits us, (2) become initiated onto that path by a perfected master of the same tradition, and (3) remain firmly committed to following that path for as long as it takes us to reach the final goal.

For those of us who would like to further investigate the prospects of the Siddha Path, with an eye toward perhaps initiating a Siddha Yoga sadhana for ourselves, the number-one recommendation is that we pay a visit to our nearest Siddha Yoga Dham. There, we can obtain a chaitanya mantra from the Siddha Guru, we can enroll in a Meditation Intensive and receive Shaktipat, or we can simply attend one or more of the free programs and discover whether or not the atmosphere feels comfortable to us. The very best way to judge the merits of any spiritual path is to spend time with others who are already committed to it, observing its effects upon them and deciding if they are the sort of people whom we consider to be good company for us.

Baba Muktananda openly invites each one of us to personally sample the Siddha Path and decide for ourself whether or not it is worthy of our time and effort. This completely non-exclusive spiritual science offers everyone a free trial with no obligation of any kind. Mantra initiation is available free of charge at any Siddha Yoga Dham throughout the world; practitioners on this path are never required to join any type of organization, contribute any funds or attend any gatherings; and no spiritual seeker is ever pressured into either beginning a Siddha Yoga sadhana or continuing one once it has been initiated. Since Baba Muktananda offers his spiritual guidance to everyone without restrictions, discipleship on this path does not require either a written or verbal contract between us and the Guru; here, the depth of our commitment to the Siddha Path may be completely confined within our own heart; it is an extremely personal decision which need not be shared with anyone else. A true guru, after all, need not be told the extent of our commitment to his path, for he intuitively knows the landscape and climate of our inner world even better than we do.

Although admittedly many of the Siddhas' claims concerning the benefits of spiritual sadhana might have once struck us as preposterous, now that we have examined some of the bases behind such assertions, it has probably become much more difficult for us to simply pass them off as completely unfounded. If then, while reading this book, we have become convinced that there is even a remote possibility that such things as death, pain, frustration, unhappiness, depression, loneliness and so on can be destroyed forever through spiritual sadhana, how much of our future time and effort are we now willing to invest in order to pursue this possibility further?

It seems that our only other alternative is to simply set this book aside and just resume living our life as we have been all along; but before we do so, it might be prudent for us to consider if perhaps such behavior would in fact be wildly irrational—the type which the sage Vasishtha characterized as "the most bewildering mystery in all Creation." In the words of Baba Muktananda:

> Listen to the immortal speech of the Self:
> O man, wake up! Come to your senses!
> Childhood days have passed;
> you have wasted your youth;
> old age has found you.
> At least now, be vigilant!
> Death's invitation is racing toward you!
> Before it reaches you, awake!
> What have you hoped to attain?
> Have those hopes been fulfilled?
> The goal still eludes you.
> O brother, arise![19]

Major Siddha Yoga Centers

All Siddha Yoga Dhams hold regular programs which are free and open to the public. Many will mail out printed schedules of events upon request. In addition to the residential ashrams listed here, there are hundreds of smaller group meditation centers scattered throughout the world. If none of the addresses below is convenient, contact one to find out if there is a meditation center operating in your immediate area.

AUSTRALIA

SYD Melbourne
202 Gore St., Fitzroy
Melbourne, VIC 3065
Phone: (03) 419-6299

SYD Sydney
1 Warrenball Avenue
Newtown NSW 2042
Phone: (02) 519-7540

ENGLAND

SYD United Kingdom
SYD London
1 Bonneville Gardens
London SW4 9LB
Phone: (01) 675-4105

FRANCE

SYD Lyon
9 Quai Lassagne
Lyon 69001
Phone: (7) 827-17-64

SYD Paris
7 Rue du Plaisir St. Ouen
Paris 93400
Phone: (1) 258-46-86

INDIA

Gurudev Siddha Peeth
(World Headquarters)
P.O. Ganeshpuri
PIN 401 206
District Thana
Maharashtra

Shree Gurudev Ashram
New Delhi
Bhatti Village
Mehrauli Block
c/o Khanna, Claridges Hotel
New Delhi

MEXICO

SYD Mexico City
APDO Postal 40-271
Mexico 06140 DF
Zamora 195
Colonia Condesa
Mexico 06140 DF
Phone: (905) 286-1676

SPAIN

SYD Barcelona
Alta De San Pedro 27-2
Barcelona 3
Phone: (93) 325-3197

SYD Madrid
APDO Correos 42 081
Madrid
Phone: (91) 448-8349

UNITED STATES

SYDA Ann Arbor
1520 Hill Street
Ann Arbor, Michigan 48104
Phone: (313) 944-5625

SYD Atlanta
1473 Fairview Road, N.E.
Atlanta, Georgia 30306
Phone: (404) 378-7932

SYDA Boston
Fernwood Rd., Manor House
Chestnut Hill, Mass. 02167
Phone: (617) 734-0137

Siddha Yoga Meditation
Ashram Chicago
2100 West Bradley Place
Chicago, Illinois 60618
Phone: (312) 327-0536

SYD Gainesville
1000 S.W. Ninth Street
Gainesville, Florida 32601
Phone: (904) 375-7629

SYD Hawaii
1925 Makiki Street
Honolulu, Hawaii 96822
Phone: (808) 942-8887

Muktananda Meditation
Center, SYD Houston
3815 Garrott Street
Houston, Texas 77006
Phone: (713) 529-0006

SYDA Los Angeles
P.O. Box 2157
Santa Monica, Calif. 90406
309 Broadway
Santa Monica, Calif. 90401
Phone: (213) 393-1491

SYDA Manhattan
324 West 86th Street
New York, New York 10024
Phone: (212) 873-8030

SYD Miami
256 S.W. 12th Street
Miami, Florida 33130
Phone: (305) 858-5369

SYDA New York
P.O. Box 600
South Fallsburg, N.Y. 12779
Phone: (914) 434-2000
        (212) 247-5997

SYDA Oakland
P.O. Box 11071
Oakland, California 94611
1107 Stanford Avenue
Oakland, California 94608
Phone: (415) 655-8677

SYD Philadelphia
6429 Wayne Avenue
Philadelphia, Pa. 19119
Phone: (215) 849-0888

SYD Seattle
1409 N.E. 66th Street
Seattle, Washington 98115
Phone: (206) 523-2583

SYD Washington, D.C.
5015 16th Street, N.W.
Washington, D.C. 20011
Phone: (202) 882-4377

WEST INDIES

SYD Trinidad
Craignish, Princess Town
Trinidad

Official Seal of the Siddha Yoga Dham of American Foundation

Notes

1. Page 71: Plato quote from L. Barnett, *The Universe and Dr. Einstein,* p. 115 (New York, 1968).
2. Page 76: St. Paul quote Ibid., p. 118.
3. Page 83: Einstein quote from M. Capek, *The Philosophical Impact of Contemporary Physics,* p. 319 (Princeton, 1961).
4. Page 88: W. Heisenberg, *Physics and Beyond,* p. 84 (London, 1971).
5. Page 89: Einstein quote from L. Barnett, op. cit., p. 109.
6. Page 90: M. Planck, *L'Image du Monde dans la Physique Moderne,* p. 129 (Paris, 1963).
7. Page 91: A. Einstein, *Out of My Later Years,* p. 26 (New York, 1950).
8. Page 97: F. Capra, *The Tao of Physics,* pp. 191, 244, 245 (Boulder, 1975). Reprinted with permission from Shambhala Publications.
9. Page 106: Kabir quote from R. Tagore, *Songs of Kabir,* p. 68 (New York, 1974).
10. Pages 108-109: Angela of Foligno quote from R.C. Johnson, *The Imprisoned Splendour,* p. 317 (Wheaton, 1977).
11. Page 113: R. Jastrow, "Have Astronomers Found God?" *New York Times Magazine,* June 25, 1978, p. 29.
12. Pages 114-115: F. Capra, op. cit., p. 19.
13. Page 118: M. Born, "Physics and Metaphysics," *Scientific American,* Vol. 82, No. 5, May 1956, p. 234.
14. Page 126: J. Jeans, *Physics and Philosophy,* p. 172 (Cambridge, 1948).
15. Page 126: A. Eddington, *The Nature of the Physical World,* p. 332 (Cambridge, 1931).
16. Page 165: Jung quote from L. Sannella, *Kundalini—Psychosis or Transcendence?,* p. 6 (San Francisco, 1977).
17. Page 165: L. Sannella, op. cit., p. 64. Reprinted with permission from the author.
18. Pages 186, 211, 266, 274, 283, 289, 295, 296: From the public lectures of Swami Muktananda Paramahansa.
19. Page 305: S. Muktananda, *Reflections of the Self,* p. 190. (South Fallsburg, 1980). Reprinted with permission from the SYDA Foundation.

Suggested Further Reading

On the subject of spiritual science as compared to Western science, philosophy and religion:

1. CAPRA, Fritjof. *The Tao of Physics* (Boulder: Shambhala Publications, Inc., 1975) A research physicist, Capra brilliantly and comprehensively explains twentieth-century physics and the striking parallels between recent discoveries and the ancient teachings of Eastern spiritual sciences. (Chapter 18 of this book may be disregarded, since the "bootstrap hypothesis" discussed therein has recently been found to be unsupportable.)

2. ZUKAV, Gary. *The Dancing Wu Li Masters: An Overview of the New Physics* (New York: Bantam Books, Inc., 1980) Written by a layman and similar in theme to *The Tao of Physics*, this book contains enough different material to warrant separate examination. Though both these books are written for laymen, understanding them will require some effort from even the well-educated reader.

3. JOHNSON, Raynor. *The Imprisoned Splendour* (Wheaton: Theosophical Publishing House, 1977) Also by a modern physicist, this very readable book places less emphasis upon the intricacies of recent scientific findings and focuses more upon the actual experience of Enlightenment, presenting a host of first-hand accounts by people throughout history who have suddenly come face-to-face with the cosmic Self.

4. BENTOV, Itzhak. *Stalking the Wild Pendulum* (New York: Bantam Books, Inc., 1979) This book contains many fascinating scientific findings related to the practice of meditation and Kundalini awakening, along with some far-fetched but mind-stretching hypotheses about the structure of the cosmos.

5. REINCOURT, Amaury de. *The Eye of Shiva: Eastern Mysticism and Science* (New York: Wm. Morrow & Co., 1981)   A valuable dissertation cataloging the essential differences between the ancient Eastern and the modern Western minds in their search for ultimate reality. Within the frameworks of science, philosophy, religion and art, the author outlines the evolution of Western objectivity and clearly describes its tragic limitations as compared to the more effective Oriental approach to such matters as the meaning of life and the essential nature of Creation.

On the subject of Kundalini:

1. VISHNU TIRTHA, Swami. *Devatma Shakti (Kundalini)—Divine Power* (Rishikesh: Yoga Shri Peeth, 1974)   A simple, lucid and authoritative treatise by a contemporary master of Kundalini Yoga.

2. WOODROFFE, Sir John. *The Serpent Power: The Secrets of Tantric and Shaktic Yoga* (New York: Dover Publications, Inc., 1974)   Though difficult to read, this book is the definitive English text on the subject of Kundalini as dealt with in ancient Eastern scripture.

3. SANNELLA, M.D., Lee. *Kundalini—Psychosis or Transcendence?* (San Francisco: H.S. Dakin Co., 1977)   A highly readable synthesis of concepts and observations from anthropology, Oriental literature and Western medical science, including fifteen medical case histories of people experiencing Kundalini awakening.

4. JUNG, Carl G. *Psychological Commentary on Kundalini Yoga* (New York: Spring Publications, 1975)   An overview of Kundalini awakening from the viewpoint of Western psychology.

5. See also the BENTOV book above, and the MUKTANANDA books on the following page.

On the subject of mantra:

1. WOODROFFE, Sir John. *The Garland of Letters* (Pomona: Ganesh & Co., 1974)   Like *The Serpent Power,* this book is difficult reading but is the definitive English text on the science of mantra as dealt with in Eastern scripture.

2. See also the MUKTANANDA books below.

On the Subject of Kashmir Shaivism:

1. SINGH, Jaideva. *Siva Sutras: The Yoga of Supreme Identity* (Delhi: Motilal Banarsidass, 1979)

2. SINGH, Jaideva. *Pratyabhijnahrdayam* (Delhi: Motilal Banarsidass, 1977)

3. SINGH, Jaideva. *Vijnanabhairava or Divine Consciousness* (Delhi: Motilal Banarsidass, 1979)

   These three important ancient texts are now available in English, all accurately translated and accompanied by an authoritative and reliable commentary.

On the subject of Siddha Yoga:

1. MUKTANANDA, Swami. *Play of Consciousness* (San Francisco: Harper & Row, 1978)   An essential text for everyone interested in the Siddha Path, this spiritual autobiography by a living Siddha Guru details the nine-year process of Self-realization which unfolded after he was initiated by his guru, and it also divulges profound information which the Siddhas have kept secret for thousands of years.

2. There is an extensive list of additional titles by Baba Muktananda, as well as many other books, magazines, home-study courses, audio and video tapes, etc., available by mail or at Siddha Yoga bookstores. For more information contact the SYDA Foundation or any local Siddha Meditation center.

Index

Sanskrit Pronunciation Guide

Sanskrit is a precise and complex ancient language consisting of some fifty separate and distinct sounds, many of which have no parallels in any modern language. Though the pronunciations which follow are in many cases merely rough approximations of the pure Sanskrit terms, they are the ones in accepted usage by most Yoga students throughout the world today.

Vowel Sounds

a = *a*bove, b*u*t   aa = f*a*ther, *aw*ful
i = s*i*t, *i*f   ee = s*ee*n, m*ea*n
u = p*u*t, g*oo*d   oo = m*oo*n, r*oo*m
e = p*ay*, *a*ble   o = *o*ver, p*oe*m

agami (aa'ga-mee)
ajapa-japa (a-jaa'pa jaa'pa)
ajna (aa'nya)
anahata (a-na-haa'ta)
Arati (aa'ra-tee)
asana (aa'sa-na)
ashram (ash'ram)
Atman (aat'maan)
Baba (baa'ba)
bandha (baan'da)
Bhagawan (baa'ga-waan)
bhakti (baak'tee)
bhuvana (boo'va-na)
bija (bee'ja)
Brahma (braa'ma)
Brahmastra (braa'mas-tra)
chaitanya (che-taan'ya)
chakra (chaak'ra)
chinmudra (chin-moo'dra)
Chidvilasananda
   (chid-vi-laas-a-naan'da)

dham (daam)
dharana (daa'ra-na)
Govinda (go-vin'da)
guru (goo'roo)
Guru Gita (goo'roo gee'ta)
Guruseva (goo'roo-se'va)
Hamsa (haam'sa)
hatha (haa'tha)
ida (ee'da)
Ishwara (ish'waa-ra)
jada (jaa'da)
jagat (ja-gaat')
japa (jaa'pa)
jnana (nyaa'na)
Kaivalya (ke-vaal'ya)
Kali Yuga (kaa'lee yoo'ga)
karma (kaar'ma)
   karmic (kaar'mik) adj.
Kashmir (ka'shmir)
kirtan (keer'taan)
kripa (kri'pa)

Krishna (krish'na)
kriya (kree'ya)
kriyamana (kree'ya-maa-na)
kundala (kun'da-la)
Kundalini (kun-da-lee'nee)
laya (la'ya)
loka (lo'ka)
maha (maa'ha)
manas (maa'nas)
manipura (maa-ni-poo'ra)
mantra (maan'tra)
Matrika (maa'tri-ka)
mudra (moo'dra)
Muktananda (mook-ta-naan'da)
muladhara (moo'la-daa-ra)
nada (naa'da)
nadi (naa'dee)
namah (na-maa')
Narayana (naa-ra-yaa'na)
Nataraja (naa-ta-raa'ja)
neti (ne'tee)
nirguna (nir-goo'na)
Nityananda (nit-ya-naan'da)
Om (om)
Paramahansa (paa-ra-ma-haan'sa)
Paramashiva (paa-ra-ma-shee'va)
pingala (pin'ga-la)
prakriti (praa'kri-tee)
prana (praa'na)
pranayama (praa-na-yaa'ma)
prarabdha (pra-raab'da)
purusha (pu-roo'sha)
raja (raa'ja)
Rama (raa'ma)
Rishi (ri'shee)
Rudra (roo'dra)
Sadguru (saad'goo-roo)
sadhana (saa'da-na)

saguna (sa-goo'na)
sahaja (sa-haa'ja)
sahasrara (sa'has-raa-ra)
samadhi (sa-maa'dee)
sanchita (san-chee'ta)
sankalpa (san-kaal'pa)
Sat-chit-ananda
  (saat-chit-a-naan'da)
satsang (saat'saang)
seva (se'va)
Shaivism (she'vism)
Shakti (shaak'tee)
Shaktipat (shaak'tee-paat)
Shiva (shee'va)
Shiva Mahimnah Stotram
  (shee'va ma-him'na sto'tram)
Shivaya (shee-vaa'ya)
Siddha (sid'a)
siddhi ((sid'ee)
So'ham (so'haam)
spanda (spaan'da)
sushumna (su-shum'na)
svadhistana (sva-di-staa'na)
swami (swaa'mee)
Trika (tree'ka)
Vasishtha (va-sish'ta)
Vasudeva (va-soo-de'va)
Veda (ve'da)
  Vedic (ve'dik) adj.
Vedanta (ve-daan'ta)
Vishnu (vish'noo)
vishuddha (vi-shu'da)
yantra (yaan'tra)
Yoga (yo'ga)
  yogi (yo'ghee) masc.
  yogic (yo'ghik) adj.
  yogin (yo'ghin) neut.
  yogini (yo-gee'nee) fem.

Additional copies of this book are available from the publisher, postpaid, @ $8.95. Send payment to Matrika Publications, Suite 1-K, 10 East End Ave., NY, NY 10021. New York residents add applicable sales tax. Please allow six weeks for delivery on orders paid by personal check. Trade discount information obtainable on request.